The Body of This Life:
Reading William Bronk

The Body of This Life: Reading William Bronk

edited by David Clippinger

Essays and Memoirs by Don Adams, Robert J. Bertholf,
Joseph Conte, Paul Christensen, David Clippinger,
Ronald W Collins, John Ernest, Norman Finkelstein,
Edward Foster, Burton Hatlen, W Sheldon Hurst,
S M. Kearns, Jack Kimball, Burt Kimmelman, David Landrey,
Tom Lisk, Michael Perkins, Paul Pines, Gerald Schwartz,
Rose Shapiro, Henry Weinfield, and Daniel Wolff

Talisman House, Publishers
Jersey City, New Jersey

Published in the United States of America by
Talisman House, Publishers
P.O. Box 3157
Jersey City, New Jersey 07303-3157

Manufactured in the United Sates of America
Printed on acid-free paper

Library of Congress Cataloging-in-Publication Data
can be found at the end of this book.

Acknowledgements: Selections from *The Collected Poems of Wallace Stevens* by Wallace Stevens, copyright 1954 by Wallace Stevens. Used by permission of Alfred A. Knopf, a division of Random House, Inc. • Selection from *Opus Posthumous: Poems, Plays, Prose by Wallace Stevens*, copyright 1989 by Holly Stevens. Used by permission of Alfred A. Knopf, a division of Random House, Inc. • "This Was a Master Spirit" by Michael Perkins first appeared in *Rain Taxi Review of Books*, Vol. 5, No. 3 (Fall 2000). Reprinted by permission of *Rain Taxi Review of Books*. • Selections from manuscript letters of William Bronk housed in the William Bronk archive of the Rare Book and Manuscript Library, Butler Library, Columbia University, and elsewhere, are used by permission of Columbia University, literary executor for the Estate of William Bronk. • Selections from the published work of William Bronk is reprinted by permission of Talisman House, Publishers. • Portions of letters from William Bronk to Robert Meyer appear with the permission of The Poetry / Rare Books Collection, University Libraries, State University of New York. • Portions of letters from Robert Meyer to William Bronk housed in the William Bronk archive of the Rare Book and Manuscript Library, Butler Library, Columbia University, and elsewhere, are used by permission of Columbia University.

Contents

David Clippinger

POETRY AND THE LIFE TO MAKE: AN INTRODUCTION

> A life to make, one might be
> more careful. Think: there is no life to make.
> Be bare in the day: a kind of life. (*LS* 194)

From 1956 till his death in 1999, William Bronk published thirty books of poetry and essays. Throughout those forty-three years, he returned again and again to a fundamental assertion that what is real—the world, truth, and ourselves—remains beyond the grasp of language and knowledge. Consequently, the world that we inhabit is a fiction of our own construction. As he writes in *The Force of Desire*:

> These are invented words and they refer
> to inventions of their own and not to a real world
> unresembled, inexpressible. (*LS* 198)

Such a stance towards the world positions the poems as well as the poet as merely self-referential inventions, thereby denying the force of the poem as a purveyor of "transcendent" moments wherein truth and the "real" can be ascertained or at least glimpsed. Bronk never wavers from this fundamental position, and the poems are a relentless interrogation of the causes, conditions, and manifestations of the inherent flaws of language, the elusive "real" self and world that remain forever beyond the knowing, cognizant self, and the propensity of humanity to accept willingly the fictive as the real.

Clearly, the philosophical and human stakes are high in Bronk's poetry. But even as his work pressurizes what and how we know, the outcome is fixed: ignorance is inevitable. Subsequently, Bronk is sometimes read as a nihilistic poet devoid of the desire for transcendence and epiphany. Within Bronk's schema, there can be no transcendence; yet there is an epiphany that comes disguised as the poem itself:

> Of course, in a sense, we aren't anyone.
> No, more than a sense. But there isn't someone across
> the galaxy either, or no one we could talk
> to, ever. Oddly, talk is what it's about. (*LS* 187)

The "Surprise Ending," to borrow the title of the poem, is the assertion of the significance of the act of talking as an act of living—"what it's about." While talking is, of course, wrong—misdirected, miscued, and misunderstood—and the idea of a speaker and a listener engaged in a dialogue is absurd since even the "idea" of a speaker and a listener is wrong, what matters, regardless, is the process, the engaging with the question of the world. In a world where nothing can be known, talking *is* the means and testament of living—bare as that life may prove to be.

William Bronk's poetry, subsequently, is more than just poems; they testify to the life that he wished to share with friends and even acquaintances through letters and private readings in his sun-room or, weather permitting, on his side porch. The poems tethered Bronk to his "ultimate reality" of "12839" in Hudson Falls, New York. More importantly, though, his poetry delineated the contours of his life that included his dialogues with countless individuals and friends—many of whom are included in this book. It is in this spirit that this collection is titled *The Body of This Life: Reading William Bronk*. The essays collected herein, which are extended versions of papers presented at the first William Bronk Symposium held at Stevens Institute of Technology in November, 1999, include personal recollections, letters, and dialogues that offer a range of insights into the poetry and life of William Bronk. All of the essays amplify the reach and breadth of Bronk's poetry and ideas while also paying tribute to the generosity and gentlemanly character that was, in my experience, the essence of William Bronk the poet and person.

In brief, the essays in *The Body of This Life* tend to fall into three interrelated but succinct categories: the relationship of biography and poetry, which is the focus of "The Plainest Narrative"; "Ars Poetica," which concentrates upon Bronk's poetry and poetics; and poetry as a vehicle for philosophical inquiry, "The Idea of Ideas." The first section, "The Plainest Narrative," takes its title from Bronk's poem that begins with the lines:

> I am William Bronk, have been raised to believe
> the personal pronoun plus the verb to be
> and a proper name said honestly is fact
> from which the plainest narrative begins. (*LS* 105)

Many of the essays in this section follow the gist of this poem, which unravels the possibility of the "plainest narrative" and therefore troubles the reliance upon biography as a critical tool of wholly explicating poetry. John Ernest, Paul Pines, and Daniel Wolff each explore the seemingly paradoxical relationship of life and poetry in distinctively different ways: Ernest approaches the poetry as a conscientious scholar arguing that the life of the poet should not be conflated with the living poetry; Pines builds his essay around his careful study of Bronk's work as well as their friendship, thereby supplementing scholarship with personal experience; and Wolff sets up his essay as a private conversation with Bronk, which is full of personal references, dialogues, and jokes. In each, the "narrative" adds to the depth, complexity, and paradoxical nature of the life of the poetry and the poet.

Michael Perkins and Burt Kimmelman, on the other hand, reveal how the life and the poetry are intimately interrelated. Kimmelman documents the extended friendship and correspondence between Bronk and Robert Meyer—tracing the genesis of specific poems and themes in relation to the dialogues between these two friends. Perkins gives an even more intimate portrait based upon twenty years of close friendship, wherein the essay reveals how many of the central poetic motifs were first actualized through highly personal letters. Lastly, Sheldon Hurst considers Bronk's poetry through the lens of his art collection, and Hurst's essay couples specific paintings with corresponding poems in order to suggest how the poems respond to the art works that were an integral part of Bronk's house and, therefore, day-to-day existence. All in all, the "narrative" of Bronk's life and poetry that emerges from these essays is an even more multi-faceted perspective of the man who wrote and interrogated the statement "I am William Bronk."

"Ars Poetica," the second section of essays, focuses upon the issues of style, form, voice, tone, and rhythm—the techné of poetry—in relation to thematic elements. Henry Weinfield's essay demonstrates how the style works in concert with the philosophical and thematic aspects, thereby emphasizing how the music of the phrasing contributes to the meditative tone of the ideational content. The relationship of form and content is also central in Rose Shapiro's investigation of the "fourteen-liners" from To Praise the Music (1972), whereby she explicates how formal poetic considerations frame the paradoxical nature of the poems. Edward Foster and Jack Kimball both draw out points of similarities and affinities between Bronk and other seemingly unlikely poets—Joel Oppenheimer in Foster's essay and Louis Zukofsky, Jack Spicer, and Gertrude Stein in Kimball's. Through these "familial" connections, Foster and Kimball reveal a continuity of innovative poetic form that includes Bronk. The charged poetic dynamic between Bronk and other poets is presented in a different way in Gerald Schwartz's discussion of reverence as a poetic mode, and he uses "The Smile of the Face of a Kouros" as a formal and ideational catalyst for his own poem—a tribute to the power of Bronk's technique to catalyze further poetic dialogues that can come as an essay or a poem—or even both.

The tribute to Bronk as a thinker is the crux of the final section of the book, "The Idea of Ideas," which offers a range of perspectives upon Bronk's relation to physics, religion, cultural history, psychology, and philosophy. In terms of philosophy, three essays read Bronk through modern and postmodern philosophical paradigms—all of which question certainty: Don Adam's reads Bronk's sense of ignorance and absence via Martin Heidegger; Tom Lisk carefully delineates the skepticism regarding reality and the modes of inquiry shared between Bronk and George Berkeley; and affinities between Bronk, Wallace Stevens, and Hans Varhinger and their use of the conditional "as if" to frame philosophical inquiry are the focus of Robert Bertholf's essay. Bronk's skepticism is also explored in a number of socio-historical contexts as well. Paul Christensen considers Bronk's prose in relation to post World War II anxiety over the concomitant dimensions of identity and reality. In this light, Bronk is read against the backdrop of Cold War angst and McCarthyism. David Landrey also examines politics and Bronk's prose—and especially *The Brother in Elysium*—but Landrey's essay explores how the concomitant themes of love and silence that dominate Bronk's poetry are an extension of his perception of the socio-political world. Burton Hatlen considers Bronk's work within a broad literary tradition of poets interested in the sublime—a point that, Hatlen argues, situates Bronk as an important intermediary within a literary history inscribed as either the Stevens or Pound tradition. Whereas Bronk is usually affiliated with Stevens, Hatlen presents a compelling reconsideration of the binary of Stevens or Pound and Bronk's place therein.

Joseph Conte's essay explores Bronk's poetic affinities with Stevens, but he also fuses together a number of previous themes including negativity and poetic form in his extended analysis of how the forms of the poems as meditative structures serve to accentuate Bronk's denial of reality. Further, this denial of reality as a governing ideational structure is central to two other essays as well. Ron Collins explicates Bronk's poetry in relation to Quantum Mechanics and theories such as Heisenberg's Uncertainty Principle, which challenge not only the nature of reality but also the act of observing "reality." My essay compares the dimensions of form and emptiness in Bronk's poetry with the paradox that resides at the heart of Buddhism—namely the insistence that, in the words of the *Heart Sutra*, "form is emptiness; emptiness is form." Bronk's poetry shares much with issues of spirituality, and the religious implications in Bronk's poetry are the focus of Norman Finkelstein's insightful discussion of the parallels between the creation of the world as described in *Genesis* and Bronk's poem "The Creation of the World." Finkelstein's analysis offers a lens to understand the religious questions implicit in Bronk's worldview. The final essay of the collection by Sherry Kearns revisits the centrality of language and metaphor in Bronk's poetry, and she reads his use of metaphor against Carl Jung's model of the unconscious and archetypes. Kearns's essay amplifies the webbing of ideas, poetry, and individual consciousness—thereby reasserting how dialogues are part of the ongoing process of delineating the "bare" life of poetry.

My hope is that these essays, which will be fundamental critical resources for future Bronk readers and scholars, will spark further conversations about Bronk's poetry and that this book will be regarded as a fitting tribute to the life and writings of William Bronk, whose poems and words are indeed bursts of light against the backdrop of a bare world:

> The light in fall but in other times as well
> can make the world so beautiful we want
> to take it all, have it take us, burst. (*MOT* 113)

In addition to William Bronk, it is important to offer my deeply felt gratitude to Edward Foster and Burt Kimmelman, who co-organized and co-directed with me the William Bronk Symposium and who wisely counseled me about this book. Moreover, without the editorial expertise of Ed Foster, this book would not have been possible. My thanks are also extended to all of those people who, out of their commitment to Bronk's work, participated in the symposium and offered their essays for inclusion in this collection, as well as Talisman House for providing its sustained support of William Bronk's poetry and for making this critical study possible.

Grateful acknowledgement is made to the University of New Hampshire Library, the Butler Library of Columbia University, and the Poetry and Rare Books Collection of the State University of New York, Buffalo for providing permission to print portions of William Bronk's letters. I would also like to extend my thanks to the various publishers who allowed use of various printed materials. Similarly, I'd like to recognize the support from Penn State University for supplying resources so that I could bring this manuscript to fruition.

Last, but certainly not least, I would like to thank Annabelle, Philip, and Tess for their patience, support, and love during all phases of this project.

THE PLAINEST NARRATIVE

John Ernest

"IT BECOMES OUR LIFE":
WILLIAM BRONK AND THE LIFE OF THE POEMS

I FIRST ENCOUNTERED WILLIAM BRONK'S WORK when I was a graduate student. I was a research assistant for a professor who was interested in a number of important but lesser-known poets, and Bronk was one of them. Wanting to know the work of the poets I was researching, I started to read Bronk's poetry, and I felt that I was reading the poems that I wanted to write but couldn't. I decided to write my Master's thesis on Bronk's work, and wrote to him. He invited me to Hudson Falls for a conversation, and that was the beginning of a friendship that grew over a period of fifteen years or so, a friendship that filled my life with warm conversations, generous letters, and many books of poetry. But I think what drew me most to William Bronk was his belief in the importance, the necessity, of poetry. Poetry had for Bronk a reality that very few have experienced, and the poetry guided his understanding of his world.

Bronk wasn't much interested in literature as a field of academic study; in fact, he dropped out of Harvard graduate school in large part because he was so frustrated with the way the scholars there talked about literature, something that I've tried to remember in writing this essay. In one of his letters, discussing how people approach literature, Bronk had this to say:

> Insofar as there can be anything about me worth writing about it would have to be the work and the importance of the work can only be to the reader who has entered into a relation with it. This is at variance with the generally—not only academically—held idea that works of art can be examined, described and assessed as though they were precious stones. Or houses. But the importance

of houses is lost in their selling price. We live in them. Or we
don't. (William Bronk to John Ernest, 13 April 1987)

Bronk spent his life trying to learn how to live in the houses he created in
his poetry. He tried, in other words, to realize in his approach to life
what he called "the permanence of ignorance." And so I have the luxury
of writing an essay in which the inevitability and value of ignorance is my
theme.

Specifically, I want to stress the importance of our ignorance about
the reality that was Bronk's whole concern, for the danger is that we will
transform the poet William Bronk into an academic industry, a knowable
entity. When I first wrote to William Bronk in 1983, looking for a chance
to talk with him, he wrote back with a characteristically generous invita-
tion, but he also noted, "I have held and still hold that my work is
concerned only with the relationship between me and the work" (William
Bronk to John Ernest, 4 April 1983). As he put it in "What Art Is," the
arts require a "private communication" that "becomes our life" ("Of
Poetry"). The life discovered in that private communication is the life
Bronk addressed again and again in his work. It is a life connected to but
independent of those personal traits and experiences that would necessar-
ily shape a biography of the man. It is the life Bronk tries to get at, for
example, in the poem "Estimation":

> The self to esteem is not any self we are
> nor the world as well, the world of the worldly world
> but only the world under the shape of the world
> and the self there under the self to be seen.

"The self under the self to be seen," the self engaged in a private commu-
nication, the self involved in a relationship with the work, the work that
requires that the reader enter into a relation with it as well—this is the
self that is central to anything we might want to know about William
Bronk.

What does it mean, then, to think, as we can't help but think, of
Bronk's life, of biography? What story can we tell about the life of

William Bronk that doesn't violate the life of the poems, that life that Bronk insisted upon and devoted himself to? I talked with Bronk once about the possibility of writing a biography, and, unsurprisingly, he would have nothing to do with the idea. In a letter on the subject Bronk said, "Just as I opposed the academic approach to literary art as a cadaver to be autopsied so do I oppose the current fashion to treat the work as a bunch of old clothes which could well be discarded but are kept to show how they are used to hide a life now being discovered" (William Bronk to John Ernest, 31 December 1996). So what *might* it mean to write a biography of Bronk, or of the poems, or of the relation between art and life? I understand that these are questions that might be asked of any writer, questions fundamental to the art of biography, and I do not mean my comments to suggest that I am not looking forward to reading the biography currently under progress.* I understand as well that many writers might resist biography, but that biography still remains for the reader part of the life of the work, and will be important in our attempt to enter into a closer relationship with Bronk's poetry, as if to spot the faded presence of someone unknown in a picture of someone we thought we knew. In fact, my conversations with Bronk led me to these questions, questions that developed when I wrote a short biographical piece on him; and like other serious readers of Bronk I've gathered a fair amount of material on his life. Still, it almost goes without saying that a biography on William Bronk, like all biographies, must inevitably fail to reach its subject. And that failure will be a large part of the biography's value.

I'm suggesting simply that even in thinking about Bronk's life we need to take very seriously the life of the poetry, a body of work that speaks clearly on the nature and terms of the "self to esteem" as distinct from the "self we are." I take seriously Bronk's claim that "to speak of us as real or to speak of us as material is not, in effect, to speak of us for it is to speak of something we are not" (*VSC* 36). Years ago, in a letter to Cid Corman, Bronk wrote, "My poetry is about all of those things of which we have concepts but which we find non-existent or unapproach-

---

*Editor's note: Lyman Gilmore has been researching materials for a biography of William Bronk, tentatively titled, *The Force of Desire: Poet William Bronk*.

able, and about our experience of finding them so" (Corman 38). We have concepts also about the documentable life. But Bronk's life, the self we seek if we are looking for "the self there under the self to be seen," is similarly unapproachable, and our concepts of that other life must similarly prove to be non-existent—and in our experience of finding them so we will be drawn into the society of the poems. As Bronk puts it in his epigraph to *Vectors and Smoothable Curves,* "reality is brought to mind by the inadequacy of any statement of it, the tension of that inadequacy, the direction and force of the statement" (VSC vii). Whatever understanding we seek of Bronk's life, then, must begin with the recognition of "the inadequacy of any statement of it," and must be sought in "the tension of that inadequacy."

That tension must remind us that one of the subjects of a biography of the life of the poems is the reader who enters into the society of the poetry, a society that includes Bronk but in which Bronk cannot be made to stand as an isolated figure, the celebrity available for interviews. The reader also is a figure in the room, and the poems guide the reader into the local discourse of this society. Our relation with Bronk, in other words, is always a triangulated relation within a larger society. Bronk once wrote, "I used to think that I talked to the reader and in a sense perhaps that was true but it is really the work that talks to the reader as it was the work that talked to the writer. The work and the artist say each other as I think lovers do and, in later contact, it is the work and the reader that say each other" (William Bronk to John Ernest, *13* April *1987*). In this mutual saying, shaped by the presence of other relations, lies the intimate and still public society of the poems. Related by shared lovers, the reader and the artist note one another's presence and communicate across the distances of the world that veils the real. Feeling the frustrations of that distance, we might even be seduced by our eavesdropping on Bronk's private communications, the lovers' conversations in his poetry. I think of the closing lines of Bronk's poem "That Beauty Still":

There are distant people nearby and, not for them,
but in their presence we feel the force of desire.
Confused, we turn to them and think it ours.

THE BODY OF THIS LIFE:

Certainly, in Bronk's presence we feel the force of desire—and perhaps that is what we seek in wanting to know more about his life, the way that one looks around a new lover's room for clues about a more intimate self unknown by others. But the confusion of desire can keep us from a more lasting relationship, as we mistake the desire for something knowable, something we can claim, as if to make of love something definite, personal. As Bronk put it in "Copan: Unwillingness, The Unwilled," "the attempt to put personal desires in place of the general want which we feel, is a simplification, and makes the problem of desire appear to be something we could hope to solve" (VSC 41). Looking for a knowable William Bronk might similarly be an attempt to control the "problem of desire."

If we are to follow the life of the poetry, then, our triangulated relation with Bronk must inevitably be one of tension and desire, of distance and intimacy. In an exchange between two who knew something about both tension and intimacy, Bronk wrote to Corman, "There are people in the world and if I assume that I speak for them by virtue of speaking only for myself it is because of the conjunction of two conditions:

1) we are encapsulated and remote from each other
2) We are interchangeable if not identical though we may appear different in different lights." (Corman 22-23)

The tension between these two statements is the tension central to the life of the poems, for the life of the poems and the life of the poet are similarly "encapsulated and remote from each other," and similarly "interchangeable." Corman suggested to Bronk that he should extend his range, write about other things. In wanting to write about Bronk's life, we similarly look to write about other things—perhaps as part of that old scholarly drive to find something new to say. After all, how many essays can one write in which one notes Bronk's distinction between human perceptions of the world and what Bronk called a "real" world that is always beyond those perceptions, a reality that both invites and frustrates comprehension? But the tension of being both remote and interchangeable is, in fact, my only theme in trying to approach Bronk's work—that feeling I had when I first discovered his work and thought it spoke for me.

In my experience, to live with that tension is to become aware of a reality of which both lives—of the poet and of the reader—are a part. Again, in "Copan: Unwillingness, The Unwilled," Bronk asserts,

> There is something which is and we are not separable from it. Then, if we want something, it is something wanted through us; we are the instrumentality of a desire which it would not be quite accurate to call external because we are part of the wanting, but neither is it right to think it personal. If something is wanted, we feel the want but we are not apart in wanting it. It is always tempting though to transmute the something wanting into personal terms, to look for, or even to find, our own satisfactions as though that were what was wanted, as it proves not to be. At any rate, our personal satisfactions, once had, often seem nothing; whatever it was that was wanted, it wasn't that, and we are puzzled by trophies that seem to have been won by someone we don't even remember. (*VSC* 40-41)

In looking for Bronk, we are likely to find a trophy life, something transmuted into personal terms, something nearly, enticingly satisfying—and something that, if we are attentive to the reality indicated by "the direction and force" of Bronk' s poetry of statements, ultimately "proves not to be."

Of course, the statements of the poems themselves suggest a biography, presenting, as they do, moments in a kind of narrative—more often, an antinarrative—of Bronk's life. But it is a crowded narrative, and a decentered one. The Bronk we seek to find is always a Bronk-in-relation—in relation to, say, Cid Corman, to Sidney Cox, to the reader, to the poems. Of course, there are moments when the poems seem to give us something so plainly and commonly autobiographical that it would be foolish to ignore it. For example, in a 1961 letter to Corman, Bronk asserted, "I am the instrument of the world's passion if I am anything at all" (Corman 22). That letter became a poem, "Of the All With Which We Coexist." Certainly, here we find one of the many direct connections between the life of William Bronk and the life of his poetry. The tensions between Corman and Bronk became the poem's statement of desire. And it is tempting to hold to these connections, as if to catalogue those moments of correspondence or intersections of life and art. But to do so is to miss the point, the desire, the passion suggested by the instrumentality. We miss the reminder of "Still Life," a poem presented in the past tense:

> Like a camera I was for the world.
> Always, it was taking thousands of shots
> of itself—different lights, different days.
> When I am lost or broken that's what it will have. (*AWWL* 114)

To focus on the moments of correspondence or intersections between life and art is to admire the instrumentality of the camera—certainly, something admirable. But the value of the camera is in what it does, not what it is. We can, of course, study the camera, and wonder what it might take to build such a camera, and we can study the snapshots, the poems themselves, for the world they indicate; but I think the real goal is to avoid the would-be tourist's reflections on the snapshots, and to think of the life one must live if one is to live in the world that the snapshots can only suggest. Bronk's was a life of response, of reception—and the particularity of reception is what the poems reveal, moments of near contact, of instrumentality.

The society of the poems is not a society formed from the resolution of tension, the bridging of distances; it is a society of tensions, of unsatisfied desire. In "Otherness," Bronk suggests that "stories of love are made up to use / love to make a story, not for love" (*AWWL* 125). The stories we make can only lead us away from the life we would know. The life of the poems can only be told in the language the poems provide, shaped by and resistant to our individual relations with the poems. As Bronk wrote, art develops its own language, and "there isn't anyone who is capable of translating that most accurate of languages into any other" (*VSC* 55).

Bronk writes this at the beginning of *The Brother in Elysium,* in his "Epistle Dedicatory to Sidney Cox, among many," and I think that there is something to be learned about biography in that book, a book that addresses the lives of three writers, and a book also that was written in part as a response to the different approaches to art that Bronk encountered at Dartmouth and Harvard. Bronk explained to Cox, and to his eavesdropping readers, "I have wanted to write a kind of essential drama, in which each of the three characters comes on the matter at hand by his own word and deed, and so reveals himself and his subject" (*VSC* 55). Bronk invites their presence, tries to be attentive to the languages of their art, looks to enter into society with three men long since dead, dedicates the book to one who was central to Bronk's creative life. "If my book makes any statement," Bronk asserts, "it must be by the relationships that are revealed, by its composition, by a form brought about to the perceptive reader, by that element which is in every line and in no single one" (*VSC* 55). The resulting book is as much about Bronk as about Thoreau, Whitman, and Melville, an autobiography of the self-in-relation.

Bronk's writing was all autobiography, a life story lost when translated into the terms of biography. One might apply to biography what Bronk says of belief in "On *Credo Ut Intelligam*": "Belief, which visas us our entry" into the real,

> comforts our incoherence, offers to teach
> some simple terms, the easy speech of the land
> as *time,* for one, in sequences, or *space,*
> as extensible, or any person *discrete*
> from any other, living a finite life,
> with *birth* and *death,* and something to build between. (*LS* 97)

The self-delusion of such translation was constantly Bronk's point. Confronted with the apparent fact of the finite life of William Bronk, we naturally want that life to survey for us "the reaches of ignorance." But the poems say otherwise. It is when we inhabit the poems, and fail to translate them into the easy speech of the land, that we become both

THE BODY OF THIS LIFE:

remote from and intimate with both Bronk and ourselves. If we find Bronk at all, we find him there.

What I admire about Bronk is that he never turned to other tasks, other themes. He willingly sacrificed the available life of the poet as public figure so as to maintain his relation with the life of the poems. "The being real," Bronk wrote, "is what is not possible / except as the mystery of what is real" (*AWWL* 82). Bronk didn't turn away from that mystery, nor did he glorify it. He simply lived there, or tried to. And here we are, in a different place, certainly, though still the same. And we are left mainly with the advice of the poem "How It Works (Or Doesn't)":

> The reader has to make it on his own.
> The writer isn't there to help him out.
> A work of art's an encounter somebody had.
> You'll know it when you meet it. Watch for it. (*AWWL* 27)

So we watch for such encounters, and if we have one we know what in Bronk's life is worth writing about. We can enter into the society of the poems, or we can invite the poems to other societies—where they will be, no doubt, pleasant guests. In my view, Bronk's poetry invites us to reimagine poetry, to reclaim it as a spiritual presence and a challenge. Bronk's poems call for love, for relation, for the awareness of distances, for the embracing of tensions—biographies that speak as much about us as about Bronk, life stories untold and untellable, or perhaps told but untranslatable. The Bronk we would know waits in the stubbornly private communication that becomes our life.

Paul Pines

Bronk's Paradox: or Trapping the Unicorn

Talk to me poem. As if we were all alone,
you are the one I listen for and to.
I don't need to speak. You speak for me.

— William Bronk

Invocation

HERE'S A MYSTERY KNOWN TO MEDIEVALISTS concerning the Unicorn: *it becomes invisible at the first sight of hunters in the wood.* Tapestries show that it is approachable only by the virgin Lady, who has no agenda, no claim on the creature she is drawn to without suspecting that its beauty and innocence mirror her own. Their relationship, one which marks the threshold between the visible and invisible worlds, embodies a numinosity that moved Medieval philosophers from St. Dionysius to Nicholas of Cusa to speculate on the nature of what they conceded could not be truly known. When William Bronk lay in Glens Falls Hospital recovering from pancreatitis, he asked if I'd heard of *The Cloud of Unknowing.* When he returned home, I brought over my copy. In the Gothic shadows of a steepled house surrounded by ancient trees, he nodded as he read the anonymous 12th-century author, recognizing in the text his own vision. The ubiquity of ignorance tempered by occasional eruptions of light were major themes of the last medieval philosopher, my friend, Sir Bill, a.k.a. The Unicorn of Pearl Street.

Enlarging the Landscape

I often sat in Bill's sun porch as he read in his stentorian voice while I found myself giving way to laughter. Take the poem "Foresight," delivered in a Jack Benny deadpan: "I lie in bed/ practicing dead; it may take some/ getting used to."

"Why do so few people get my jokes?" he'd asked.

It may have been a way of asking why so few people bought his books. I recall finding him hunched over a royalty statement that indicated a dozen books sold.

"Thank god I'm an amateur," he'd sigh.

Bill liked to separate himself from those whose livelihood and career ambition depended on literary efforts. Much of his daily life had nothing to do with writing. Almost every morning Bill walked to the Post Office on Main Street, then to McCann's pharmacy where he picked up his *New York Times* before leaving through the back door. Anyone who accompanied him knows something about the peculiar paradox of "Bill" the man vs. "Bronk" the poet. At every stop he exchanged nuggets of local gossip. People greeted him as Bill, the man who'd spent his life on Pearl Street and inherited the Coal & Lumber business by the railroad tracks. Few recognized Bronk the poet.

Bill liked to gossip about the locals. He knew the skeletons in every closet and spoke easily about generational patterns and fated genealogies. When Richard Elman, under the pen name of John Howland Spyker, used nuggets collected during his long friendship with Bill as the basis for his darkly humourous fiction, *Little Lives*, set in Washington County, Bill felt betrayed. Public use of private matters embarrassed him. There are still those who believe only Bill could have authored this book. But such stories were not the fare of his writing life. People and localities in themselves could not penetrate the "cloud of unknowing." Bronk the poet was not interested in human behavior, however exotic, for its own sake."

In spite of his self-proclaimed "amateur" status, a growing pile of literary correspondence littered the sun porch, some of it from those doing critical studies of his work. He enjoyed the attention. But his initial pleasure was often replaced by the wariness of a woodland creature alerted by a predator. Usually the hunter was one whom Bill had encouraged. Much to the bemusement of Bronk, who became invisible.

Bronk's invisibility was especially evident around the issue of "literary influences." Hunters bumped into each other stalking his affinities. Some compared him to Wallace Stevens or Robert Frost. Many tracked him to the watershed of Cid Corman's *Origin*. (This, after all, is how Pound taught us schools were made.) Others discussed his relationship with George Oppen, whose sister June co-published *The World, the Worldless*.

("She promised to make me famous if only I'd cooperate," recalled Bill.

"Look what she did for George," I said.

"Ah, yes. I never thought of that." He flashed his most fetching unicorn smile.)

But nobody sniffed out Reuel Denny, the obscure Yale Younger Poet whose Craneish verse Bill read by the coal stove while waiting for his bread to rise. *Listen to this,* he'd say, his voice quivering with the yeast of Denny's language.

Fleshing The Paradox

He was fond of saying: "*Our lives are fictions. We make fictions of our lives.*"

My excursions with Bill through Hudson Falls taught me that his position on this had to be understood in terms of his paradoxical nature. Bronk had ceased to be artistically attracted to these fictions *per se*, but was fascinated by the fact that we created them and, having done so, believed they were true. If "our fictions" were of limited importance to Bronk the poet, they were endlessly interesting to Bill the local observer. In time I came to see how Bronk the poet crept into the life of Bill the man, and Bill the man winked at me through the protocols of Bronk the poet.

Nevertheless, in an age shaped by confessional poetry, he declared that we misread subjective experience, suffered it as a collective delusion. As long as we believed we were the subjects of our sentences, even the vaguest apprehension of Unknowable Reality eluded us. There's nothing comforting here. It's a Buddhist situation with an Old Testament punchline. For Bronk, the proposition was compelling and moved him to embrace what others shunned.

"Something is living. It is not we," he stated in "The Plainest Narrative." The proposition is a paradox within a paradox: one who eschews narrative uses *the plainest narrative* to declare the subjective experience a false one by appealing to subjective, indeed, archetypally subjective experience.

"Is it wrong?" he asks. "Not wrong. Just that it isn't true./ No more than its opposite is true. That 'I'/ . . .were willed. . . ."

In "Canaletto's Venice," he compares Turner to Canaletto, painters whose differences are rooted in a singular affinity. Both recognize objects which appear solid as functions of light. Bill, like Turner, was dazzled by "the concentration of light." Bronk, like Canaletto, measured the landscape to "set it down 'the way it is.'" The poet's ability to have it both ways is a tribute to his cunning as an artist, and his recognition of a quantum universe in which chaos is revealed to be an unstable order of startling complexity: ". . . what some used to say they heard/ as music of the spheres . . . but they, as we,/resonate only as silence."

What reconciles the man and the poet is the Platonic *eros* Keats called "unheard music." Bill Bronk listened until the message became audible: "Voiceprint": *I overhear the poem talk to itself/ Is that what it said? I write it down to try.*

The Drift Of The World—

Bronk listened. Bill remained "in the drift of the world." Poems were temporary anchors. Even so, In a piece called "The World," he wrote:

I thought that you were an anchor in the drift of the world;
but no: there isn't an anchor anywhere.
There isn't an anchor in the drift of the world. Oh no . . .

Poems came at night, before sleep, or at dawn, in the afterglow of dreams. He'd wake to write what he heard in a composition book, or type it on the old Royal at the foot of his bed. The rest of the day followed a routine which allowed friends to drop in through doors that were never locked. If Bronk the poet rued his anchorless condition, Bill the man took pleasure in what washed up on his sun porch. An Englishman who'd published twelve books of poetry wrote that Bill was the first metaphysical poet since the 17th century and enclosed a cassette of his own poem, "Starting With A Line From Bronk."

"He also calls me 'the poet of sweet rigor,'" Bill observed.

A Boston-based Lithuanian requested a Bronk blurb. He'd first encountered Bronk's work in *Manifest; and Furthermore*, which he praised for its *irreverent impudence*.

"What do you think?" he asked.

"He never read it," I replied. "Are you going to blurb him?"

"Why not?" Bill shrugged. "It's journeyman work. I've seen worse."

I suggested he hail the Lithuanian's *impudent irreverence*.

Dr. Geisel, from Houston, sent Bill grapefruits and dirty jokes, which were prized more than literary obsequies. The crusty doctor, known for his dedicated treatment of over-heated venereal seamen, inspired in Bronk the *bonhomie* of "Good Friend": "In a room full of loud boasts he tells/me again some quiet jokes we used to hear."

Next to his art, Bronk placed a premium on friendship.

One sunny summer afternoon in the early 1970s a group of Hudson Falls High School students kicked a soccer ball from the woods bordering the house onto a picnic table set with food. Instead of yelling at them, Bill invited the boys to join his guests assembled on the lawn. The boys remained for lunch. And returned regularly to listen to Bill read his poems or eat homemade soup and Bronk bread. He was for them both a refuge and a portal. Three decades later many of them traveled to speak at his graveside. For a while they were for Bill (as he was for them) "an anchor in the drift of the world," though Bronk continued to deny such a *punto fijo*.

Bronk watched friends grow up or distant, while Bill continued to embrace them. Friends asked for help. He commented on their work, wrote publishers in support of them, gave them blurbs. One day I confessed despair about the fate of my work. He told me: "If I sent my poems out signed Joe Blow, no one would give them a second look."

There were moments when Bill despaired, too. But Bronk knew success did little to slow the drift of the world. After his friend Stephen Mitchell sold a translation of Lao Tzu to Random House for $130,000 he wrote: "For Stephen Mitchell," "The enlightened stumble and fall:/ no flashlights in the dark, blindly daytimes also."

Flushing The Unicorn

"We come to art expecting to find something else than we eventually do," he would shrug philosophically. "It's not what we expected. Poetry is a private thing between the writer and the page."

A grasp of the process that existed between Bronk and the page is crucial to understanding his poems. The way the poem got there was not merely private, but essentially mysterious and, often, haunted. A favorite metaphor compares the poet to a house (like his own) inhabited by a ghostly tenant. Another links dreamlife to backstage props and pulleys, whose effects we accept as real from our seats in the waking world. The rational mind, he wrote, is a placebo we believe in ". . . well beyond the limit of its application."

Here he locates the conundrum central to medieval philosophy: *credo ut intelligam.* Cusanus concluded in the 15th Century that there was no understanding without belief. Bronk finds both belief and reason among the fictions we create to sustain the illusion that we are the authors of our acts and that these are of some importance. Advancing the discourse, he concludes that the world lives us. We are the unwitting vocabulary of *its* intentions, not our own. A deceptively simple proposition, there seems to be something in it for everyone: the Buddha's *shinyatta,* Hindu *samsara,* Christian *via negativa* and dark night of the soul, epistemological ambiguity, transpersonal psychology's non-discursive consciousness, existential post-modernism, the implicate order of theoretical physics, and a revisioning of Jungian archetypal ground. If these can be read into his work, so can their refutations.

Bill never said, "If you see Buddha on the road, kill him." He did say, "I envy, more than honor, those of a mind/ to invent a grounded scheme," and entitled the poem "Enticement." The reality of the self is as unknowable as the reality which contains it. Unlike Buddha's response to impermanence, Bronk advances neither system nor anti-system.

Discussing *Job*, I once asked him if the voice that gave him his poems was not the voice from the whirlwind, the unheard nightingale, transcendence.

"It's what we know of it," he nodded. "We've no direct apprehension of it through reason. We know it in suffering, in exaltation, in wonder."

But couldn't we draw from it some foundational knowledge?

"Every culture posits an all powerful force that has answers to our condition, the knowledge that can eliminate suffering. I don't believe it. Suffering is real. We suffer because there's suffering. We don't know the answer. Even Reality may not in the sense we mean 'to know.'"

Only the voice could penetrate unknowing, the voice which came to him in suffering, wonder and exaltation to deliver his poems.

Engaging The Unicorn: Paradox And Process

Observing Bill's devotion to the voice, it seems callow to ascribe external influences of substance or style to his work. One might as easily cite the laconic speech patterns of Washington County, NY, or his affinity to Nezahualcoyotl as invoke Frost, Stevens, or Oppen. Bill's process was too *inner* to be so ascribed. His poems leaped from latent consciousness into the light like the manta in "A Fish Mosaic In The First Basilica In Porec":

> Or for all that, I don't know much about
> the manta, the giant ray; but I have seen
> this hoverer, this wide reacher, this sky,
> horizon stretcher, waverer above
> and under, bottom plunger, swimming wing,

THE BODY OF THIS LIFE:

this leaper! I should use him. I have seen
him leaping, the top torn from the sea and the sea,
high, holding, a wide sail set
and snapping in no wind, its own wind.

This is Bronk's description of the invisible erupting into the visible
world, the voice from under tearing the top from the sea to stretch the
horizon. In telling us he'd prefer the manta to some more familiar fish as
a symbol on his basilica, he claims it for himself, lets us know that he's a
poet "snapping in no wind" but his own.

And what a wind it was!

While images like the manta leap from his pages, he cleaves as often
to gnomic statement or simple narrative. Metaphor is fundamental
because, as Nicholas of Cusa puts it, "the quiddity of things, which is the
truth of beings, is unattainable in all its purity." The poems are them-
selves metaphors for incompletion qualified by the process through
which they came to light, the mantic voice "flapping in its own wind."
Here is the central paradox of Bronk's work: *statements about the
indifference of Unknowable Reality rise from its embrace.* To be sur-
rounded by the voice that spoke to Job, to hear it through suffering,
wonder and exaltation, is to be a chosen one.

Sir Bill admits as much in the latest publication of his work, *Lines &
Smudges*, by his long time friend and publisher, James Weil. But the title,
"Conceding," is pure Bronk:

We discover the story that life's been telling us
all along is a story about life, not us.
The story is interesting and probably
important.
      It's been a privilege to hear.

The Unicorn can't be trapped. It remains visible only to the Lady whose uncompromised devotion allows her to draw near. Jung might call her *anima*, or soul function. She bridges the known and unknown, visible and invisible. Through her, the immeasurable slips into the mundane. It was she for whom he listened. His poems were her "voiceprints." She was his best beloved. The legend on her tent reads, *"To my only desire."*

After reading a poem that used the building of a cathedral as a metaphor for the numinous aspect of human creativity, Bronk offered this disclaimer: "We think we do these things. Just because we draw the plans and execute them, we believe we have built the cathedrals. We don't! Something uses us to do these things and we don't know what it is."

Pound, looking back at the edifice of his work, asked us to forgive what he had made. For Bronk, there was no master plan, no grand, Canto-like structural intention. His cathedral emerged as evidence of his devotion to a voice that allowed the Unknowable to tell its story through him.

Warming a pot of homemade lentil soup on the coal stove, Bill once spoke to me about himself and his work in a way that, unlike Pound, seemed genuinely reconciled. If it survived, he said, all well and good. If not, it didn't matter. We thought things important that really were not.

"Even the Holocaust. As much as I hate to say it, didn't matter. No more than the hundred-thousand dead in the Middle East, or starving in the Sudan. No more than the thousands killed by Stalin. We just don't matter in the larger scheme of things." Then he went on to slurp his soup as he always did, with gusto.

In the early days of our friendship, we talked about a life devoted to a voice that came and went like "the wind that bloweth where it listeth." In those days, he lived in fear the voice would abandon him. "It's gone," he'd say. Or, "It's back." When it left him, he became listless, silent, depressed. But later, he'd pull out a folder and read a group of new poems. After his nearly fatal bout with pancreatitis, he stopped worrying that the voice might abandon him. It never did. A last poem was found by his bedside the night he died. It read:

> *Art isn't made, it's in the world almost*
> *unseen but found existent there. We paint*
> *we score the sound in music, we write it down.*

Daniel Wolff

A Guide to Death

T|HAT'S FUNNY. The part about you dying, I mean. Did you figure I might stop writing to you after that? Oh, I think not.

After all, you left this trail of poems behind. When poets die, it's no different than anyone else (or as different, I suppose), except they've probably written about it—you did, anyway—and that means we have what amounts to a guide: a guide to death.

I want to try to talk about that without going into your life too much. We knew each other, what? Fifteen years. Long enough for me to hear you bark about privacy. About friends, for example, using your letters to analyze your work. You didn't like it when they stepped over the line that separates. . . . I wanted to say the personal from the public, but you obviously used the personal in your writing. You have poems about your house, your friends, your hometown. But they were a means to an end, a metaphor. You barked when people stepped over *that* line, mistaking the man for the work.

So, I'll just cover the basics. The name you were given: William Bronk. Where you lived: Hudson Falls, upstate New York. Your father ran a lumber and supply business, which you took over after he died. (I remember you saying that, while the business meant nothing to you, really, the act of running it may have affected the voice in your poems. They have the sound of someone who's been in what you would laughingly call "the real world.") Anyway, the family bought a house—big, pretty Victorian house—on a nice, elm-lined piece of property in Hudson Falls. That happened when you were two years old. And you basically lived in that house until you died, this past February, 1999.

Enough of that. The first book of poetry, *Light and Dark,* came out in 1956, when you were thirty-eight. You dedicate a long one (anything over a dozen lines was long for you) to that English teacher you liked so much at Dartmouth. There you are, in your thirties, already on the subject: "The Arts and Death: A Fugue for Sidney Cox."

Death dominates my mind. I
do not stop thinking how time will stop,
how time has stopped, does stop. . . .

I don't know if I believe that: believe that death can be so all-consuming at such a relatively young age But I don't have to believe it. I just have to ask why you wrote it and what you meant by saying "time has stopped." We all know it does and will. But do you mean it already has stopped for others? Or, that knowing it will stop and having that fact dominate your mind means, in a sense, that it already has? Death is right there: always in the way. Towards the end of the poem, your reaction is to start speaking directly to the world. (You wrote that way a lot. A kind of interior monologue, but not really. As if talking to the next door neighbor. Or a tree. Or someone who's dead.)

. . . World, world, I am scared
and waver in awe before the wilderness
of raw consciousness, because it is all
dark and formlessness: and it is real
this passion that we feel for forms. But the forms
are never real. Are not really there. Are not.

I should get this right—and early—because you keep coming back to it. The fear surprises me a little. I don't see that much in the later work, but it makes sense. It's the emptiness—what you call the wilderness—that scares you: the great unending rawness of it all. "We live in a world we never understand," you say in the poem's second to last line, and that's the unavoidable, unchanging, and frightening fact The passion we have to fix that feeling—to have form—that passion is real. But the forms we come up with never are. As soon as we think we've made sense out of the world—given it shape—that, too, dissolves. So the final line, the last note of your fugue, reads: "Our lives end nothing. Oh there is never an end."

In a backwards way, aren't you talking about what continues after death? I don't really get it, but I don't feel too bad about that, because I don't think you "got it," either. Or, if you got it, you spent another forty years getting it better.

You called your third book of poetry, *The Empty Hands*. The title comes from a poem called "The Smile On the Face of a Kouros." I assume that's a reference to "Ode on a Grecian Urn," where Keats sees the urn's painted figures and decides, famously, all we need to know is that beauty is truth, truth beauty. What you see on your kouros is a painted boy, approaching death with his strength and virtue intact: "the prize with which// his empty hands are full." But not so fast! Because you also say that there is no—can be no—form ". . . forever beautiful and whole." Not in a formless world. Classic beauty is (you don't say this, but I think you're just being polite) a fake. So, you turn, and you start one of those dialogues, again, this time directly with death. I can picture you doing it, the light flashing off your glasses as you raise your deep voice:

I tell you, death, expect no smiles of pride
from me. I bring you nothing in my empty hands.

The same way you aren't actually talking to death (I mean "actually"), it seems to me you aren't talking about death, either. Death isn't the question; it's a way into the question.

For example, you wrote a poem called "The Elms Dying—and My Friend, Lew Stillwell Dead." You were approaching fifty—the age I am, now—a time when friends and family start to die. That's the subject, but you see past the death (or, into it, maybe). I can still hear the fear, but it's gone through some change, as if you've caught it and held it and looked it over:

. . . the riches of the world are infinite and it
is prodigal. What is terrible is

—not any death diminishes the world.

What is terrible is, in your own words, the "raw consciousness" goes on and on. In the last lines of the poem, you cry out, but it's a more controlled cry, now. No less fearful, maybe, but riding the fear, only raising your voice so much.

> . . . Always. We have it. That there is no
> diminishment. Never. Nothing. Help us. Help!

I read those lines, and part of me is convinced they aren't poetry at all. "Never. Nothing. Help us. Help!" doesn't sound like poetry. It sounds like something you'd say to yourself, in solitude, walking around the big house, expecting no one to hear you. Plainspoken, it sounds simply like the truth. And unless that *is* beauty. . . .

I'm teasing a little. But out of admiration. Because the sound of the poem corresponds so neatly with what it's doing. The straight forward words convey a straight forward gaze. It makes me think of that flat, gorgeous, upstate light that you wrote about. And the straight forward gaze is to determine whether the world, or your friend, or death itself actually exists.

You had an Uncle Will, right? That's a dumb question; sorry. In the poem by that name, you have him gardening right up to the end, past when he could manage to eat what he grew. But the growing, you say, is:

> . . . the choicest fraud we know:
> whatever we mean by growing, whatever it makes
> a symbol of for us. . . .

There's something almost mean about that. Pointed, anyway. As if to say we can't help but be frauds—make metaphors we know aren't real—because we need some way of holding back the emptiness. And then comes the end of the poem, where I picture you mimicking the local accent—mimicking your own, flat, Hudson Falls accent:

He kept a cat would eat cooked corn
and raw tomatoes. In May he fixed the first
asparagus for it, which only shows we find
someone or something to seem to do what we can't.
The last I know, the cat was still alive

I love the punch line. And it's the same joke, isn't it? We find forms
to fill the formless world, and it's that passion that survives, prowling the
overgrown garden.

I don't know who you thought you were fooling with that "aw
shucks" voice. Except maybe . . . . What more glaring example of trying
to put structure to the world than a poem? If you write it so it doesn't
sound like poetry, maybe it sneaks in there, fixing an unfixable moment
before it disappears.

By the time you get to the one called "For Peter Kaldheim," your style
has gotten even plainer, even more declarative. "Look, we die," you say.
Point blank, like that. Of course, from there, you go on:

Well, we live and whatever way we live
it happens
                    —a result perhaps, but anyway,
it happens:
                    and nothing changed. Result the same.
So no result . . .

It—life and death—happens. If I apply those words not abstractly
but directly to the fact of your death, they seem cold blooded. "Nothing
changed." Is that right? I drove by your house a few weeks ago. There's
a "For Sale" sign out front. So, that's changed.

"Result the same. // So no result" seems unfeeling. At the same time,
I can read it as the opposite: actual feeling instead of how we're taught to
react. You wrote a poem when you were in your sixties called "Igno-
rance." It reads in its entirety:

I am concerned about our deaths as we all are.

There may be a real world (as I think there is)
of which we know as little as we do of our lives.
We don't know our deaths are not in that world.

Parse that! (Oh, and please pardon me: I know you can't paraphrase
or explain the poem any more than you can the world, but you can take
it apart and turn it over and try to figure out what's ticking. That is, if
the light's good enough.) You say you're "concerned" about death, but
you say it in such a distant voice. Then, you commit an act of faith: you
declare your belief in a real world which we can't know. And there is the
possibility, if I read the double negatives of the last line correctly, that
our deaths are in that world. Not our lives, mind you—the one thing we
do know is they aren't "real"—but our deaths. Isn't it that which in-
trigues you? Which explains your slightly chilly concern? The possibility
that death might be real.

They collected what you'd written so far in *Lift Supports,* which
came out in 1981 and won the American Book Award. (Not that we care
about such fleeting rewards, right?) You added some new poems, too,
that push forward this whole equation. "Reality Not Described" begins
with one of your flat declarations:

Death is to remind us how temporal
we are.

Fine. But then comes the almost laconic rebuttal: "Well, maybe not.
. . ." And we're off

. . . death says no matter what we think
it may not be what is thought: we only do
it for a little while whether we do it or not.

I counted: that's three lines with not a word over two syllables. So,
how come it's so hard to have them settle down and make meaning?
There's this rattle as they keep bouncing against each other. Turns out to
be the negatives: it's not easy thinking in terms of what things aren't. In

the end, all you can rely on is that "it" only lasts "a little while." Death is the great spokesperson for that.

There's something funny about all of this. Or, anyway, you're almost always funny about it. Like the jokes soldiers tell on the way into combat. For example, if this real world isn't, then, when we try to discover where we are:

> . . . we don't come back
> with the grids and reference points, the altitudes.
> We go over the edge of the world and disappear.

Boom! Like the end of some silent comedy. Only thinking about it, later, does it occur to me that this disappearance might be death. And as I picture us sliding over the flat edge of the round world, it *still* makes me smile.

In your sixties, you start writing more love poems. Which might seem odd (I've made you out as such a sober chronicler of death and dying), but it comes as a logical extension of these logical constructs. "Mortal Loves" actually explains the phenomenon of love (kind of) in terms of death:

> My last elm is gone and I had many.
> Oh, there are seedlings: little trees come up
> and live for a while as though they expected life
> to last forever. Well, it doesn't—at least
> not theirs. Or ours either. I
> don't think it will nor do I want it to.
> Love acknowledges it lives in time.

Here's where I need to go past the personal. I picture your "real" house, and those real elm trees that you grew up with and which are now dying. To love is to acknowledge such things happen. So, to not love (I'm using your ax, here: thinking in negatives) would be to expect to live forever. It seems to me you're at least implying that eternal beauty—that old classic—represents a kind of hatred of this world where things, by nature, perish. You don't say you want that to happen; you *do* say you don't want life to last forever.

I guess it's not surprising that the end of life begins to play a larger and larger role in the collection of poems that includes "Mortal Loves." You were, after all, almost seventy when they were published. So, "Foresight," in its entirety, reads:

I lie in bed
practicing dead;
it may take some
getting used to.

If you believe this is poetry (and I do), then the formal aspect of a poem and a joke have a lot in common. It has to do with the build-up and the surprise twist at the end. The joke (or poem) is that we think we know what's coming, and we don't. And we do! Look how this little four-line thing teeters between matter-of-fact and profound. I read it as a kind of take-off on those aphorisms—"Home Sweet Home"—that people put into needlework. Imagine "Foresight" stitched on linen and hung in the master bedroom. What did the classical painters call it: *memento mori?*

The book you published in your seventy-first year is called, simply enough, *Death Is the Place*. The title comes from a three-line poem, "The Time Observed," which seems to me to reverse the logic we've seen so far. So far, you used death to prove that we live in a world we can't understand. Here, isn't life used as proof that death exists?

Death is the place I want to go to
again. Not now. Not yet awhile. But I'm sure
it's there. The days and nights observe this.

The days and nights convince you that death is the place. Which I understand as a metaphor: that the longer one lives, the clearer it becomes that all this leads to death. Love, as you said, acknowledges this, and you even sound eager to get there, although "not now," thanks. But what gets me is when you say you want to go "again." I'd like you to explain that. When were you ever at the place called Death that you want to go again? It sounds like we're born from a place that we die back into—with this confusion in-between. That's a pretty mystical set-up for such a logical man. The closest I can get is to picture you sitting in your kitchen. On your beloved coal-burning stove is a tea-pot full of water. You're in a straight-back chair, waiting for the pot to boil, knowing it will because you've seen it happen before.

In "Elder Brother," death is the brother, "born again with each of us," and your language goes a little Victorian with the conceit: a tongue-in-cheek nod to the poetic tradition you're almost following? This isn't exactly John Donne, but, for a poet who's told us metaphor is fraud, a change of voice seems in order when you start addressing death as "the one immortal."

> . . . old
> already, older than anything and death
> will be chief of mourners to mourn our dying, death
> is our guide and we quarrel and argue against him but thin
> the life without his ready company.

Death is the guide to what? To that other, real world, wherever and whatever that is? Or to this world, where friends and elm trees pass, where we simply go till we fall off the edge? I think that's more likely. Our guide, then, is here to show us just how lost we are.

"It is important that we die," you say in a poem published a couple of years later, "only to show its unimportance." Is it unfair of me to say that sounds like whistling through the graveyard? Maybe that's my reaction, not yours. Take the three-line poem, "Surmise," (which I think of as a kind of sister to the one about lying in bed "practicing dead")

> Horizontal doesn't matter, it
> will drain out through my feet and I'll lie
> there, empty bottle with no deposit to collect.

The Body of This Life:

Now, there's a comprehensible, manageable event, apparently without any vestiges of fear or even bother. Although I would have thought that if death is the place where you go *again*, then there is a return policy.

It's still funny, except by 1994, when the book called *Our Selves* is published, you're seventy-six, and there isn't just death to be faced; there's also sickness. So that, in "Caller," you've gotten a little angry at the joke—or, more accurately, angry at Death, the stand-up comic, who keeps extending the build-up to the punch-line you know is coming

> So laugh, comedian, it wasn't you
> again as I half believed it might be. . . .
> It's not funny you send somebody else.

But if you've gotten tired of the preliminaries, you still seem ready for it to arrive. In another poem from the same book:

> I'm for you, death, you have a right one
> when you come at me. Neither eager, we'll know
> on sight the other and meet without surprise.. . .

That, in another era or with another poet, might be called getting ready to meet your Maker. But I don't think of you as preparing to meet death. Or not in the traditional sense. Because that supposes a way of looking at the world which your whole body of work argues against. That supposes a definition of "self" and "death" which you don't buy. Instead, there's the dense logic of the three-line "Self Destruction," with its one-syllable words and all its echoes:

> The life that doesn't die when self dies
> is all the life self ever had
> and all the self it had was in that life.

How do you get ready for that?

You'll forgive me if I go slowly here. we're coming to the end. Something doesn't die when we do: you seem sure of that. You, who have been mostly sure that we couldn't be sure of anything. And the thing that doesn't die is all we ever had. The soul? Again, the traditional term doesn't quite apply. It's too . . . noble. Too embellished with meanings. Metaphysical as all this sounds, you steer clear of that vocabulary. You don't characterize "all the life self ever had" as beautiful or corrupt or holy. No, I think *we* do that. Out of habit We're used to thinking of anything that doesn't die as automatically majestic or, at least, special. Maybe one of the reasons you keep going back over this is to try to break that habit. In us and in you. Certainly, I could read these poems as saying that what continues after we die is simply the stuff we never understood. You're not crying "Help," anymore Aren't you saying, quietly enough, that what's left after we wrestle for meaning is not meaning but whatever we wrestled with?

We have arrived at *The Cage of Age*. The title poem of the collection is this brief and beautiful rumination:

> In the cage of age
> days are slow
> nights the same
> it's all been
> it won't end.

Which is not that much of a shift from the fugue you wrote forty years earlier. But you never claimed variety was the spice of anything. The issues remain; the poems change some but are always circling the same area. At one point, in "Testamentary Statement," you poke fun at yourself for that, for the repetition and the constant monitoring:

> I have watched the world get to where
> it could get along without me. I'm pretty proud
> as if it couldn't always have. I think
> I'm going to leave it everything I've got.

There's the slip on the banana peel, the grin on the death mask! If it strikes me as brave, it doesn't seem to have struck you that way. Bravery wouldn't seem to enter into it, not when a life is—as you call one poem—"Visitor's Day at the World." "I spend my time here;" you say in your best tourist voice, "isn't it beautiful!" Still joking and, still, the jokes all serious.

That tone runs right into the last book you finished, *All of What We Loved*. There's one in there called "Occupation Therapy," which reads in its entirety:

If someone asks you
what it is we do
just say we die.

The joke is in the brevity: of the poem and of the life. If that's your attitude towards dying, how can there be such a thing as grief? It feels almost like a betrayal of the poems to be sad that you're gone. It is, after all, just the emptying of a container, just a "For Sale" sign in front of an old house. At the same time, in "Laura Gone," when you write about the death of someone you loved, I hear you rising up through grief to defiance.

Death contradicts. Beyond its "NO",
its tone says further, "You never had a life."
What life we thought was life wasn't death's to kill.
Impostor death, you are illusion, too.

With a roar, you gather in what you've had. Death is an impostor, and I can read that two ways. Since we never really understood the life we lived, death can't affect it. It's a figment we created and, so, is both inaccurate and untouchable. And/or, death has missed the "real" action: the life which we always knew was beyond our incomprehensible one. Either way, death ends up an illusion. Which is a backhanded way into eternity, but it does get you there. I think I should say it gets you and Laura there.

In one of your last investigations of this thing that comes at the end of the thing we call life, you use the container metaphor, again, but with a variation that the title underlines, "The Coupling":

It's only me as life and itself as death.
No one is watching us. We agree we aren't
antagonists and needn't pretend to be.
Each is a glass the other is drinking from.
No need either to hurry. The bottle will last.

I picture you in the living room (and have to laugh a little at that name), alone and still in that big house. Laura gone, and, out front, the elms gone, too. You are sitting down with death, and you're engaged in an impossible coupling: mouth to mouth, is it? Drinking from each other. But drinking *of* something else, something beyond definition, except to say that it will last.

Can I leave it there? Of course not. Not quite. Since the poems have told us again and again that this isn't about "you" or "me," it only seems fair that the work itself should get the last word, uninterrupted and un-interpreted. After all, if we don't get it by now. . . .

The poem is called "In Pacem." It reads, in its entirety:

Sing me no requiem.
Sing us one.
Celebrate loss.
Not ours.

Michael Perkins

THIS WAS A MASTER SPIRIT

WILLIAM BRONK LIVED IN THE SAME HOUSE IN HUDSON FALLS in the North Country of New York for most of the twentieth century. His faith in his work was so strong that although he traveled widely, he felt no need to take part in the literary life of Manhattan. This faith gave him great independence. The world came to him, and he received its callers with open arms.

Bill's Civil War-era house on Pearl Street was never locked. It was newly-painted when I first visited over twenty years ago, and I found it quite notable. For me it is impossible to think of Bill without thinking of his house, his great lawn, his street, his village, and his county. This was his world, which I stepped into for a week or so every season in the years that followed.

Entering by the side door on the driveway, I often found Bill facing me, standing at a counter kneading bread in a 1930s kitchen featuring an antique refrigerator and an Aga coal stove with soup bubbling on it. We would embrace and sit down to lunch, resuming our talk where it had broken off on my previous visit. Afterwards we sat in his sun room amid a clutter of potted plants, art works, and piles of chapbooks, manuscripts and books by friends. He showed me his correspondence, and caught me up on news about his many friends.

After he napped—on the same worn living room couch where he died—we would go for a long walk along the canal that ran near his house, out into open farmland, with the Green Mountains on the horizon. He loved the summer light and the natural world, and he was an indefatigable explorer of Washington County hills and thickets and railroad tracks. We swam naked in the canal at "Bronk's Beach," where we once were graced with the sight of a Great Blue Heron lifting heavily into flight.

Because he was the most important man in my life—first as a father figure, then as a mentor and intimate friend—I made notes of many of our conversations in my diaries. Similarly, Sidney Cox, Bronk's Dartmouth teacher and mentor, was the most important man in *his* life.

"I lived for Sunday evenings at Sidney Cox's house. I think I loved Sidney Cox more than any man in my life." (Bill was a very loving man, which was why his cry from the heart, "Sometimes I wonder if I've ever loved anyone," a month before his death, was so surprising.)

I was present when Robert Ross, a Dartmouth classmate and English teacher there, came to interview Bill. Bill had been hurt by Dartmouth, but he was polite. Ross asked him about influences. None of the names or currents of thought cited in essays about his work were confirmed in his responses. He wasn't a Buddhist, nor an existentialist. He didn't know the Vienna Circle. He laughed at post modernism in all its guises; he scorned the deconstructionists. He didn't read poetry in translation. He said he "couldn't read" Pound or Williams ("What are they talking about?") He dismissed the work of his old correspondent, Olson.

"My first influence was Conrad Aiken. I drew a twenty-five cent pamphlet of poems by him at random from a bunch offered us in high school English class. Oh, Auden and Frost, of course, and Stevens—but I'm not Stevens! I envied Samuel French Morse. I think perhaps my favorite poet was Reuel Denny."

The name of Dartmouth grandee Richard Eberhardt came up.

"He's my *least* favorite."

I pressed him about translations, feeling that he missed much by avoiding them.

"Language is not only the vehicle of feeling but its subject," he replied.

Spiritual influences? "I'm a religious poet, though not formally anything. I love *The Book Of Common Prayer* and *The Cloud of Unknowing*. I'm not a negative poet. I just write what is. No matter what is said, I say 'even so, but. . . .' What critics don't understand is that my ideas are not as important as the feeling I create—my ability to move the reader."

After dinner we sat in the parlor and he read his work, in his rumbling, expressive North Country voice. Hearing him read aloud was to hear him explicate his poems—and to experience his ability to move his listeners. But he also read aloud the stories of Thomas Mann, other poets, and his favorite obscure novelist, Thomas Hal Phillips. He loved to gossip, and one lazy summer afternoon, outdoors after a picnic, he entertained us by reading passages from the sun king of gossips, Saint-Simon. To him, the greatest writers were Shakespeare and Proust.

When I learned of Bill's death, I didn't turn at first to his poems for solace, but to his letters. The poems were in my head, every one of them, in Bill's voice. But his brief letters, written in a tightly elegant hand, full of wit, weather, opinions about the literary life, and unpublished poems, are a more personal consolation. They are warm with the passionate sweetness of his soul. Bill's first letter to me arrived in 1969, the year I offered to become his publisher after reading *The World, The Worldless*. (He thanked me, but James Weil had claimed that privilege.)

26 May 78
"This is the ruling theme of *The Force of Desire*: that the desire we feel is neither ours nor for its objects—its apparent objects."

6 Oct 79
"I feel very molted and soft-shelled and look sideways as if at some exoskeleton I would like to walk away from. Like the crabs, we end up with the same shell again—a slightly different size but no real change. But I hanker for the wholly unlikely boon of a new name and zip code. Why does reality have to be 12839?"

12 March 79
"Traditionally, we have approached a person's life and nature by way of historical narrative as though we could know it that way. I wonder if this is ever so."

3 March 80
"Ross Feld says, 'I gave a copy of *The Empty Hands* to Philip Guston, the painter; he became so excited after reading it that he wanted that weekend to make an expedition from his house in Woodstock to yours, to meet you.'"

24 Oct 80
"I read proof for the Collected. It was a strange experience: as though someone else had written them and I don't know who he is. I only faintly get an idea of him. And, of course, this was true as early as when I wrote *My Father Photographed*. Still unsure who sits there. . . ."

14 Feb 81
"I am always ready to believe in darkness and despair. I need the sun and my friends to show me the light that isn't in me. Your shining restores me."

16 April 81
"In the last few days I have had copies of *Paideuma*, *Credences* and *Text*. . . . My two theater poems were in *Credences*. What was I doing there? I'm in the wrong house. No place else to go but who can I talk to at this party? About what?"

18 June 81
"I am pleased that you want to write about me. I'm like the cook who has cooked a big dinner and is more interested in having other people eat and enjoy than in eating myself or, I feel, with the collected coming out, like a crab swimming blithely in naked freedom from his old shell. I've shed it; it hasn't anything to do with me anymore. Or, maybe like the child just off the potty looking at the turd with pride and pleasure before going off to play elsewhere, dismissing it. Write about the turd not the child. Time enough to write about him when you outlive me. Neither of us knows much about the child anyway."

29 July 81
"We live in cages. Are there any free men?"

4 March 81
"The (slight) satisfactions of recognition that it seems to you *Life Supports* must be rolling up make me realize how much I have inwardly wanted them for a long time and also how trashy they are and how wrong to want them. I resist regretfully; we do not want trashy things even in the face of the real satisfactions which are the work itself and the love and response it brings from Michael Perkins and a handful of others. Fuck the prizes and the public regard of people who couldn't be bothered to read the work or care about it. What good is praise—if that's what it was—from Hayden Carruth who doesn't know what I'm talking about in the *NYT* which doesn't care. And how should I not want it?"

* * *

William Bronk was a major poet whose work will find its rightful place in the great tradition of English and American poetry. The work was what he cared about, and what he wanted others to care about. "It's all out there," he would say. "It will either survive or not. Who I am is not important."

Of course he's right. He almost always was. But I think it is worth noting that in my experience of him he was not only a great poet, he was also a great man, a fully realized human being. This was a master spirit.

Burt Kimmelman

"ART AS A WAY": ABSENCE AND PRESENCE, AESTHETICS AND FRIENDSHIP IN THE WILLIAM BRONK–ROBERT MEYER CORRESPONDENCE

WILLIAM BRONK AND ROBERT MEYER CAME TO REALIZE the significance of their correspondence over the course of some thirty years; they even planned for both sides of it to reside in the same archive.[*] Hundreds of letters passed between Bronk and Meyer, a German Jew who fled nazism to settle in Manhattan as a school teacher, which attest an important insight into the nature of artistic expression—one they developed together, to a considerable degree. This insight helps to comprehend Bronk's overall notions of beauty and form, and most of all his poetics, and leads inexorably toward Bronk's final poem, discovered by his side in death, which begins, "Art isn't made; it's in the world almost / unseen but found existent there."[†] Indeed, as these lines suggest, art provided

---

[*] "Since [Robert] Bertholf [i.e., the Curator of Poetry / Rare Books Collection at State University of New York Buffalo] has the bulk of our correspondence already I suppose we may as well keep it all together" (Letter from William Bronk to Robert Meyer, 2 May 1985) Logistics would dictate otherwise, however. Bronk's letters ended up at the State University of New York at Buffalo, Meyer's at Columbia University. Formal acknowledgment is here gratefully made to these copyright holders for permission to reprint copyrighted material: the Poetry / Rare Books Collection, University Libraries, State University of New York, permission to print portions of letters from William Bronk to Robert Meyer; and, the Rare Book and Manuscript Library, Butler Library, Columbia University, permission to print portions of letters from Robert Meyer to William Bronk housed in the William Bronk archive.

[†] Untitled poem, William Bronk, *Metaphor of Trees and Last Poems* (Jersey City, NJ: Talisman House, Publishers: 1999), 147. All further poems by Bronk mentioned in this essay come from William Bronk, *Life Supports. New and Collected Poems, New Edition*

THE BODY OF THIS LIFE:

Bronk with the most reliable threshold onto what he called the reality of worldlessness; art allowed him, figuratively in his writing—and, in his personal life, actually—to approach the fecundity of a "worldless" world he could never ultimately even touch. Art also provided Bronk and Meyer with the lingua franca of their close communication. They each saw art as uniquely valuable; art articulated something all other human expression failed to achieve. To be sure, their letters constitute the most substantial evidence of Bronk's philosophy and poetics, beyond his published work. Often containing poems well before their publication, the letters hold phrases and ideas in their evolutionary stages, which appear later in poems and essays. One wonders why Meyer, no poet, artist or philosopher, should have become the recipient of Bronk's explanations of his work and reports of his daily reading as well as attendances at the theater, concerts, museums and galleries. Most unlikely as it may first seem, he was Bronk's intellectual soulmate throughout his mature life.

Meyer and his wife Irma had made trips to Latin America and elsewhere with Bronk and his sister Betty—a great companionship flourished, and along with it a quite rarefied discussion. It was not all agreement, however. Meyer tended to see the arts as functional, insofar as they provided solace, education, and social cohesion. Bronk, conversely, saw poetry especially as a kind of counter-self or alter-force he lived with and at times against. Nonetheless, both men believed in the phenomenon of art as the most prized human manifestation, one that could, moreover, deliver them from the world's irrelevancy and even cruelty. What especially emerged out of their dispute was the joint recognition, and mutual affirmation, of *absence* as being the absolute foundation of art. Absence sustained the sense of openness vital to architecture's built environments, the negative space critical to painting and sculpture, and the silence that nourishes all poetry and music.

Early on in their dialogue (in 1957), Meyer lays out his working principle: "The study of the 'What is' (despite my earnest delving into

---

(Jersey City, NJ: Talisman House, Publishers, 1997), hereafter cited as *LS*.

Throughout this essay I shall endeavor to point out the correspondences, in the letters, to Bronk's published poems.

philosophy and psychology) seemed never quite worth the same effort as the striving for "What ought to be" and I still feel, since one can never solve fully the riddle of human existence and essence one better addresses oneself to a normative humanism" (quoted in Bronk's letter to Meyer of 12 June 1957). Bronk replies that Meyer's outlook seems

> To be the equivalent of saying that one should turn his attention from the unsolved riddle of [ancient Mayan] bannerstones [*sic*] to good useful building stones. Of course that's unfair but I have never claimed even implicitly to be a fair-minded person. It is true that the direct contemplation of man (as opposed to turning one's back on him) solves no riddles but what else do we have to do? And beware of striving for any "what ought to be" (which probably includes all what ought to be's) that doesnt take full account of man as an unsolvable riddle. If one has an equation in two unknowns all the real equations would have to include more than two—one doesnt really solve it by assigning an insufficient value to one unknown and deriving the consequent incorrect value of the other.́ It has been demonstrated mathematically that squaring the circle is impossible. I would not advocate devoting oneself to that riddle to the exclusion of solvable problems. But I dont *càre* about squaring the circle and I do care about man. One reason that I care about man is that he is likely to sit with his eyes blank, his mouth open, and his belly sagging, contemplating an unsolvable riddle when by all rights he ought to be making the world a better place to live in.

Four years later, Bronk writes to Meyer to say that, while the answer to a riddle may not be forthcoming, he can

> recognize the question. The reason which gives order. Why can we no longer accept it? And why at the same time, and in that light, do we nevertheless feel that it is a kind of barbarism to be free of the *need* to accept it? We have to do this thing (to believe in order-giving

---

˙Cf. "How Indeterminacy Determines Us," *LS* 56.

reason) which we know we cant do. One recent approach I took to the question is in this poem.

Here Bronk writes out his poem "The Failure to Devise a Better World,"* then paraphrases its theme, and comments:

> As you know, I too am obsessed by the fragmentation and disso-lution of reality, by Prospero's "insubstantial pageant," and "baseless fabric" and the recent direction of my thinking has been to attempt to win beyond it by first accepting it wholly—but not finally. (14 June 1961)[†]

Less than a month later, he enlarges his difference with Meyer:

> You think we could devise a better world by will and decision. I dont trust our will and decision. (Am I, in effect, agreeing with you by making that statement?) No, I mean to say I find it in the nature of things that we are not able to devise a better world. It is not intended that we should, though it is right and proper that our failure should disturb us. Our failure is built in. Will and decision are clumsy and false and insensitive and dishonest. God save us from a savior! (11 August 1961)

Bronk's skepticism is no mere intellectual exercise. In 1960, Meyer receives this letter:

> Life continues to surprise me and it is with wonder that I think of the difference in our lives—you the deraciné the object of the violence of our times, and me the continuously rooted in an apparently placid and sustained environment—that only so late it should seem to you that this is not a real world, to whom in the past it should hardly have appeared credible. And this incredibil-

---

*Cf. *LS* 75.

[†]Cf. "To Prospero, Afterwards," *LS* 75.

ity, this unreality is the basis of anything I think. Plato's figure is one of the deepest human perceptions. As near a thing to a certainty as I have is this negative one, that whatever reality may be it is certainly not what we have, collectively as humans, pretended it is[.] Things can't be what they seem to be. In order to get from one end of the day to the other we assume that they are (we even assume that there are such things as one end of the day and the other)[.] But they cant be that. They just don't go Together [*sic*] that way. This is not a world that we understand. It may be in some scheme rational but not if we mean by rational comprehensible and responsive to our reasons.

Maybe it is the ultimate rational heresy and humanist heresy that I have sometimes been glad that this should be so on the assumption that reality is more rather than less than we could comprehend it to be.

But it also comes to me that you had to believe in a real world, a world that can be made better and more rational by our efforts; that you could not otherwise have had the courage to move out from under a political madness and make a new life in another country.

I reproach myself for saying these things to you, incoherent and comfortless as they are, however opposite I wish that they might be. But when I read your remark that the world doesn't seem real to you I could only say Yes. What else has my poetry said for years? What else have I thought?

And I wanted to tell you this—tell someone this—irrelevant or maybe relevant as it may be,˙ that a few days ago for the first time in months I was able to look at some of my poetry without cringing and even to think of the possibility that sometime I might even write something more, that it might be barely possible to say *something* to *someone* or to pretend successfully that the possibility existed. We get used to living with impossibilities.

˙Cf. "The Tell," *LS* 174.

Robert, I am no help to you. Damn it I wish I were. I wrote it; I'll send it. Don't count it against me. (6 August 1960),

Eventually, Bronk will write the poem "My Shoulder for Robert. Help Us Both," which distills the thoughts in this letter, in his volume *To Praise the Music* in 1972:

What, this world? Of course. It is
that terrible. The curious thing,
—we come back and back to think or pretend to think
there was some mistake, some fault, and it isn't so.

We think our attitude was wrong: no trust
or too much trust, lazy or not relaxed
enough. Did we have the chances? Did pampering
spoil us? We refuse to believe it really is.

It is, though. So what do we do? There must
be something to do, some way to make it right.
We refuse to believe there isn't a remedy.

Well, we may be right. You know though
I don't believe we are. You know my mind
is somewhere else. Another world. No world.

(LS 142)

Bronk's reference in his letter to Plato conveniently posits the basic situation, as Bronk and Meyer see it, of phenomena and their perception, which will allow finally a concord between the two men regarding art's reliance on absence—although Bronk, I would argue, does not describe, in his poetry and essays, the Platonic construct as such. It is worth a pause to consider his distinction. His thinking actually differs from Plato's in one important way. Bronk's notion of worldlessness "would cease to exist if there were no world, and so there is a stronger bond between" the unreal manifest "world" and the real, "worldless" world "than what we find between Plato's Ideal and his world of shadows." For that matter, Bronk's assertion is also unlike the Buddhist conceptualization of the universe in which the world supposedly rests upon a void.

> The void may not need the world for its non-existence in the way worldlessness does, but more importantly, the void is nothingness, whereas worldlessness is a fullness or presence albeit one that cannot be known; as well, the void resides beyond intuition. It might follow that the intuition of worldlessness is the realization of one's vitality, and that to intuit the real that is worldlessness is to know one's own genuine state of being. Worldlessness cannot be intuited, however, unless there is a world one can experience; this world allows for the telling of another world that is real if finally unattainable (i.e., the world Bronk knows is a false [world but still] a world that leads him to a sense of the real). When Bronk reflects upon the fact that he, first of all, apprehends the falsity of the actual world, and that, secondly, he intuits a realness that is *not* the actual world, then he achieves ontological plenitude. (Kimmelman *"Winter Mind"* 178)

So, the realized world must also include its opposite—presence is supported by absence. All forms, and most of all forms created by humanity, disclose that absence, to one degree or another.

Bronk, therefore, consistently celebrates *form* by noting the limitations of conscientious human shaping, and the potential of randomness. For instance, in his poem "The Smile on the Face of a Kouros" he likens the desire for perfectly shaped form to "wanting death" (*LS* 26), whereas, in "The Beautiful Wall, Machu Picchu," he finds the Incan stones of the wall to be "abstract austerities," "unimitative" and "self-absorbed in their unmortared, close / accommodation, stone to different stone, / exactly interlocked, deep joined. . . ." Bronk is attracted to this primitive edifice because he perceives in it a "grace inherent more as idea than in the world," the love of "simple soundness in a just joint, / and the pieces together once though elsewhere apart." Looking at these Incan stones, he

THE BODY OF THIS LIFE:

sees that they "say of the world there is nothing to say" (*LS* 41). In his 1957 letter that mentions the Mayan bannerstones, which were apparently shaped but for some unknown purpose, he observes that "Those stones have that perfection and sophistication which lead me to doubt the common sense or at least, near-sighted idea of time which lays it out in an increasingly meaningless accumulation, and by its cluttered and trivial foreground, removes us so far from those who are actually perhaps our contemporaries in other sense than the common" (12 June 1957).

Both time and space can be trivial, meaningless, inert. Or they can be dynamic, substantial, even life-sustaining. Meyer, who has now been sent a copy of Bronk's essay "The Occupation of Space—Palenque"* writes in 1958,

"Time and Space" are indeed the 2 basic concepts underlying Mayan society and that you have outlined remarkably well. It always struck me that only an artistic approach, only an esthetic philosophy could unlock the secret of the Mayas. . . . Opposite to their cities I was even wondering what basic cultural "ground plan" was behind them, why the buildings were standing just so, what "order" could be detected in this seemingly willful and gratuitous "disorder"—I knew the contents of their culture (Time, Space, an hierarchical religion) but why they took the shape of Chichen or Uxmal or Labuá I still can't fathom. I am not satisfied with Ben Shans [*sic*] tautology that "Form is the shape of content," but I do feel the Mayan cities are like the creative act of a painter who transforms the image of his into lines, colors, forms on the canvas—I only want to know why *this* form and not *that*. On reflection it struck me that many of their cities have one outstandingly high or large edifice. . . . Could this be the focus the axis of the whole complex of buildings? Even if it is not in the centre, is seemingly disconnected or off-middle or

---

*Cf. William Bronk, *Vectors and Smoothable Curves: Collected Essays, New Edition* (Jersey City, NJ: Talisman House, Publishers, 1997), 21-29.

solitary? You know of course van Goghs paintings, in particular the ones of the garden of the insane asylum in Arles, where a tree on the lefthand or righthand carries holds the whole whirl of buildings and greens together, or Breughel's vast canvases where one group of people or buildings on the side are nevertheless the focal point of the whole mass of goings on. . . . . (30 June 1958)

In a similar vein, almost a decade later Meyer quotes from Kafka's "'Parables' [in which there is this sentence:] 'how the Sirens have a still more fatal weapon than their song, namely their silence. And though admittedly such a thing has never happened, still it is conceivable that someone might possibly have escaped from their singing; *but from their silence certainly never*'. A prophet he!"(25 October 1967). Fifteen years later, Bronk is enumerating his favorite composers to Meyer; what is it about their music? Perhaps recalling Meyer's comment, he observes that "Silence is the term for the unspeakable which is what we are always talking about but never are able to say. It is what we come from and go back to but, attentively, we never really leave it. No need to wait for the time. I think our lives would be unbearably trivial without it" (22 February 1982).

In 1961, speaking of individual creativity and community, Bronk had opined that we "value art not because it summons up for us the artistic experience but because it summons up for us reality, our most intense experience of the world. I think I sent you The Stairs at Korcula˘ which bears somehow on this." Bronk then includes a copy of his poem "The Greeks, the Chinese or, Say, the Mayans,"[†] after which he asks,

If art is . . . timeless and art is the essence of, not the artistic experience, but the human experience, is man the only feeler the sufferer of the eternal experience? Is there nothing else to do, to be done? Are we not to have a time? I admit to you privately that

---

˘Cf. *LS* 78.

[†]Cf. *LS* 71.

my eyes also go straying and lusting after it. I hanker for a time world a made world a world which can be manipulated and reshaped and listened to, and taught, and believed in, and made to stand alone and repay our love and devotion—an ego world, a world in time. (19 October 1961)

For Bronk, space can suggest that absence, as well as timelessness, and this suggestion is an intellectually and spiritually ultimate provocation. In one letter, referring to his poem "The Real Surrounding: On Canaletto's Venice" (*LS* 104), he writes, "What interested me was his ability to paint enormous volumes of empty space coupled with his matter of fact acceptance of the most mundane and unprotesting details of naturalism" (26 June 1966). Three years later, he quotes Harold Rosenberg's criticism of the painter Barnett Newman to the effect that he "'works with emptiness as if it were a substance..... His program is to induce emptiness to exclaim its secret; in short, he wishes to grasp the absolute through painting....' I thought, of course, of my Canaletto poem and what different ways we take to say the same things" (22 April 1969).

The importance of the negative, in structures, is perhaps a given, although not everyone can see in them how they are realized by it. Yet space and silence, indeed, like any metonym in a language, are what Bronk seizes on in trying to find his locus within an ephemeral world. From that world, art stands forth. Art is a buoy in the sea. It is the realization that artistic expression is substantial. This understanding eventually prompts Meyer to advance the concept of "art as a way" (a phrase he borrows from his friend, the Buddhist painter and author, Frederick Franck, also the title of one of his books). Bronk, of course, begs the question. Meyer argues for "'truth [as residing] in poetry'" (quoted in Bronk's letter of 30 January 1981) and hence for poetry's efficacy beyond its own existence, and receives this reply in 1981: "You are generous to think that . . . but I think [poetry's] truths like those of mathematical systems or any articulated schemata are all internal: 'all measures measure themselves, none measures the world'" (30 January

1981).' Over the next several years, Bronk begins to focus, in his letters, on the question of the arts a bit more than before: "I am sure there are artists whose intention and even experience it is to be 'enriched' by their art and . . . to whom art is the spoonful of butter swirled in the sauce just before serving to finish it. It must be a pleasure to eat at their tables. What concerns me is not the sauce so much as the sustenance, that it was some other animal or vegetable life before it sustained mine, that it turns into tissue and bone and feces, that it aches and decays and loses itself in oblivion. [Some people] may know of the elegant uses of art but nothing of its compulsion, absurdity and terror" (24 March 1981).

In another letter, Bronk continues to see art from the creator's point of view, in which, for him, art becomes a "jailor." "Art as a WAY? as your friend Franck says. What sort of an artist could say this? Probably he is not an evil man though I considered for a moment if that old-fashioned obscene sin of simony could have popped up again in new style. A naif, I guess. A dabbler" (23 August 1983). A month later Bronk adds, "When Franck talks about Art making the Way easy and full of celebratory comforts I think he must be talking about something other than all I have known" (28 September 1983).

Meyer responds:

Dear Bill, but of course, I never understood Frederick to mean "Art as a Way" to be a signpost, a prescription, a tranquilizer for you, the poet, the writer, the painter and all of your fellow-artists. It was I, who felt addressed, the committed reader, the passionate, loving listener to music, the visionary viewer of art and all those, for whom "Art" is a solace in and a deliverance from this mad world. The creative spirit in Man is for me the only manifestation of the Divine; "Grace" is not "revealed". As in all religions, we have to "look up to the mountains, the summits, from where the grace and salvation cometh." (1 October 1983)

'Here he is referring to his poem "On Divers Geometries," *LS* 92.

THE BODY OF THIS LIFE:

Not long before Meyer's death, Bronk returns to this constellation of thoughts about art:

> That I am at a different pole from your friend Frederick Frank [*sic*] and remain there didn't preclude my being touched [...]. None of us knows really the pull and propensity to respond to the terror and horror of human experience as our responses may be different at different times. That there are polarities includes the idea that polarities may reverse and reverse they do in our uncertainties. (21 September 1985)

"Art as a way," for Meyer, meant a salvation, especially since art reached and seemingly touched the truth of ideal existence where nothing else could. Bronk might come around to Meyer's way of thinking on occasion, but only when he could get beyond his relationship with his own art. At times they disagreed about the function of art but never about art's authenticity in an otherwise inauthentic world. "Art As a Way" represented for them both the path through that world. Meyer could feel hopelessness, would reassert an optimism. Bronk, the skeptic, never hoped for much but delighted in the arts, and in the natural world, and did, I think, derive solace from them. Yet he was loathe to admit this—which we see reflected, for example, in his letter where he is at pains to explain his view of reality, in part by paraphrasing "The Failure to Devise a Better World" that he suggests exemplifies the "recent direction of my thinking"; he then warns, "it is a little wrong to speak of the recent direction of my thinking because it hasn't any" (14 June 1961).

Meyer proved to be a great foil for him but also a loving and supportive friend. As if he is summing up the relationship between the two of them, he writes, toward the end of his life,

> Dear Bill, I showed last night to Claire [Meyer's second wife] the few woodcuts by Eugene Canadé—she did not know the where-from and the how of your connection. So we got lost in rereading you and both were struck by the thought, that "the grim poet of Hudson Falls, who sees the dark side of life" and the "American

voice of darkness" always and almost always only praises the Music in meeting the trees through which the light shines, the flowers and plants in our garden and your life supports derive from Nature. At that moment a past event lighted up in my memory: It was in Cozumel, when I "gave" you a beautiful palm tree, we passed often on our way from town to the beach for your next poem. (I obviously did not know then much of your poetry.) After a few days you said "I give it back to you, Robert". The loneliness of that single tree seemingly distressed you. I must tell you something of the great modern Balzac Romain Gary, whose Goncourt prize [book] you may have read. . . . His last published novel . . . closed with the words: My consolation is my knowledge, *that I am not alone, being alone!* (11 October 1983)

W. *Sheldon Hurst*

The Poet as Collector:
An Introduction to the William Bronk
Collection at Adirondack Community College

Art isn't made, it's in the world almost
unseen but found existent there. We paint,
we score the sound in music, we write it down.
                    (*MOT* 147)

I N THE SUMMER OF 1997, William Bronk indicated his desire to leave
his art collection to Adirondack Community College. He wanted the
collection to be where students could see it, live with it, and study it. He
was eager to have it not hidden away but in public places, so that the
community as a whole would be able to enjoy it. And he wanted the
college to have this gift with no strings attached.

This was a significant moment, both for Bronk in his life and for the
college. For Bronk, the intended gift was the result of a process that, in
his 2 November 1997 poetry reading at the college, he referred to as a
"reconciliation and embrace of mortality," an idea which finds expres-
sion in "Testamentary Statement":

Shortcomings maybe, but as though it were my child,
I have watched the world get to where
it could get along without me. I'm pretty proud
as if it couldn't always have. I think
I'm going to leave it everything I've got.
                    (*COA* 67)

For the college, "everything [he'd] got" was a gift not only of an art
collection but also of a new vision. At this point in its history, Adiron-

dack Community College had only a few works of art, scattered about the campus. Bronk's intended gift set in motion serious conversations about the role of art in the campus community, the nature of the relationship between the arts and other disciplines, and the responsibilities the college would embrace by accepting this collection. It is a vision which has continued to enliven the campus, even as the campus community itself has begun to be changed by what is now "in [its] world almost / unseen but found existent there."

The significance of the William Bronk Collection rests not only in the vision and thought which it has inspired at the college but also in the quality of the art he collected and in the nature of the relationships he had with the artists whose work he enjoyed living with. There are works by eighteen artists in the collection, and just over 130 pieces. Approximately one half of these works are prints; in addition, there are twenty paintings, ten drawings, five broadsides, twenty sculptures, and miscellaneous artifacts. The artists whose work is in the collection include painters and print makers whom Bronk knew early in his life: Vincent Canadé, Eugene Canadé, Shirley Clarke, Herman Maril, and Gobin Stair. In the 1970s a group of young men were mentored by the poet; their paintings, prints and sculptures often became his: Daniel Leary, Loren French, Peter Homer, Dan Fleckenstein, Stephen Perrone, and Frank Rayno. In addition, he collected works by James Weil, Henry Lyman, Henry Elinson, Calvert Coggeshall, Bradford Graves, Guy Langevin, and Jo Ann Lanneville.

For the most part, Bronk knew these individuals as friends as well as artists. He collected their art because he valued their friendship, a concept he explored early on in his book *The Brother in Elysium*. His friendships were rooted in trust and honesty, in mutual respect and a common commitment to the creative act. This unwavering bond was reaffirmed in the last poem he wrote, found near his body when he died: "We paint, / we score the sound in music, we write it down." The collective "we" is a testimony to the creative community of poets, writers, composers, musicians and artists to which he belonged.

The arts have something to tell us.
It is not what we wanted to hear;
but we listen.
It is a very private communication.
It becomes our life.

(*MF* superscription)

Bronk has shared this communication and this life with the college community in the act of bequeathing his collection to the college. What was his private world is now an invitation to the larger public to be drawn into the exploring, hearing, seeing, and thinking which were fundamental to him.

William Bronk's last public reading of his poetry was at the college's Visual Arts Gallery on the occasion of an exhibition of works by his longtime friend Herman Maril: *Related to Paper: Herman Maril*, 19 October–13 November 1997. One of the works in the show, *The Flats* (Figure 1), be-

Figure 1. Herman Maril. *The Flats*. 1967.
Oil on canvas, 36″ x 48″

longed to Bronk and had been lent by him. The reading honored his friendship with Maril, and it included the poem quoted above from *Manifest; and Furthermore*, which Bronk had read at Maril's memorial service. He introduced his poetry reading on the afternoon of 2 November with the words: "The arts have two proper subjects: death and desire." These subjects were not new interests of his. In "The Informer" he had written:

What I think I mean is, against our death
our lives are nothing but become something when we think
of death. Temporality. We are here too short

to change things and anyway it isn't ours
to change. Our minds are directed otherwhere
by death. It comes up behind us to show us things.
                    (*MF* 27)

This theme is one he explored again and again. Death provides insights.
Life is marked by loss upon loss, but the piece by piece paring away of
concern about the superficial can lead to that which is worth perceiving,
and maybe even to the unknowable. Such paring away of the non-essen-
tial is a characteristic of Maril's painting, and it is an element of the
mystery of life and death about which Bronk contemplated in "The
Mind's Landscape on an Early Winter Day":

What makes the senses feel is loss, and not less loss
for being neither final nor complete.
The senses and the mind agree it seldom is.

For loss is what we live with all the time.
                    (*LS* 27-8)

Living with loss is the human condition; Bronk's response to this was to
affirm:

and we open our eyes and feel our
way in the dark.
                    (*LS* 27-8)

A painting by Vincent Canadé, *Self
Portrait* (Figure 2), is one of the earliest
works Bronk collected, and is, perhaps,
indicative of the connection he felt be-
tween the ideas he explored in poetry
and the insights he saw in the art he
lived with. In this painting, the artist
depicts himself with open eyes, not

Figure 2 Vincent Canadé. *Self Portrait*.
nd. Oil on board, 9¼" x 7¼"

unusual for a self-portrait. But it is precisely the openness of the eyes and that they are looking which the poet played with in "On a Picture by Vincent Canadé" (referring intimately to the painter as "Pop"):

> But all
> Pop's heads looked like him, each in its own way.
> Practice in looking at painting shows us how what
> we see can be said to look: as painting looks.
> And this is the reason for painting, to say it so,
> to limn the real, limit, illumine.
> (LS 94-95)

This is a wonderful play on "looking" and its possible meanings. It does seem to suggest that one can trust what is seen, for the painting looks as if to say it's so. And just then comes the admission of the way it really is:

> Ahh! Flummery! Pop knew more than that,
> knew better than try to say the world or himself.
> Those heads, like glances out the window, are to say,
> "Listen, I have been here looking all day, all day
> and every day; I have been here looking, all day."
> (LS 94-5)

It is the looking that matters. It is one of the legacies of Bronk's poetry, and it is one of the legacies of the works of art he collected and gave to the college: an invitation to open one's eyes—time and again, in the face of loss and darkness, in the expression of one's humanity, in the possibility of experiencing the ineffable.

If it is the looking that matters, both to the poet and to the artist, then one of life's necessities is light. Bronk and the artists he esteemed recognized the metaphoric power of light. Vincent Canadé emphasized light and its partner, shadow. Maril accented the luminescence of color. In works by Eugene Canadé in Bronk's collection, the relationship between light and object is explored in a number of different ways. Several of his works were created with a Cubist sense of light—splintered reflections and interactions with shadow. In *Still Life, Fruit and Shells* (Figure 3), there is a more traditional rendering of objects in which light serves to define each one. It is in relationship to this work that Bronk, in the poem "Annihilation of Matter," might have considered:

Figure 3. Eugene Canadé. *Still Life with Fruit and Shells* 1979. Oil on canvas, 14″ x 23½″

> Here it is always the light
> that mattered, and only the light. Once, it had seemed
> the objects mattered: the light was to see them by.
> Examined, they yielded nothing, nothing real.
> (*LS* 42)

The objects, fruit and shells, only seem real as light illuminates each. But what appears because of the light is not reality; rather, what is enabled by the light is the possibility of seeing a different essence.

> They were for seeing the light in various ways.
> They gathered it, released it, held it in.
>
> In them, the light revealed itself, took shape.
> Objects are nothing. There is only the light, the light!
> (*LS* 42)

This metaphor of light, explored in the poet's poems and in the poet's art, continues to invite the world to change the way it perceives itself. There is a very basic tenet to the work that accepts the unreality of what is frequently considered real and the necessity of searching further for what matters. There is the challenge of recognizing what can never be known.

In his poetry, Bronk repeatedly returned to this problem of knowing and not knowing. One looks, one seeks, but in the end, what does one know? In "On *Credo ut Intelligam*" he clearly stated, "I plead the permanence / of ignorance, that we acknowledge it" (*LS* 96-97).

This view recognizes limits and failure: awareness leads to belief, which leads to a constructed way of knowing, which is then deconstructed. A scaffold falls apart; a snowman melts. Each seeming to "know" only proves its own limitation.

> That world which asks
> our belief, and offers us understanding back,
> has cost too much in what it shuts away
> of all our awareness, the reaches of ignorance.
>> (*LS* 96-97)

> Reality is what we are ignorant of.
>> (*LS* 96-97)

Yet, the realm of unknowns is like a magnet, and the artist responded in "Holy Orders": "What counts is that we write it down or paint, /dance, compose, the way we are given to" (*MF* 63).

In *Portrait of Bill* (Figure 4), Shirley Clarke created an image of the poet when he was 20 years old. Her interpretation has him looking over the top of a geometrically configured body. The slanted shoulders, the angled arms, the crossed legs—the image is conjured up in yet another of the poet's reflections on the incapacity of the human to know. In "Something Matters But We Don't," Bronk wonders that:

Figure 4. Shirley Clarke.
Portrait of Bronk 1939.
Oil on board, 30″ x 12″

In man, I can see no substance solidly;

it is as if what we call man were no more
than an oddly angled look at something else.

(LS 139)

The "oddly angled look" of the poet in both the painting and the poem is the expression of limits and ignorance. What he sees is what is there:

Let me leave off speaking, unknowing as I am,
but not before I speak of the limits of speech,
or tell of man there is nothing to tell,
or tell of what we discern perhaps there could be
to tell that we know too little except it is there
and, if anything happens, it must be it happens there.

(LS 139)

The connection between painting and poem is one of the characteristics of the William Bronk Collection which is both personal and powerful. While both the paintings and the poems are complete in and of themselves, the overlapping of themes suggests the influence the paintings had on the poet, and perhaps that the poet had on the artists whose works he collected. Each work of art is a construction, Bronk would say—nothing more, nothing final in any ultimate sense. But for Bronk and his artist friends, there was a common obedience to the compelling force of making art and a belief in its power.

The power of the art is one of the experiences that the Adirondack Community College community is now privileged to enjoy, thanks to Bronk's generous gift. The presence of this art collection at the college will help those of us who knew Bronk and counted him as a friend to remember his extraordinary persona, to reminisce on our visits with him, and to recall his house where the paintings were hung throughout. But more than that, his collection also provides to a much wider audience new possibilities of seeing: of seeing art, of seeing art in the context of his poetry, of seeing and reading Bronk's poems in the presence of the art he lived with. His valued relationships with visual artists are reminders of the integrated nature of all the arts, and the gift he gave is a celebration of all that is creative in the human spirit.

Ars Poetica

Henry Weinfield

Bronk's Heroism: The Style Makes the Poet

B RONK IS USUALLY APPROACHED THEMATICALLY: as a philosophical skeptic for whom "ideas are always wrong"; as a religious poet of desire and of nothingness; as the most recent in the long line of American transcendentalists. The thematic approach to Bronk has borne fruit, but in remaining at the level of content it is has been unable to explain what makes him so distinctive a poet. There is a mystery at the heart of Bronk's work, a mystery woven of darkness, distance, and irony; and in order to penetrate it we have to proceed by a different route, along the pathway of Bronk's style. I want to make a few preliminary remarks on Bronk's style in this paper, and then at the end, move from stylistic to thematic or philosophical issues, so as to make some headway in drawing the two together.

Consider a very short poem, "A Long Two Way," from Bronk's penultimate collection, *All of What We Loved* (1998), which came out in the poet's eightieth year:

> There is a going down into the dark
> but, getting there, we turn around, come back.
> The solstice comes before the winter comes.
> It isn't winter. Only slowly spring. (*AWWL* 78)

Bronk's strength as a poet resides in his phrasing, and in the way his phrasing is pitched against rhythm and syntax, the horizontal movement of his lines and the vertical movement of the poem as a whole. "There is a going down into the dark" has an abstractly impersonal rhythm that is very different from "We go down into the dark"; the elimination of grammatical agency (accomplished by the old-fashioned gerundive construction) allows the line to imply not only "We go down into the dark" but also "The days become shorter," without being limited to these meanings. The mysterious opening line is then countered, uncannily, by a second line which seems to imply that it is our will or intention to turn around and come back—although obviously it has nothing to do with us. It *does* have something to do with us, the line seems to say, and maybe on some level beyond our powers of apprehension it pertains to a will with which we are in accord. The opening line has the connotation of death, but there is no turning back and coming around with death—only with the seasons; and thus there is a mysterious mixing of the linear movement toward death with the cyclical and circular movement of the seasons and what one might call seasonality. This is a poem written in strict pentameters, and my sense is that Bronk is very often at his best when his prosody is most formal and regular. The tonal convergences in *down* and *around,* in the off-rhymes *dark* and *back* (Bronk generally eschews end-rhyme, but makes much use of off-rhyme, internal rhyme, and assonance), and in the alliterated g's and d's, contribute to the power of the first two lines. And in the final two lines, which could not be more simply or straightforwardly phrased, the slowness of the movement is marked by the repetitions of *comes* and *winter,* and by the convergence of *solstice* (a word denoting a point of demarcation which in reality, of course, is a fiction) and *slowly.* The poem ends, unexpectedly, on the word *spring.* It is a poem that enacts what Mallarmé called "the Orphic explanation of the earth."

It is also a poem that could not have been written by any other contemporary poet writing in English, or, for that matter, by any previous poet in the history of English poetry. It cultivates values which are now out of fashion and which are no longer being cultivated, a morality of craft which is not even understood in the present cultural context. It is a small poem, but one that is made to last—and now more than ever, there is a danger that poetry of this kind will be swallowed up and lost among all those things that are not made to last.

We can trace the origins of Bronk's style to the poems in *My Father Photographed with Friends,* his first book (although not published until 1976). In most of these poems, Bronk has not yet broken free of his earliest influences (the dominant voice is that of Frost), and his use of rhyme and meter is sometimes heavy and awkward. But there is one poem, "Benedicite Omnia Opera" (it is the first poem included in my edition of Bronk's *Selected Poems*), which, though not particularly ambitious in what it attempts to encompass from a technical point of view, seems to me a fully realized work of art:

See the fish
in the sea
deep down
deep down
density.

Bird-colored
flower-colored
dark;
grey, wild hunger
of the shark.

Heavy, heavy
water lies,
moulds the body,
bulges eyes.

Open eye
and open mouth
search the water
north and south.

Pectoral fins
calm the floor,
hover quiet
close to shore.

There are mountains
in the sea;

oh, deep down
deep down
density. (*LS* 17-18)

The strangeness and intensity of Bronk's phrasing are already in evidence here, and we can connect the peculiarities of his diction to his mature vision, which in this poem has apparently already taken hold. In the second stanza, for example, the dark is "bird-colored" and "flower-colored." Of course, there are colors but no birds or flowers in the sea; but the reason birds and flowers are mentioned is that they contribute to the darkness, which (literally and figuratively) takes precedence over them and all other entities—as if to say that birds and flowers, with their variegated colors, function not to eliminate the darkness but to delineate it. By the same token, what is emphasized is not the shark but its hunger—as if the shark existed to define the hunger rather than the hunger to define the shark. Water, inchoate like darkness, "moulds the body, / bulges eyes." The repetitions of the last stanza are magnificent, and the poem's final word, "density," continues to reverberate after the poem has been spoken or read. What is the relationship between the poem's title and its vision? We are left to ponder. "Bless all things," says the title, but the poem emanates from a vision of depths and darknesses that nothing—certainly not an anthropomorphic God—seems to penetrate. But perhaps we are in the context of the Book of Job ("Canst thou draw out Leviathan with a hook?").

Now, having paid some attention to Bronk's style, where what is important is the *micro-level* of phrasing, let us turn to the *macro-level* of the poet's philosophy, his ideas. There is a sense in which Bronk is the most extreme example of the "philosophical poet" (a term that needs to be interrogated) that we have ever had in English; and yet, paradoxically, he is a philosophical poet for whom "ideas are always wrong"; and so I want to turn to the poem in which he expresses this idea, "Blue Spruces in Pairs, A Bird Bath Between" (from his 1964 volume *The World, The Worldless*):

Seen by starlight from the window, fat
blue spruces patch the lawn with darker dark.

Arranged in pairs. People no longer plant
these trees in pairs, with bird baths set between.

Fashions in ornamental planting change.
Houses and yards lose style in twenty years.

Seen by starlight. The universal stars.
Something here is certainly laughably wrong.

Ideas are always wrong. Their separateness
causes a threat to neuter each other out

and leave us without a world as it does here:
heavens and styles collide meaninglessly.

The unsubmissive mind has freedom to be
nothing, worldless—not to exist at all.

Because the various world we sense is not
ever apprehended as one, or formed as one,

ideas are always wrong, always unfixed,
and often their power to make the world real is lost.

Huge factors stand ready to leap in
to alter or destroy a world we defend alone. (*LS* 41-2)

The poem begins with a phrase that will later be repeated: "Seen by
starlight." That phrase has the metaphorical significance of *under the
aspect of eternity,* and this is a perspective that will remain constant in
Bronk's work and against which our ordinary, earthly perspectives will
continually be measured and found wanting. Under the aspect of eternity
our ideas are always wrong, but there are ironies accruing to this perspec-
tive that go beyond the mere articulation of its skeptical thesis. For one
thing, Bronk is a poet of ideas, for whom ideas are always wrong; and for

another, he is a poet and not a philosopher, and therefore all ideas, including the idea that ideas are always wrong, never exist in themselves in his poetry but are always mediated by what we can only call its music. Although the philosophical statements contained in his poems have to be taken seriously in and of themselves, they do not mean what they would outside of their contexts. The statement "Ideas are always wrong," for example, has a different tonality, and therefore a different meaning, in "Blue Spruces in Pairs" than it would have in a philosophical treatise or in another poem.

The elegantly distanced, meditative quality of a poem such as "Blue Spruces in Pairs" (with, for example, its pronominal references to "we" and "us" rather than to "I" and "me") offers a kind of stylistic protection not only from the nakedness of the utterance but from the fierceness of the poet's existential stance toward the world, a stance that embodies a kind of solitary heroism. "The *unsubmissive* mind has freedom to be / nothing, worldless—not to exist at all." Bronk refuses to submit to any sort of fragmentary, factitious identity or relationship to the world, to anything on the order of what Sartre calls the "in-itself," and this solitary refusal is what gives the poetry its dramatic tension. Bronk's poems present themselves, by and large, in intellectual terms, but they are the product of an often camouflaged internal agon.

The last eight lines of "Blue Spruces in Pairs" enact (or reenact) a series of paradoxes that are characteristic of the modern mind (perhaps since *Hamlet)* and that Bronk has probed more deeply than any other contemporary poet. The unsubmissive mind, refusing anything less than the truth, refuses to accept a "world" and hence a "self" on which to hinge it; but that refusal of a world in effect constitutes a world, which the self that has been reconstituted by negation must "defend alone." The world that we defend alone is easily lost, but the heroism of this poetry is never to lose touch with that loss, never to let the tension of its pathos go slack.

Valéry once wrote that the mark of a poet lies in the rigorousness of his refusals. And in the poetic world that Bronk defends alone, the refusal to submit, to be submissive, is marked, stylistically, by the beauty of his phrasing. But though the world of Bronk's poetry is governed by solitude, it is not a solipsistic world. "Huge factors stand ready to leap in," writes the poet, "to alter or destroy a world *we* defend alone." There is both a modesty and a generosity to that pronoun, and Bronk seems almost alone among his contemporaries in using it. His use of the first-person plural suggests that the loneliness of the quest for truth is a shared loneliness, that it can therefore be communicated, and that the potential for such communication is what constitutes the potential for poetry.

Rose Shapiro

"Questions It Would Do Me No Good to Ask": Voice and Form in William Bronk's "Fourteen-Liners"

The boldness of language supervenes our actual experience. It means to say what we don't know. It creates the world as if the world were. Its whole necessity is metaphor.

—William Bronk, "Costume as Metaphor"

B RONK'S SONNETS, POEMS HE HAS REFERRED TO AS "FOURTEEN-LINERS," offer a singular window into his singular poetic world, for they seem to be working at an odd angle to the conventional rhetorical structure of the form. Rather than asking a question or establishing a situation and then responding to it, Bronk's sonnets ask questions that do not seem to want to be answered; only rarely does a sonnet end with the kind of resolution one expects from the form (and even then it is an ungraspable statement). That quality will be familiar to every reader of Bronk: the essential unanswerability of his poetic proclamations and propositions. Edward Foster tells us that "Bronk's work is certainly guided by a pressure for traditional form, . . . and there is a strong pull toward closure and resolution, but within the poems themselves, one often finds a struggle against formal restraint and toward the recognition of what Bronk calls 'unvesseled light'" (Foster 78). Bronk's sonnets throw into high relief the tension that Foster delineates.

The absence of rhyme-scheme in these poems, for instance, highlights their apparent lack of artifice: in Bronk we find ghosts of rhymes or, more often, the sense that a rhyme *might* have been there but was decided against. The highly variable meter he employs not only allows him to develop unfettered the simultaneously conversational and transcendent poetic voice that is the hallmark of his work but also allows him further

THE BODY OF THIS LIFE:

to elasticize the form rhetorically. By reformulating in a variety of ways the stanzaic structure of the sonnet (both English and Italian) Bronk again seems to be working through the unanswerable within the poems themselves—not seeming to know where to stop himself, where the questions are taking him. The result is an astonishing display of the poet thinking, presented to us as the process itself (while these are carefully worked poems and could never be called "stream of consciousness" in the way that term has come to be used).

By virtue of their radical adaptation of all the micro-formal and rhetorical conventions of the form, we may concur that his sonnets are truly "fourteen-liners"—but that is not to say that they do not perform an intimate *dos-a-dos* with tradition. In fact, the processual quality in his sonnets raises them to the level of a true variation of the form—a variation, perhaps, like Hopkins's "sprung sonnets," destined not to be repeated but one that is not merely representative of the half-hearted foray into form seen amongst so many contemporary free-verse poets. As Henry Weinfield points out, "The mysterious relationship between form and content is in a certain sense more advanced in Bronk's work than in any other contemporary poetry . . . because the paradox that obtains in all lyric poetry is *thematized* in his work" ("Cloud"144). This essay considers his volume of "fourteen-liners," *To Praise the Music* (1972), looking closely at "His Poems" and "The Real World," in order to assess one of the manifestations of that paradox in Bronk's work.

In their introduction to *The Sonnet: An Anthology*, Bender and Squier call the sonnet "virtually the only important verse form in English poetry" (Bender and Squier xxvi). They also make clear the criteria they consider when distinguishing sonnets from any "fourteen-line poem": "In general, a sonnet should retain a pattern of rhyme or a division of thought consistent with the history of the form. . . . Not every fourteen-line poem is a sonnet, but we must pay some regard to a poet's intention and be willing to grant the flexibility of the tradition" (Bender and Squier xxvi). The sonnet's rhetorical structure, I would argue, its most salient feature. Thus, if we are to consider the poet's "intention" with respect to Bronk's sequence, we need first to ask what sorts of variations he makes in the form and how (indeed, whether) those variations come together in a legible pattern that can be contextualized within the tradition of the sonnet in English. (The fact that *To Praise the Music* is presented as a sonnet *sequence* figures importantly in such an evaluation, though I will not be investigating that issue here).

Perhaps it is significant that *To Praise the Music* contains fifty "fourteen-liners": a half century of sonnets (Bronk was 54 when it was published). We are reminded of George Meredith's *Modern Love*, another half century of not-quite-sonnets. In the last poem of the Meredith's sequence, the bitter husband mournfully declares: ". . . what a dusty answer gets the soul/When hot for certainties in this our life!" "Certainties" are the stuff of sonnets, and sonnets are the stuff of English-language poetry: the sonnet, a traditionally didactic form, is the most thoroughly practiced fixed form in the language. Thus Meredith's *Modern Love* engages the venerable tradition of the sonnet sequence (in particular, of course, sonnets of love) to dramatize the dissolution of a marriage, the dissolution of romantic ideals, and the dissolution of poetic "certainties" along with them.

Bronk takes an altogether different approach: poetically unconcerned with the details of human relations, he *celebrates* his own curiously wrought certainties, though these are neither subject to summary or analysis nor available for debate or, indeed, for any apparent didactic use whatsoever; they simply *are*. Foster notes that "Bronk is unlike many of his contemporaries in choosing to stay, at least marginally, within the limits of traditional prosody" while "many of his contemporaries have looked for new poetic forms imbedded in the structure of the spoken language" (Foster 62-3). Bronk has a limitless talent for expressing in "the spoken language" what no one would ever *say*; that his prosody engages in a delicate dance with tradition only makes this feat more astonishing.

Bronk's prosody in these sonnets is not easily characterized. While there is no doubt that he works almost exclusively with the five-stress line, his adamantly conversational syntax means that these poems float in and out of a recognizable pentameter. In fact, many of the sonnets begin with a line of regular pentameter, belying the array of variations to follow. When rhyme occurs it is so slight that one would be hard pressed to call it even off-rhyme; in fact, the most common method of rhyme in this volume is the exact repetition of an end-word—'You want a rhyme? I'll give you a rhyme,' the poet seems to be teasing. The effect of this strategy in the poems ranges from pathetic to humorous, but its chief function is that it underlines the didactic ambitions of the sequence.

The rhetorical "turn" in the sonnet is one of the major criteria—for some, the primary criterion—in determining when asking whether a fourteen-line poem is indeed a sonnet; it is the axis of the rhetorical balance often deemed necessary to the form. Indeed, his handling of the turn is the most highly variable feature of Bronk's sonnets—and the most indicative of his innovation in the sonnet form. Throughout the volume the turn is, by turns, repressed, delayed, parodied. He asks questions in many of his poems, but often the responses have no obvious correspondence to these questions. Yet these sonnets manage to achieve the didactic unity associated with the form: there are answers, legible or not, and these poems are a most demanding instructor.

The Petrarchan sonnet "His Poems," a moving and playful parody of the mystery and paradox of his unique body of poetry, is all about the turn.

> To say I only listen isn't true
> but neither is it conversation really: in the end
> whatever is said is theirs. If I hold back,
> their stubborn assurance, their patience, waits for me.
>
> It might be a long wait; apart from the times
> I fight them, there are times I wasn't even wrong.
> I discover later what they said. Or, prompted by that,
> I look for other things they, maybe, could say.
>
> There are some they hold back: answers I want
> to questions it would do me no good to ask. And I don't.
> Not really. But I want to know. Are the answers there?
>
> Alone sometimes, I remember how certain things

were said: that's what we were talking about
and the statement was made that—and then, oh . . . yes! (*LS* 140)

"I discover later what they said," he claims in the seventh line, setting us up for an expected turn so that we, too, can discover what they say. But we are frustrated in this desire; the "turn" seems to yield only a further delay in our knowing: "There are some they hold back: answers I want/to questions it would do me no good to ask." One line later we are set up again—"Are the answers there?"—but we get only the ecstatic "oh . . . yes" as any kind of response (and wonder whether the ellipsis is hiding something essential from us). "Questions it would do me no good to ask" are the very stuff of his poetry. He might as well say "Sonnets it would do me no good to write." Yet one of the functions of the sonnet is to ask questions and to provide "answers" within the delicately structured rhetoric of the form itself; no matter that the answers have no applicability outside the structure: the structure moves to resolve itself. In the case of Bronk, the reader is left to do the work of connecting the questions and the answers; the poems are either unwilling or unable to provide that bridge. The didacticism of the sonnet form thus becomes a radical education.

Any reader of Bronk knows that an effort to answer these questions not only would do "no good" but is nullified by the questions themselves. We might say, for instance, that in "The Real World" the question is "What can we say about the real world?" and that the answer is "Nothing"—that in this carefully crafted English sonnet the question and answer are not didactically developed through the structure of the sonnet but are rather stated and repeated in each of the three quatrains and again in the "couplet." But that precis denies the subtle movements in the poem, movements that show it to be a both a parody of and homage to the traditional English sonnet.

The real world is no world though without
our knowing it may well be. We can't
say anything about it: how it is

or why, what way it may, but it is there.

They studied the animals, how they react,
earth sciences, measured the interplay
of energies, money matters, how man
treats man, or has in time,—his history.

Nothing we say makes sense, finally.
All right: we believe certain things.
There are things we can say within that belief unless
they negate it. None of them deals with a real world.

There is a real world which does make sense.
It is beyond our knowing or speaking but it is there. (LS 145

In the first line we learn that "The real world is no world"; the first
quatrain tells us that "We can't/say anything about it" but assures us that
"it is there." The second sums up the ways in which "they" have at-
tempted to say something about a postulated "real world," its "history."
The third quatrain introduces the paradox that believing leads us away
from the "real world." Thus we can't speak of this "real" world, can't
study it, can't believe in it. That is what we have learned.

But the couplet, in its bold and bald proclamation, forces us to
rethink the terms by which we have been reading the poem until that
point: "There is a real world which does make sense./It is beyond our
knowing or speaking but it is there." The assertion that "it is there" (a
handy credo for reading all of Bronk's work) has become both resignified
and unsignified in its repetition in the poem. Whereas its first iteration
occurs in a context of something like despair, its resurgence in the couplet
is celebratory: in spite of our bungled efforts to "make sense," the "real
world" persists. Thus the title itself changes valence at each division of
the poem: it is by turns nostalgic, ironic, and perfectly present. In this
case, Bronk's reliance on the traditional structure of the English sonnet
explodes its didactic capacity by telling us at the outset that it is impossi-

ble to learn anything about the subject he presents but teaching us about it nevertheless.

The last sonnet in the sequence, "The Stance," stands both as a manifesto against the rhetorical presumptions of the sonnet and as an explanation for why we cling to it: "We maintain the stance the model does stand/for us, were perfect if only we knew how." "There is disorder," he proclaims in the last line, "it's what, anyway, we see." If we can make a "model" like a sonnet work, he says, "it isn't us." Bronk has a chosen a model that prizes wit and clever rhetorical manipulation to house a poetic language that relies fundamentally on proposition and that rejects conceit and, indeed, almost all figurative language to an astonishing extent. Edward Foster tells us that "[Bronk's] point is to be as precise as the language and the poetic conventions he has adopted will permit" (Foster 62); it is possible, however, to reverse this assessment: the very precision of his language is the first term, and it dynamically engages with the poetic conventions within which he has chosen to work. Samuel Retsov [Edward Foster] says of Bronk's "baroque" poetry: "There is great joy in the sheer complexities of syntax and the shape of words" (Retsov 92), a joy we see expressed frequently in his repetition of words and phrases. Syntax, in fact, seems to substitute for figurative throughout his work and is certainly one of the chief rhetorical devices in his poetry.

As a didactic form, the sonnet has an ethic of sociability written into it, an ethic furthered by its traditional status. In an examination of Bronk's sonnets, in the context of a body of the poetry of deceptively unrhetorical declaration, one of the most important questions we must ask is whether that didactic spirit has survived his experiments with the form. I hope I have shown that his sonnets are indeed powerfully didactic: their poetic revolution is that they teach without demonstration within a formal convention that is essentially demonstrative. What we witness in *To Praise the Music* is a sort of burlesque of the sonnet, though a burlesque of the most refined nature. The Bronkian sonnet is a true variation in that, no matter how unsonnet-like an individual poem may appear to be, we intuit the tradition behind every one without necessarily being aware of that intuition—and without necessarily being aware of what we are thus being taught.

Much has been written about the role of form as an overarching philosophical concern in Bronk's work, for form is certainly an obsession in this poetry. Bronk, in his essay "Costume as Metaphor," posits desire in general as an anguished desire for "shapes," and he movingly delineates the paradox of that desire: "How uneasy our lives are: we are denied those shapes and spaces of desire by our desire which rejects them. Shapeless and impalpable ourselves, we want that reality which has no shape to occupy" (*VSC* 51). Music, claims Burt Kimmelman, "teases Bronk because it imparts a sense of the absolute through its utter formality" (*"Winter Mind"* 163)—a formality that is, finally, unavailable to him. This frustration may be the motivation for his experiment with the sonnet. Weinfield's assertion that Bronk's "work represents what is perhaps the most radical confrontation with the limits of poetry in our time" ("Cloud" 137) can easily be brought to bear when considering Bronk's sonnets, for he is clearly testing limits in this sequence. The strong poet knows that however neatly the rhetorical structure of a sonnet resolves itself, the "conclusion" reached is always tragically contingent, provisional, answerable to and in only the world it has itself created, "as if the world were": the "real world"?

Gerald Schwartz

ENCOUNTERING REVERENCE WITHIN WILLIAM BRONK'S POEM, "THE SMILE ON THE FACE OF A KOUROS"

AKING A POEM IS A PROCESS OF DISCOVERY, not self-discovery. It is a movement toward a quality of reverence,—a fidelity towards one's own beliefs that is the central fact of a human condition—that is what must be discovered. It is what must be learned. By reverence, I mean this paying of strict attention to what's there and how you feel about it. Language is a vital, wonderful tool for that act. All of art is. I'm conscious of the almost playfully visionary, romantic, perhaps impractical impulsion of reverence as the central engine of all art—even in an era of indignation, outrage, and intolerance where language has become a tool of aggression, hostility, and criticism (in the negative sense of the word).

Yet language is such a strange thing because we share it, we all share it. Any gesture you make in it is manipulation of stuff that you find. After all, you're not putting paint on a canvas; you're not arc-welding steel together, you're using nothing that isn't there for everybody. Your work is clear: you are to respond to the material you're working with, and so respond to the people you're stealing it or borrowing it from, that it isn't spoiled for them, that it isn't wrecked for them, and all the while, you're giving something back. And that is a thimble-full of what I mean by reverence. I'm interested in what comes out of language, what that reverent interaction between William Bronk's own feelings and the everything-else conditioned by language produces.

Most of the horror of this century came not from earthquakes and apparent, obvious demons, but from strange misapplications of logic from which the only thing that could protect us would be a kind of reverence. If you revered complex, living systems, for example, you would be unlikely to solve your problems by killing one. I believe these moments are exigencies of mind, and it does seem as though we are having more and more of them, when good intentions launch intentionally into bad action. This "salient moment" when good intentions unintentionally make bad actions is also "the exigency of poetry": when a poem is made a poet stands in veneration before the original concept of some subject—or a prospect to the realization of which the apt skills are only the tools of language, however necessary. So too—for those of us who take up a poem: a poem is something you enter, seeking the form of a poem that stands before you somewhere. You move towards words, but we have only an intuition of what they are.

Both the making of a poem and the taking up of it are based on the universal experience of the self and others as persons. These two acts become a vehicle for the understanding and communication of the experience of human transcendence through this artistic and analogical elevation. Both acts construe the relation between involvement in the ordinary world and the specifics of life. Poets speak from their innermost depths for from that part of us issues forth the primordial words. And yet, these ultimate words possess only that "simplicity" which conceals within itself all mysteries. These are the primordial words which form the basis of our existence. In every primordial word there is a signified piece of reality in which a door is mysteriously opened for us into the unfathomable depths of true reality in general. It means only that primordial words reflect us in our dissoluble unity of mind and body, transcendence and perception, metaphysics and history. It means that there are primordial words, because all things are interwoven with all reality and therefore every authentic and living word has roots which penetrate endlessly into the depths. The poem "The Smile on the Face of a Kouros" is composed of primordial words—they are the words of an endless crossing of borders. They are the words on which in some way our very reverence—and perhaps our redemption depends.

One way to understand this powerful cluster of charged words—indeed, perhaps a way of expressing reverence in return, is the act of interwriting. Robert Kelly had applied this technique in his book *Mont Blanc*, where he wrote into Percy Shelley's "Mont Blanc: Lines Written in the Vale of Chamouni." This process is simple: you take a poem and write into it. All of the original poem must occur and all of the original poem must retain its ordering.

To this exercise of "interwriting" I would add the following guide or strategy: 1.) A specifically urgent understanding of transcendence should be the conceptual stream-bed of the poetry; 2.) The controlling proposition in this linguistic field should be that the poet transcends the difference between himself and others; 3.) Nevertheless, procedurally we should begin with "our" experience of transcendence, identifying in it "lines of stress and pressure" that we can then trace to our original focus. So in this practice, I would seek to establish the general intuitive conditions for the saving import of any particular; then I am in position to affirm such import, categorically, of the particular reverence. Bronk's poem begins this way:

> The boy, of course, was dead, whatever that
> might mean. And nobly dead. I think we should feel
> he was nobly dead. He fell in battle, perhaps,
> and this carved stone remembers him
> not as he may have looked, but as if to define
> the naked virtue the stone describes as his. . . (LS 66)

That's the first few sentences, so to say, the first six lines of the poem. This is a poem I wrote, in which all of Bronk's poem occurs in its order. So my poem begins this way:

> This boy, far in place, but not thought,
> of course ancient beyond, was dead,
> stagnant as dead air, whatever that might mean,
> destitute of acumen. And nobly dead,
> edifice possessing eminence. I think
> we should feel though, receive that
> he was nobly dead. And in noble death,
> delivered from age's continuos failures,
> its rank frustrations, delivered through death

from self-limited successes, the awful
banality of life. He fell in battle, perhaps,
looking to the state to solve his own
personal deficiencies, and, this carved stone
remembers him not as he may have looked,
his face may have been more special-featured,
but by accouterments a figure asserts itself;
we see it all as if in an illustration, a gesture
indicated as boldened and underlined,
but as if to define the naked virtue the stone
partly carved, partly mapped—abstract
concept of human form onto rectangular block,
describes as his. One foot is forward, the energy
of stance, a natural rhythm, the eyes look out,
a glance of large-eyed wonder, the arms
drop downward past the narrow waist to hands
hanging in burdenless fullness by the heavy
flanks, fleshed roundness of limbs prevailing
over distilled construction reigning in space.
The boy was dead, where dead bones outlast
the living ones for we begin to die when we live,
and long life is not but a prolongation of death;
our life is a sad composition; we live with death,
and die not in a moment. How many pulses
made up the life of this boy, his days must
have become considerable like petty sums
by minute accumulations; where numerous
and those days of span equal to little,
and the stone smiles in his death, the stone
brought under an artist's hand to the beauty
of form is beautiful not as stone, but
in virtue of the form—its idea introduced
by the art, the form not in the stone; but
in the artist before it enters the stone—
and even this smile shows itself upon

the face of this kouros not integrally, with
entire realizations of intentions, but only
in so far as it subdues the resistance
of the stone, lightening the lips with
the pleasure of something achieved: a
successful revenge? Restoring order in
its original, ritual form? Some act,
a deed heroic, admirable? An end?
To come to an end. To come to death
as an end, the great mutations of this world
acted, rendering time too short for our designs,
and in coming, bring there intact, full weight
of his strength and virtue, the prize with which
his empty hands are full. The unreal life? A life
forever unconsummated? This boy standing apart
from effects, unable to give himself to them,
receiving payment in kind; because his relation
to them is forever external, these things in turn,
withholding their full reality from him? No,
not this boy. None of it lost, safe home, and
smile at the end attained. His occurrence
of life unbroken, that it "meant everything"
to him; alive as subject within object, a life
lived in otherness as well as low within itself,
a life firing, complete, drive to force. Now death,
of which nothing as yet—or ever—is known,
leaves us alone to think as we want of it,
and accepts out choice, shaping the life
to the death. We are as farmers wise with
understanding when we see the fruits
have ripened well, harvest them at once,
that they may not be spoiled by rank damage.
Do we want this knowledge? Do we want
this end? All vanity personified is amply
accompanied by an unheeded figure, whose

sinister presence makes stark mockery
of whatever satisfaction is to be had
from gratifying such a vice, a reminder
of a life hastening toward decay. It gives
us; and takes what we give and keeps it;
and has, this way, in life sufficiently itself,
a kind of treasure house of comely form,
achieved and left with death to stay and be
forever beautiful and whole, as if we are
cleared of all wrong beginnings, and may
never; but at the total emptiness for ever,
the sure extinction traveled to and shall
be lost in always, as if to want too much
the perfect, unbroken form from where the same
as wanting death, wanting to be always
lost in always, wanting not to be here, not
to be anywhere, wanting nothing more
horrendous, nothing increased veridical,
as choosing death for an end. There
are other ways; we know the way to make
the other choice for death: unformed
or broken, not in contrition, the good
not done, love not given, but in time
torn off, unused, less than whole, puzzled,
we live in a formless world, one we create
to pretend we never die. Endless, we hope
for no end, believing no rational being
can fear a thing it will not ever feel. I
tell you death, expect no smile of pride
from me, having small content in
the common satisfaction we somehow
survive or live, incarnate in another life.
I bring you nothing in my empty hands.

I have found a tremendous answer to the question of reverence, to the question of the complexity of the text, by this exercise. Simply it is the writing into another text, preserving it, entering it with your own voice.

I take on this act as simply a fact of language in which you can speak, just as, when you are a child, you have to learn to bob and weave your own way through a conversation. I consider the text as a conversation, already there, into which I must speak. This project was, for me, an investigation into the subject of consent . . . the themes of expression and individuality.

The minute you work with another text, when you are doing something which seems to obliterate (and mine obliterates Bronk's poem, because you no longer hear it as a Bronk poem after I've gotten done with it, you hear my poem instead) that represents the nature of an ordinary engagement with language: the sum of words and their housing, their very occupation of space.

This engagement with language is a conversation and it can be especially rewarding since it can throw light upon the manner in which expression patterns, self-conceptions, reference groups and others are related. With this kind of engagement we attempt to create and comprehend new expression, we not only use poetry but also constitute poetry as a collective phenomenon—an intersubjective accomplishment. We are, in essence, affirming the facticity of the world as given by a natural attitude. We are also using those facts to generate and constitute activity, social and artistic and questioning and searching. In doing what I have done I have not meant to make it less or more. It is still there. William Bronk's "The Smile on the Face of a Kouros" continues serene, spanning years, and perhaps mutability. There you see it. Nothing is going to happen to it, that is the beauty of it. This was just a way of taking this poem and making it my own by writing my way into it.

Edward Foster

OPPENHEIMER, BRONK,
AND THE EDGE OF IMAGINED SPACE

I.

[I]N WILLIAM BRONK'S *Some Words*, originally published in 1993 and reissued in 1999, one poem, in its entirety, is as follows:

> Come into the poem, reader. The door will close
> itself behind you. You can leave whenever you will. (*SW* 58)

The poem is called "Bid," and indeed it bids us enter, although the phrasing "Come into the poem, reader" may feel less cordial than coercive, even intimidating, and no one should be reassured by the sentence with which the poem ends. The poem is a seduction, and its gentleness is a mask, for if the poem works its will, it will root itself within us, and we will not be able to leave it; it will be part of whatever we are.

"Bid" can be understood in another way: as a gamble, for Bronk and the poem are playing with high stakes, and if you truly understand what the poem says, and agree with it, it wins the game. The victory is dual; you cannot leave that to which you assent.

Bronk's late poems experiment with tone and the appearance of an easy-going, almost careless sensibility, but it is the carelessness of the song "Careless Love," the title of which Bronk borrowed for the title of one of his books.

In *All of What We Loved* (1997), Bronk says

> . . . in my mind
> are kept intricacies of ones gone
> who'll then be gone again. (*AWWL* 13)

What are these "intricacies," these things that "we" loved? What is this seemingly casual, careless, if quite seductive, love?

II.

When Joel Oppenheimer was teaching at New England College, he invited Bronk to do a reading there, although why he did so Bronk considered a mystery. A poet in such positions, Bronk pointed out, usually invites poets whose work is in some fashion in sympathy with his own, and, he added, his own work had very little in common with Oppenheimer's. Substantively, in fact, they seem as opposite as two poets can be. "There is no person," says Bronk. "The person never was." But Oppenheimer's poems are peopled explicitly with girlfriends, children, wives. Oppenheimer says:

> i am happy now
> alone tonight still
> there is a woman
> real and loving
> she wants me
> as i want her. (Oppenheimer 193)

Bronk, on the other hand, says:

> I suppose there may be a line between us (an us?)
> and the where we live (a where?). I look at the terms
> —the we, the where, whatever—we speak in
> and wonder whether they have to do with the stuff
> there is, whether they is a stuff as we say. (*LS* 213)

It isn't that Bronk does not want a world in which "there is a woman / real and loving," who "wants me / as i want her," but his mind leads him to ask what "wanting" is, and although he believes the *experience* of wanting is universal, the objects of that wanting are found in mirrors and echoes. Oppenheimer says the woman wants him; Bronk says, "I am the other I love" (SW 10). Bronk's poems name those whom he loves, but he knows that beyond the names, they are, in the poem, essentially what he believes them to be.

That is the fundamental condition of lyric poetry. We will in fact never know much about Shakespeare's Mr. W. H. or Petrarch's Laura. Mr. W. H. and Laura are not important except insofar as their authors imagined them in the poems. The same is true, it may be, of that woman who "wants me / as i want her."

Nonetheless, if one truly believes there are selves we desire other than those whom we imagine, one can construct an exquisite space in which it is possible to say:

> i remember only
> there was a woman
> of rare beauty
> > a wife
> who bathed herself
> so slowly in my tub
> that i wrote poems
> about it. (Oppenheimer 316)

The wonder is that Oppenheimer can say this so casually—as if we all should know, whether we are women or men, exactly what it means to have "a wife / who [bathes] herself / so slowly . . . ." But do we respond in the same way if we imagine the speaker, like the bather, to be a woman? How in fact does one read the poem if one is not, as the majority of readers necessarily are not, men with wives? This may belabor the obvious, but the question is essential. Oppenheimer's poem seduces us into a vision of relations between people that he clearly enjoyed but one that depends upon a private perspective. It asserts a pleasure and wonder that is deeply solipsistic; it is in fact as much a matter of mirrors and echoes as "Viva la Compagnie."

Oppenheimer can be seen as a Pre-Raphaelite, or late nineteenth-century male poet. His imagined women have affinities to those in, say, Dante Gabriel Rossetti or, to choose someone less obvious, the American symbolist Stuart Merrill. The following, from one of Merrill's late poems as translated by George Eugene Odom, could as well have been written by Oppenheimer:

> Today you gave me your body. And the sun has stopped in the sky, and winter has burst into flower, and the rivers have retraced their courses, and nothing is more real in the world outside the embrace of your bare arms. (Odom)

As conventional as these sentiments are, they assumed a new life in the late nineteenth century but were then generally eschewed by American High Modernists. Early Pound, still under the influence of Rossetti, was drawn to them but not the later poet. Nor, for the most part, was Eliot or Stevens, and although Williams reinvoked them in "Asphodel," they were not central to most of his work.

In short, Oppenheimer was summoning things that his century had largely ceded to movies, musicals, and other forms of popular culture.

III.

Petrarch's and Shakespeare's love poetry involve solitude and the frustrations of the poet in getting his lover's attention. But even the subjects of the poets' attention seem solitary. We may know little about Mr. W. H., but we know at least that he is very much in love with himself, for the poems tell us that. The subject of Oppenheimer's poem is solitary, too—bathing slowly, caressing herself, self-absorbed, alone. Publishing the poem, or even writing it, breaches the solitude—as happens in, to cite an instance from another art, John Everett Millais's iconic painting of Elizabeth Siddal as the drowned Ophelia. If the poem concerns the poet's solitude, then presumably he has the right to make it public, if he wants. But if the privacy is the self-destructive Siddal's or the bather's in Oppenheimer's poem, the issue is more complex—unless, in Bronk's words, "There is no person. The person never was."

IV.

One way to move Oppenheimer out of the nineteenth century and its archaic (archaic in poetry) notions of women is to consider his definition of metaphor. In "For Tom Blackburn," he says,

> metaphor is all
> and all
> when come to
> metaphor
>
> "to bear over"
>
> the one act
> which makes us
> conscious also
> brave deceitful
> and the like. (Oppenheimer 229)

That "metaphor" be "the one act / which makes us / conscious" is obviously not true—there are many acts that make us conscious—unless he means that the mind knows only representations, that it knows strictly the things it imagines, metaphors for whatever is filtered through the senses.

The poet, he says,

> . . . must
> start by baring self
> then move to
> things bearing on our
> selves and make those
> things and self
> more in the world. (Oppenheimer 229)

The poet, that is, weaves and asserts correspondences, so that words and the world they presume to represent become a grand knit of relations. This suggests that the world can be known as such, or at least differentiated, objectively, from the self. In fact that would seem impossible, but Oppenheimer's belief at least allows him to see the poem as an imagined construction rather than as a transcription of something impartially and objectively perceived. He goes on, however, to say:

> words for things
> for words for things
> and still have them things
> and still have selves
> and have the world. (Oppenheimer 229)

But what are those "selves" and that "world"? Are they appropriated or imagined? The answer is not clear from what Oppenheimer says, and one is left with the possibility that Oppenheimer believes that the woman of whom he writes is truly in and of the world—and that what he does is then appropriate her. Oppenheimer can, then, "still have selves"—possess them, that is—and not merely desire them. If so, his poetry must be read as fundamentally nostalgic for a poetic vision that Rossetti and Merrill took for granted.

V.

At times it seems as if "selves" exist literally in Bronk. He writes, for instance, in "The Wall,"

> Watching the curve of the long line of your back,
> desiring, I said in my mind that each of us
> is alone forever, forever. We live with this. (LS 83)

But Bronk, although believing the world may be composed of infinite selves, resolutely insists that what we know is, exactly, our desire for them. The rest—that which we desire—is invention.

If Oppenheimer seems Pre-Raphaelite or generally nostalgic for the nineteenth century, Bronk is rooted in the Kantian dilemma that marks the beginning of modernism—the recognition that things are not knowable in themselves and that the terms through which they are perceived, time and space, are products of the mind. Kant's positions were fruitful for poetry, making the poem more than an Aristotelean imitation of a real and insistently calling into question the belief that affective communication is possible—for how can I know that the you I desire is other than what I imagine—other, that is, than the significance I project onto your form ("the curve of the long line of your back")?

VI.

Oppenheimer's bathing woman might be flattered, like a Laura or a Stella, to find herself in his words, but it may be that for the rest of us, although we may love the poem, the woman herself does not matter; even her name becomes an encumbrance. What we care about are the poet's perceptions in his words. The subject, as something outside those words, vanishes before the ink is dry, and in fact this has been repeatedly recognized by poets working in the conventions of romantic love poetry: "O that you were yourself" says Shakespeare in sonnet 13; "But, love, you are / No longer yours than you yourself here live." The real subject is not the self but desire and the metaphors through which it is manifest.

Bronk writes:

We know nothing of the world and will never know. All we say is metaphor which asserts at once our unknowing and our need to state in some language what we don't know. How we love clothes; plain clothing or even our nakedness, speaking the silence of the world, or fanciful costume in which we praise some aspect of the world we mean to praise. Clothing as metaphor, not to dress ourselves nor to say what the world is if we knew but to praise that world however it might be. Rich fabrics and fine leathers, ruffles and satin, silver and lace, glorious colors and the fragile purities of clean whites: none of these is the world nor are they all together the world. Songs only that sing its praise, the earnest entreaties and importunities of our desire. (*VSC* 49)

Here he and Oppenheimer appear to be in agreement: "metaphor is all"—at least as far as our "knowing" is concerned. But the differences, I think, are deeper than the similarities. Oppenheimer may be isolated in his wonder and his desire and so creates a world in which his desire can find expression. But he does insist that his imagination live among wives and children. He is nostalgic for metaphors of the past, and I think that nostalgia goes a long way in explaining why most of his readers and critics are male. The past is powerfully resilient.

There is great benefit in not seeing things within Oppenheimer's terms, but at the same time, something is lost. "Belief in nothing," says Bronk,

is a positive belief apart from relieving us of partialities; and, even in that respect, it is a liberation. The world is not partial. Nothing is all and the world is nothing as we are. What should we say? Nothing to say of ourselves and the world tells us nothing. The world is a silence. But we talk of it and to it. (*VSC* 49)

Oppenheimer's nostalgic determination, even if it leads only to what may seem to us a metaphorical configuration, is heroic. Bronk, enticing his readers into a space from which they can less easily extract themselves, may seem by comparison demonic; he wants more than to have his reader share a perception or an insight. He would in fact terminate worlds like Oppenheimer's. And, in his language, he does.

And yet those worlds, in *their* language, go on, though now understood somewhat differently than has been the convention: in Bronk's words, "things / may be beautiful but things are the sight not the things.

/ What we desire may only empty desire" (*AWWL*, 95). What is left to Oppenheimer is the power of nostalgia, and it gives him the authority to insist that what he sees is true and not merely a private version. And with that comes the heroic recovery of something we find that we might still feel and used to believe.

Jack Kimball

WILLIAM BRONK AND FAMILY

P OETRY THAT QUESTIONS WITH CLARITY IS RARE. Poetry that questions such certainties as time and place and, more, deploys an abbreviated linguistic code to accent uncertainty—this sort of poetry appears discontinuous and alien. Writers of this sort, like William Bronk, seem amused by their very connoisseurship of discontinuity, occupied by their own methods and objects of avulsion from known qualities, the knowability of qualities, indeed, the whole apparatus and artistry of knowing.

A lineage of discontinuity

To demark a lineage for such discontinuity within twentieth-century American verse, in addition to Bronk, one might suggest Gertrude Stein, Louis Zukofsky and Jack Spicer, as well as their late-century descendants associated with a "language" poetry whose aim is to undermine passive reception of conventionally logical discourse strategies. Even though Bronk favors stark language that obliterates prosodic conventions, as do Stein, Zukofsky and Spicer, Bronk's standing in this lineage can be debated on grounds of his unsubversive syntax and transparent testimony. His verse is not so experimental; it is far simpler in its discursive organization and argument than that of the others. With regard to experiment, for example, compared to Zukofsky's frenetic appropriation of Marx, Shakespeare, Mallarmé, et al., Bronk's discursive techniques are markedly conservative. Bronk makes disciplined assertions, sometimes in poems of no more than three or four lines comprising the cool and classical: embedded anaphora ("Whether what we sense of this world / is the what of this world only, or the what / of which of several possible worlds /—which what?"); aggravated apophasis (". . . there are worlds

but . . . no world. . . ."); rampant paradox ("The carelessness of love is
we take such care."); and antimodernist vocabulary that borders on the
devotional in its embrace of "the world," of "we," of "man," of "God."

Mentalist search

Bronk's methods are nonetheless governed by an expansive bedlam
of the psychically discontinuous and unknown, an anarchy which renders
his poetic objects utopian. In the fourteen-line "Unnamed" Bronk reduces
uncertainty to an agnostic purity housed in a slender sonnet, entered into
by way of curt anapests leading directly to dark, iambic qualifiers:

In the narrowest and most immediate
view, we are named and identifiable
as persons, noted and notarized as such.*

---

*Scansion is how we live and breathe (to coin a phrase) into and out of lines. And this
in turn is linked to upbringing and a sense of where we're heading at given points in time,
as well, these are flowing matters of how we enunciate, elide, hem and duck from syllable
to syllable in a music that should reflect versions of how we talk or might talk in a
moment of some drama, or in a poetic crisis, say, rather than how a lexicographer
inscribes a given word to encode the convention. I scan the three lines of Bronk's as
follows, with (a) standing for anapest, (i) for iamb, (t) for trochee and (d) for dactyl·

a, a, i, /a, (—or—a, a, i, /i,)
a, i, t, d,
i, i, a, i, i.

1: in the NAR / r-est and MOST / im ME / di yete ..

2: VIEW, /

(—or—in the NAR / r-est and MOST / im ME / dyete ..
VIEW, /)

2 (Cont'd): we are NAMED / and I / DENT i / FI a ble

....

From this entry perspective, readily discernable because it "is a way we live," Bronk's mentalism gives way in his second stanza to the less usual view "from a long way back and away." Here, time-dependent wires of life and death get crossed. The knowing stance of "a way we live" evanesces into a brazen, alternate pattern, a utopia out of time where we are just "bones," and "cells shed from the skin." Quite gleefully, "there isn't even a body to shed from." The staggering truncation in a third and last stanza tips Bronk's anarchist hand.

> But feel vitality. Plenitude.
> Untimed. Nothings, we share in it.

The "we," Bronk's synecdoche for mankind, participates in a nothing so power-packed that "it" is "nothings" not subject to rules of syntax, expository proposition, timing or time. Similarly, within six lines from "The Imposition of Measure" time and place "thin away . . . beyond survey. / Beyond our here, likewise we are there." Again, Bronk is providing clarity and giving shape to a mentalist search in its many aspects, what physicists might call a quantum phenomenon present in all its instances, and what zennists describe as conceptualizing mind, provisional, time-bound, imposed wakefulness to—for lack of a better term—the ineffable.

---

3 as PER / sons, NO/ ted and NO /ta RIZED / as SUCH.

The first line runs onto the second, with two likely scans for the run-on: an anapest or a slurry-speech iamb—more the case in upstate New York and upcountry New England where it could be plausibly pronounced as "dyete." The second line ends in pattern variation, trochee and dactyl; other lines seem consistently given over to anapests and iambs.

Another point. The run-on from line one to line two is key to the clippedness I sense throughout, one of the controls over an anger that underpins most of Bronk.

The Body of This Life:

With texts like "Unnamed" and "The Imposition of Measure" Bronk holds up time in celebration of discontinuity, a programmatic stand midpoint between Stein and Spicer. All three reach through language to demonstrate possibilities of choreographing the timeless and ineffable. Spicer in *After Lorca* alternates between textually self-referential accounts in prose and in poetry of the "time mechanic." Spicer, though, relies on appeals to an "ideal" readership, the people to whom he dedicates his poems, for instance, and this strategy frequently sidelines his chance-taking in the direction of amiable pleasantries and received sentiment. Stein has suggested more opaquely than would Bronk that in her improvisations she "was groping toward a continuous present, a using everything a beginning again and again" ("Composition as Explanation"). In a phrase, Stein's choreography is all but too much chance-taking: repeatedly drawing the reader into a now-fresh, now-obtuse no-time and no-place in the "continuous present."

Bronk's chance-taking is cogent if predictable ambiguity that casts time and perception of time into the scientifically-correct category of relative fact or, in Bronk's terms, uncertainty, as time is only a specter of the "untimed" real. Shorter works from Bronk toy with untimed reality as paradox and enigma: "The life that says me poems . . . doesn't say

---

Regarding the "ideal" reader in *After Lorca* Spicer dedicates each verse to youths, friends, lovers, and in his epistolary "asides," to Lorca himself. These are bold and wonderful gestures, generosities, really, that allow him to say things like· "When you are in love there is no problem. The person you love is always interested because he knows that the poems are always about him. If only because each poem will someday be said to belong to the Miss X or Mr. Y period of the poet's life. I may not be a better poet when I am in love, but I am a far less frustrated one. My poems have an audience" (*Spicer* 38-39). Spicer is right, he has an audience; this is an expectation fulfilled, justifiably so. And Spicer saying he has an audience *in* and *to* Lorca is instructive. But the point I am attempting is that such declarations and gesturing ultimately delimit Spicer's time game by imposing courtly conventions on the paranormal experiment entailed in tinkering with time's machinery. Spicer's dedication to his audience self-consciously reminds the reader that this is, well, poetry with an affectionate demeanor fixed in social ambitions; so in that respect, *After Lorca* is meditatively relaxed as it is merely, seductively remarkable, not miraculously or even revelatorily *beyond* a received and, as I say, sentimental intent.

itself." Slightly longer pieces cycle in dialectics: (a) fake concession to a version of perceived reality propped up by well-formed syntax and stolid metonymies ("the general want," "the evasive," the "something" that "wants through") and (b) the fated breakdown of pretext. That Bronk's estrangement from certainty is so *certain* exposes his poetry to attack as dogma and to parody by paraphrase. Despite a whittled diction and minimalist formality, there are excesses: patchwork pronouncement ("our now is always . . . having no past or future[.] Here's an eternity."); plain talk on a grandiose scale ("Sky, trees: / earth is believable."); stoical wordplay ("Our lives corrected prevalent errors. / The corrections prevail in irrelevance.").

Program, excesses and all, Bronk is rigorous demonstrator of such errancy. Once his flaws are conceded, resistance evaporates, because Bronk's is a discontinuity not merely spoken, but specified. In fine, his clarity trumps other criteria:

> We are in the real world as ghosts are in this world. . . . The matter of the real world passes through us . . . the link may be a projection without conforming, like the relation between an airplane and its shadow on the earth, which in following the lateral, or better, circumferential flight of the plane, goes up and down with the contours of the ground, or glides across the water though the plane climbs or descends. (*VSC*)

The real world. And this world. Bronk's ambiguity raises the alien prospect as a perspective and discipline, while his psychic transparency—a "projection without conforming"—mimes how these worlds collide. Ever-specific in depicting this collision involving the "circumferential" and the shadow that "glides," Bronk is unwilling, too scrupulous, I would stress, to make larger claims for our link to the real, viewing it without exaggeration as what "passes through us."

Resistance and centrality to other poetries

One consequence of Bronk's projection of untimed reality gliding over our world is his meditative hauteur sustained and circumferenced by profound liberation and solitude, a self-imposed condition that has carried over to his relationships with other poets and their poetry.

> I don't feel close to any poet's work. There are poets I've been close to personally . . . but I don't think there is any real connection between my work and their work. We've gone separate ways. (Bertholf, "Conversation")

Bronk's felt separation from others is not so much blanket objection to being categorized as fair notice that like any "strong" poet, he opposes adoption, and bears responsibility for his own place with or without a lineage.

Notwithstanding his denial of "real connection" to others, Bronk is a central figure within a family of the discontinuous, a group including such economists of language as Stein, Spicer and Zukofsky. As for temporally constrained story line, linear argument and whatever symbolic coherence narration and argument imply, Bronk, Stein, Spicer and Zukofsky behave badly, along with other twentieth-century poets. By abbreviating or abandoning discursive constructs, realigning representational modes with nonrepresentational contexts—in short, composing a verse-in-shards—poets of the discontinuous foreground and recontextualize the jigsaw enactment of invention, the poetic moment, the now.

Bronk and Zukofsky

To consider fuller Bronk's 'family connections' to other poets of the discontinuous, it is particularly helpful to compare him with Zukofsky, because these two pair off in poetic temperament as well as linguistic strategy. Both poets maintained a distance from their contemporaries, an outgrowth of their mentalist epicurism. There is Zukofsky's exactitude, for instance, to "detail, not the mirage . . . seeing . . . thinking with the things as they exist" (*Prepositions*). Zukofsky's concern for detail is complemented by Bronk's focused gaze on perceived reality (which is unreal!) and on reality beyond (which is imperceptible!), an incongruity exemplified in this segment from "The Dream of a World of Objects":

> . . . the waking world,
> the object-poor, the edgeless. We dream of touch,
> of weight, of the definite frame, but rather this.
> As it is . . .

With respect to jigsaw enactments of invention, Bronk and Zukofsky recontextualize the now, the poetic moment within a *languaging process*, which in turn results in new roles, as well as new measures for time, relative to text and readers of text. In Zukofsky's verse language is rendered as material for voice and mind. Phonetic and syntactic particles emerge as conspicuously interactive objects by means of which readers participate in a "linguistic etiquette" that can connect "new meanings of word against word contemporarily read"; moreover, Zukofsky composes the poem as "precise information on existence out of which it grows" and "information of its existence, that is, the movement (and tone) of words" (*Prepositions*). "Information" in Zukofsky's sense represents a departure from modernist and romantic belief that reading a text necessitates acquiring meaning back-authored from some past or pasts. For Zukofsky, text in its present form as information is emphasized; likewise, textual "existence" deflates notions of a compulsory linkage to either tradition or forms of mythic or poetic history predating the text. To be sure, in contrast with Zukofsky particles of language and other formal liberties—such as slangy off-rhyme, ventriloquism via collaged citation of diverse texts, lexical japery and misassociations mixing mathematical formulae, classical reference, political rant, botanical notation, etc.—Bronk's forms of lyric look less shard-like. But Bronk's lyrics, in effect, are shards writ whole in that they reinvent that most formidable of linguistic puzzles, the riddle-as-invocation, the rune. Bronk accomplishes the nearly incredible within a demagnified language for mind and no-mind (or, if you will, for a form of meditative mind) in fleeting, syntactically cohesive verse-assertions and verse-inquiries about secrets, desire beyond poetry, belief in nonbelief, the unreality of the tangible and the natural. These are half-visions to engage the reader's capacity for focusing the invisible, invoking proximities of the unknown.

Engaging with Zukofsky or Bronk, readers thus assume responsibilities based not so much on taking in a text's a priori information as on collaborating in its immediacy and development for the future. The text "exists" as readers enact the poem. While this insight seems as though it should be universal—applicable to poetry entire—the distinctive feature of a lyric by Zukofsky or Bronk is that a reader's enactment of text is the poetic subject matter, that is, the poem's language invites reassembly for processing sense and meaning.

Formal urgency

Bronk's poetry is formally urgent at two linguistic and semantic levels. With regard to diction, Bronk's runic compression shepherds what seem like familiar terms into close and remarkable environs. To unpack the riddle we enter an oddly refractive microworld calling for necessary and sufficient reflection. Consider the four lines of "A Stayover"—

> Soul's the one we came with. When we go
> It's on our own. Great to live with,
> soul was loved and lover, the landscape.
> Let's leave it at that. Get along.

There are at least a dozen potentials here for conceiving "the landscape." Working backward from the term itself, we find that it is lover and loved, the soul. Also, in reading backward and forward, we see that it's part of us, yet it's independent of us, prior to us, something to live with, travel with, something to leave, as in departing from and/or leaving as-is, and—from the title—it's something that hangs on, perhaps only for awhile. The poem's last two words encourage us to consider moving on and/or going along.

At another level of analysis, Bronk's diapason resonates with tonal gravity. Bronk seems serious because his premises are pedagogically unevasive, direly imparted with syllogistic definitude that gives no quarter to extraneous literary device. His poetry "says what it means," refusing to "take roundabout, concealed ways" (Weinfield, "Conversation"). Poem after poem grapples with an unattainable nonexistence or absence, knowable only through "feelings" that, according to Bronk,

> seem not to have the habit of reality . . . come from beyond our skin like approaches to us, like messages; and we respond, trembling and shaking, or vibrating in tune as though we were instruments a music were played on. . . . (VSC)

In this light, Bronk's is a poetry of passions, transmitted not by shocking metaphor or bold experiment, but by postulate and derived consequence.

A *didactic scale*

Bronk's compressions coupled with "trembling" *gravitas* establish a didactic scale for various formats of the psychically discontinuous. For example, through Bronk we may weigh Zukofsky's reliance on "historic and contemporary particulars" (*Prepositions*) as constitutive of "information on existence," cited earlier. If we do, we might regard Zukofsky's direction as radically different from Bronk's—for Bronk, the particular is "dismissed" and existence is perpetually bracketed as unreal. Zukofsky's prosodic surface is more textured and conceptually more experimental than Bronk's, but also, to the didactic scale, less germane, less daring. History, existence, indeed all time frames are reduced to irrelevance by Bronk's utopian gamble. With Bronk, the stakes are always the same: rational speaking to and for a discontinuity engendered by the real world v. this.

That Bronk's reductions do not lead to parsimony of vision or the implementation of despair is disturbing. Current convention anticipates dour results from a lyric of nonbelief. Instead, in Bronk's streamlined meditative regime, ephemera of experiment, those of Bronk's and others', meet a measure of desire preserved beyond trends, beyond fiction, a longing for "nothings" unfiltered by approximations. Such longing, even for the "nothings," is a metaphor of "a material world" but "nothing more"—as Bronk puts it in "My House New-Painted." Bronk stays home, holed up in his cloister, as it were, but he maintains the alien perspective, looks out his window, beyond its frame, toward the "real world" across space and time. One reward for Bronk's gazing into the real is that he feels its message and conveys this "as though we were instruments a music were played on." This is desire secured but transmuted as common prayer, a kind of humane and even familial chic. We share in it.

THE IDEA OF IDEAS

Burton Hatlen

WILLIAM BRONK AND THE SUBLIME

"[I]N THE SUBLIME," SAYS TERRY EAGLETON, "the 'real' itself—the eternal, ungraspable totality of things—inscribes itself as the cautionary limit of all mere ideology, of all complacent subject-centeredness, causing us to feel the pain of incompletion and unassuaged desire" (Eagleton 89). This sentence describes, with uncanny accuracy, a nexus of experiences and emotions around which William Bronk restlessly, even obsessively circles, in dozens, hundreds of his poems: perhaps, indeed, in all of them. Thus Eagleton's definition invites a reading of Bronk as a poet of the Sublime, and it is such a reading that I will offer here.* As Eagleton himself reminds us, the Sublime enters history, hand in hand with her sister the Beautiful, in the eighteenth century. Together the Beautiful and the Sublime claim to offer a space of human freedom within an increasingly closed world-system based upon commodity production and exchange. In particular, the Sublime, like Art in general from the Romantic period to the present, attempts to preserve a sense of the sacred in a time when the traditional religions were becoming either empty social rituals or bastions of an "orthodoxy" threatened by new scientific discoveries, or simply by the recognition that religious "truths" vary from one culture to another. Thus to read Bronk as a poet of the Sublime is to place him within some broad cultural currents that extend from the eighteenth into the twentieth centuries.

But in particular, I hope that my reading of Bronk will help to clarify his relationship to his immediate poetic predecessors, all of whom were

---

*I am not the first critic to link Bronk to the Sublime. In particular, Norman Finkelstein, in a series of essays from 1982 into the 1990s, has sought to position Bronk as a poet whose "recognition of an infinitely remote and unknowable order becomes the ground for the negative sublime" ("Bronk, Duncan, and the Far Borders of Poetry" 38). However, I want to pursue this argument in a new direction, by placing Bronk within the history of the Sublime as a historical phenomenon.

also engaged, if in quite different ways, with the Sublime. As Norman Finkelstein has pointed out, it is difficult to place Bronk within one or another of the dominant currents in modern poetry, for while his work emerges from the poetry of Frost and Stevens, it has found its chief admirers among "such figures as Creeley, Olson, Oppen, and Corman," who "trace their origins back to two very different modern poets—Pound and Williams" ("Bronk, Duncan," 33). We can resolve this apparent paradox, I want to propose, if we recognize that what I will loosely call the "Stevens tradition" and the "Pound tradition" explore overlapping but different modes of the Sublime, and that Bronk is engaged with both modes. The poets writing in the Poundian tradition, I will here argue, have pursued, metonymically, what Kant called the "Mathematical Sublime," while the poets in the Stevens tradition have been attempting, primarily in their self-reflexive engagement with metaphor, to ground themselves in Kant's "Dynamical Sublime." The Mathematical Sublime carries us to the limits of the Sayable, and the poet that pursues the metonymic path pushes language toward the point where it disintegrates in an impossible attempt to take on the material solidity of the Otherness that it reaches toward. On the other hand, the Dynamical Sublime allows poets to turn back, via a metaphoric displacement, from the radical indeterminacy of the unbounded Sublime, to reground the self upon the very Otherness that had previously called the autonomous self into question. But Bronk refuses both the totalizing gestures of the metonymic

---

Marjorie Perloff has summed up the opposition between these two poetic lineages in the title of her essay, "Pound/Stevens: Whose Era?" In practice, to critics such as Helen Vendler and Harold Bloom, who see Stevens as the pivotal figure in twentieth-century American poetry, what Perloff calls "the Pound tradition" is simply invisible; and, conversely, critics such as Hugh Kenner or Perloff herself see the first half of the century as "the Pound era," and they tend to dismiss Stevens and company as incurably retrograde late Romantics. Puzzling over the paradox of Bronk's apparent links to both of these traditions, Finkelstein juxtaposes Bronk with Robert Duncan, and he suggests that the Stevens tradition (as represented by Bronk) and the Pound tradition (as represented by Duncan) might constitute two very different but finally complementary ways of moving toward the "far borders of poetry." In addition, Finkelstein suggests that in both cases this pressing of poetry toward its limits might have something to do with what we convention-ally call "the Sublime." In these respects Finkelstein anticipates my argument here, although we develop these themes in quite different ways.

poet (I am thinking of Whitman as well as Pound) *and* Stevens's aestheticization of the Sublime. Instead he insists, in poem after poem, that we press ourselves up against the limits of the Sayable, to the point where we must acknowledge the absolute Otherness of the Real. In so doing, his works constitutes a rigorous and unflinching critique of *both* the Stevens tradition *and* the Pound tradition—and thereby draws these two traditions together at last.

I

Kant draws a sharp distinction between the Beautiful and the Sublime: "The beautiful in nature is connected with the form of the object, which consists in having definite boundaries. The sublime, on the other hand, is to be found in a formless object, so far as in it and by occasion of it *boundlessness* is represented, and yet its totality is also present to thought" (Kant 82). The Beautiful and the Sublime elicit very different responses in us, says Kant. The Beautiful " brings with it a feeling of the furtherance of life, and thus is compatible with charms and with the play of the imagination. . . . Natural beauty brings with it a purposiveness in its form by which the object seems to be, as it were, preadapted to our judgment, and thus constitutes in itself an object of satisfaction" (Kant83). The pleasure of the Sublime, on the other hand, "arises only indirectly; viz. it is produced by the feeling of a momentary checking of the vital powers and a consequent stronger outflow of them. . . . Hence it is incompatible with physical charm; and as the mind is not merely attracted by the object but is ever being alternately repelled, the satisfaction in the sublime does not so much involve a positive pleasure as admiration or respect, which rather deserves to be called negative pleasure. . . . [T]hat which excites in us . . . the feeling of the sublime may appear, as regards its form, to violate purpose in respect of the judgment, to be unsuited to our presentative faculty, and as it were to do violence to the imagination; and yet it is judged to be only the more sublime" (Kant 83).). For Kant, then, the sublime is always *beyond*: "no sensible form can contain the sublime properly so-called" (Kant 83-4). "We call that *sublime* which is *absolutely great*," says Kant (Kant 86). The absolutely (as distinct from the comparatively) great transcends the capacity of the human imagination to grasp or contain the object it confronts. For Kant, the experience of confronting the absolutely great evokes "*astonishment* that borders upon terror, the dread and holy awe which seizes the observer at the sight of mountain peaks rearing themselves to heaven, deep chasms and streams raging therein, deep-shadowed solitudes that dispose one to melancholy meditation" (Kant 109).

Recent theorists of the Sublime, such as Thomas Weiskel and Harold Bloom, see the Romantic poets as resolving the anxiety aroused in us by the "absolutely great" through a metaphoric bridging of the gap between self and world. In this respect, these critics are describing what Kant called the "Dynamical Sublime." In this form of the Sublime, says Kant, we experience nature as overwhelming *power*. The contemplation of such power reminds us of our own weakness, but it also "raise[s] the energies of the soul above their accustomed heights and discover[s] in us the faculty of resistance of a quite different kind, which gives us courage to measure ourselves against the apparent almightiness of nature" (Kant 100-1). In effect, we triumph over the natural powers that we confront by affirming a counter-vailing power within ourselves. This power is, I would propose (and here I am going beyond Kant), the metaphor-making powers of the imagination, which allows us to triumph over nature by identifying ourselves with it. But Kant also distinguishes a second form of the Sublime, the "Mathematical Sublime." A simple form of the Mathematical Sublime is the number series itself: we can add one to any number we can conceive, and thus by definition we can never arrive at the end of the series. But Kant also points to the pyramids of Egypt and St. Peter's in Rome as examples of the Mathematical Sublime. In the presence of these human creations too "there is . . . a feeling of the inadequacy of . . . imagination for presenting the ideas of a whole, wherein the imagination reaches its maximum, and, in striving to surpass it, sinks back into itself" (Kant 91). Thus we encounter the Mathematical Sublime at the moment when the imagination arrives at its limit point, and discovers that there is something *beyond* anything the imagination can conceive. If the Dynamical Sublime resolves itself in an imaginative identification with the powers of nature, the Mathematical Sublime finds its resolution, for

Kant, in an act of rational reflection. Confronted by a "magnitude" that "goes on without hindrance to infinity," "the mind listens to the voice of reason which, for every given magnitude—even for those that can never be entirely apprehended . . . —requires totality. Reason consequently desires comprehension in *one* intuition. . . . It does not even exempt the infinite (space and past time) from this requirement; it rather renders it unavoidable to think the infinite (in the judgment of common reason) as *entirely given* (according to its totality)" (Kant 93).

I will here rename Kant's Mathematical Sublime as the "Metonymic Sublime," because in it we move toward the Unsayable by increments: this + this + this. The metonymic poet—and I would include here the Whitman who defines himself, not as the loyal disciple of Emerson, but as Emerson's poetic antithesis, along with Pound and Williams in the twentieth century—seems to be impelled forward by the hope that if he can name every individual thing in the universe, one at a time, he will arrive finally at the One. But, of course, the Whole remains Unsayable—all the questing poet can do is to point *toward* it, as the n~ recedes constantly before us. So too, I will rename Kant's Dynamical Sublime as the "Metaphoric Sublime," because writers like Wordsworth or Shelley or Whitman's great opposite Emerson seek, through an act of verbal substitution (centered, commonly, on such figures of the infinite as the sea), to incorporate the Unsayable into the self, and to resee the Other as our humanity writ large. Kant's distinction between the Dynamical and the Mathematical Sublime thus corresponds to Roman Jakobson's distinction between the two great poetic master-tropes, metaphor and metonymy. In turn, these tropes correspond, for Jakobson, to the two axes of language itself, the paradigmatic and the syntagmatic—and, indeed, to the two fundamental modes of human cognition, the spatial and the temporal (esp. 95-114). In the twentieth century, as Mutlu Konick Blasing has proposed, Stevens inherits the metaphoric tradition of Emerson, while Pound inherits the metonymic tradition of Whitman. Stevens locates the imagination firmly at the center. "After the leaves have fallen," he tells us, "we return / To a plain sense of things," with a sense that "A fantastic effort has failed." "Yet the absence of the imagination," he declares, "had / Itself to be imagined" (*Collected Poems* 428).

For his part, Pound invents what he calls the ideogrammic method, grounded in the faith that by piecing together the particulars of the world, one at a time, we will arrive finally at the moment when we can declare, with Herakles in Pound's translation of the Sophocles play, "What splendor! It all coheres."

The Modernism of Stevens and Pound represents an extension of the Romantic Sublime, in that both poets display a continuing longing for the moment of closure in which the mind bridges the gap between self and world. But since the late nineteenth century this moment of closure has become increasingly problematic. The art of our century still points us toward the unspeakable, *the beyond*, but no longer does it presume to contain the unspeakable in concepts such as "the infinite," or in symbolic images such as the mist-haloed mountains and the shadowy gorges of nineteenth-century painting. Acutely aware of the inadequacy of the nineteenth-century rhetoric of the Sublime, both Stevens and Pound admit into their work, in different ways, a measure of unresolved indeterminacy. In Stevens these moments are likely to come at the ends of poems, where the stately eloquence of the poet's discourse gives way to a simple act of pointing, as at the end of "The Motive for Metaphor," which arrives finally at a vision of "The vital, arrogant, fatal, dominant X" (*Collected Poems* 257)—or, perhaps most famously, the ending of "The Man on the Dump": "Where was it one first heard of the truth? The the" (*Collected Poems* 186). In Pound's case, indeterminacy enters the poem primarily via a formal method that leaves the moment of closure to the indefinite future. Until near the end of his life Pound assumed that someday he would "finish" *The Cantos*: draw together all the drafts that he had been composing since the 1920s into a coherent grand design. But he never did so, because his poetic method itself—which both allowed and required him to begin anew, again and again—precluded any such moment of closure. Thus, despite the visions of the gods scattered through the poem, the one truly sublime moment comes at the end, when Pound admits that "I am not a demigod, I cannot make it cohere" (Pound 796)—and then adds that "it coheres all right / even if my notes do not cohere" (Pound 797).

THE BODY OF THIS LIFE:

Stevens's efforts to reach beyond the music of his own rhetoric to grasp an Other that remains Unsayable issues in a pervasive ironic distancing from the very formal resources that he mobilizes with such skill. No poet of our century has reinvented so persuasively the music of the Grand Style of English verse, as it passes down to us from Milton and Wordsworth. And yet Stevens seems compelled to interrupt or even mock that music, in the passages of often-cacaphonous nonsense syllables that erupt again and again into his verse. In the poetry of Pound and his closest associates and successors, the opening toward an indeterminate Sublime issues in a progressive disintegration of syntax, as language seeks to take on the material immediacy of the physical object. Throughout his career Pound aimed at an absolute immediacy in presentation. In practice, this search for presence undermines the grammatical logic of the discursive sentence, which increasingly gives way to juxtaposed noun phrases: "The apparition of these faces in the crowd: / Petals on a wet, black bough" (*Personae* 111). We may see an analogous impulse to open up the structure of the sentence in Williams's "Rain," where the poet "spreads ///////// the words //////// far apart to let in ////////// her love" (*CP* I, 345). And in the later poetry of George Oppen, heir of Pound and Williams and sometime friend of William Bronk, the glue of syntax softens to the point of melting entirely; as the phrases slip and slide indeterminately over the page, a good many gaps open up where the mystery of What Is may leak in. All of these poets in the Pound tradition seem to share an impulse to push language as far as possible toward the Unsayable, even at the risk that in the process language will become not only as material but as unreadable as the things of this world themselves. At this point, enter William Bronk.

II

No poet that I have read explores so resolutely the borders of the Sayable, or points more insistently toward what lies beyond this border, than William Bronk. "Reality," says Bronk in one of his few programmatic statements, "is brought to mind by the inadequacy of any statement of it, the tension of that inadequacy, the direction and force of the statement" (*VSC* preface). And if, as Eagleton proposes, the limit point of the Sayable is also the moment of the Sublime, than I think it can be said that no poet addresses himself to the Sublime more consistently than Bronk. We may begin our exploration of the Bronkian Sublime with a passage from the poet's conversation with Henry Weinfield and others, published in the special issue of *Sagetrieb* devoted to his work. Bronk is here describing the way poems come to him: "But its like, all right, you walk out the door, and you hadn't been paying too much attention to the weather, and there's a tremendous light. The sun may be going down; it's been a cloudy day, and it's been dark all day, but there's this clear area just above the horizon and you're astonished: here's this light. You didn't invent the light and who the hell did? Nobody did it; it wasn't planned; it just happened" ("Conversation" 39). The poem, any poem, Bronk is saying, comes to him as something "tremendous," "astonishing," a light out of the darkness. The poet does not choose the moment when such an experience happens, and he certainly does not create the light; it simply comes to him, from somewhere "out there," beyond. The experience that Bronk here describes is, archetypally, the experience of the Sublime as described by Thomas Weiskel: we are living locked up in ourselves, in an "habitual, more or less unconscious . . . , harmonious" relationship with the world, but then suddenly "the habitual relation of mind and object breaks down. Surprise or astonishment [Bronk's very word] is the affective correlative, and there is an immediate intuition of a disconcerting disproportion between inner and outer" (Weiskel 23-4). Even Bronk's gesture of lifting the eyes toward the distant horizon, where the light breaks through, is archetypally Sublime, reenacting countless nineteenth-century landscape paintings. And no less archetypal is the sense that at this moment of vision something of vast importance has been revealed to us.

In telling this representative anecdote, Bronk is purportedly summing up his experience in writing his poems, but I am struck by how many of his poems tell a similar story of a man who is suddenly struck with astonishment, as a light from somewhere "beyond" breaks in. Here is a well-known example, titled—serendipitously for my purposes— "Metonymy as an Approach to a Real World":

THE BODY OF THIS LIFE:

Whether what we sense of this world
is the what of this world only, or the what
of which of several possible worlds
—which what?—something of what we sense
may be true, may be the world, what it is, what we sense.
For the rest, a truce is possible, the tolerance
of travelers, eating foreign foods, trying words
that twist the tongue, to feel that time and place,
not thinking that this is the real world.
Conceded, that all the clocks tell local time;
conceded, that "here" is anywhere we bound
and fill a space; conceded, we make a world,
is something caught there, contained there,
something real, something which we can sense?
Once in a city blocked and filled, I saw
the light lie in the deep chasm of a street,
palpable and blue, as though it had drifted in
from say, the sea, a purity of space. (LS 36)

The first half of this poem judiciously but skeptically assesses the possibility that something of what we sense may be true of a "real" world. "What" and "which"—these words are both shifters and pointers: their reference shifts depending on who is speaking and where, but "what" is not only a question but also an emphatic affirmation of the immediate givenness, the quidditas or whatness, of things. But the best possible outcome of this sifting process seems to be a "truce," as we agree to accept that we are always "worldless," aliens in any world we inhabit: no food is the right food, the food of home, and we are never allowed to speak our true and natural language, a "real" language that would give us the "right" names of "real" things. But we can grope our way forward, as long as we don't delude ourselves into thinking that this makeshift structure we've nailed together is the "real" world. Nevertheless, even as we acknowledge that we spend our lives in such structures, the possibility remains that there might exist a "real" world as something that we can, if not lay hold upon, at least approach, metonymically. The breakthrough moment comes with "Once in a city." The city may be "blocked and filled," but nevertheless the light breaks in. Where did this light come from? Does it come up from below, since we see it—not at the distant horizon, as in the anecdote quoted above—but in the depths of a "chasm," an abyss? Or does it come from "beyond"—the sea, or even outer space? We don't know. And what if anything does the light tell us—about, presumably, "something real," since that is what we have been talking about. Bronk offers us no explanations: "Nobody planned it; it just happened," as Bronk says of the light in the anecdote quoted above. The only possible source cited—the sea, a traditional metaphor of the unbounded Sublime—is clearly fanciful, and is surrounded by qualifiers: "as though," "say." Is the light material, "palpable and blue," or is it an emptiness, "a purity of space"? Clearly, we have here come up against the Unsayable: there are no words that can define and encompass the light. It is wholly Other, simply There, as it forces itself upon us—or, depending on your point of view, offers itself to us, an immaculate gift. In either case, we have, it seems, approached the "real," although we cannot grasp, lay hold upon, or even name It.

For Bronk, any world that we can talk about is not, by definition, the "real" world:

> It is unspeakable, that which exists.
> All I ever said was spoken of what
> is not, by one who is not. We do not speak
> of that. Oh, we say. Make speeches, love.
> And it is in place of what we would say,
> what will not ever be spoken, cannot: is. (LS 147)

"Unspeakable" suggests not only the impossibility of putting the "real" into words but also the horror that the "real" therefore evokes within us. If the "real" "is," then by definition we "are" not. Of course, we talk, make speeches and make love, but we do all this to avoid recognizing that we can never speak the primal word of being. The isolation of "is" after the colon drives home the point: what is will not and cannot ever be spoken. "At Tikal" addresses the same issue, with an overpowering pathos:

> It is always hard like this, not having a world,
> to imagine one, to go to the far edge
> apart and imagine, to wall whether in
> or out, to build a kind of cage for the sake
> of feeling the bars around us, to give shape to a world.
> And oh, it is always a world and not the world. (*LS* 32)

World-making is the great human task, and Bronk is often lovingly appreciative of our ingenuity in making a home for ourselves within this cosmos. The hard work of world-making happens out at the "far edge," where the Sayable meets the Unsayable, and there is something heroic about life at that edge. But Bronk also insists that we acknowledge the limits of the "ideological" (in Eagleton's terminology) worlds that we construct. In building a home for ourselves, we've also walled out the Unsayable, and in this respect every such wall becomes a cage in which we have imprisoned ourselves. The "pain of incompletion and unassuaged desire" that Eagleton refers to sounds through clearly in the "oh" of the last line. Desperately, we want *our* world to be *the* world, but always, ineluctably, the Unsayable Real presses in.

What does Bronk make of our inability to escape the cages that we build for ourselves, our continually frustrated effort to lay hold upon "what will not ever be spoken, cannot: is"? Some critics, including John Taggart, have argued that the dominant feeling in these poems is "frustration and despair" (Taggart 33). However, other critics, including John Ernest and Louise Chawla, have seen in Bronk's engagement with the ineffable an ultimate religious affirmation; and Henry Weinfield, in a more nuanced exploration of this issue, suggests that Bronk is moving perhaps not toward God, but at least toward the place where God might be, "along a path that is parallel to the *via negativa* of the mystical tradition" ("Cloud" 143). But I cannot read Bronk either as a poet of cosmic despair or as a poet of religious faith, and I would hope that approaching him as a poet of the Sublime might offer an alternative to both of these positions. The Sublime, as theorists since Burke have emphasized, offers itself to us as at once terrible *and* wonderful. The Sublime radically challenges the capacity of the self to master the world, either through an imaginative leap or through rational reflection. At such moments the self is, in the most literal sense, annihilated, "nothinged," and it responds with horror. Yet at the same time, the discovery that there is truly something "out there," something great that transcends our imaginative or rational grasp, is exhilarating. The word "awe" comes closest to suggesting the mixed character of the encounter with the truly Other: as noun, "awe" retains a sense of religious wonder, but as adjective it becomes "awful," which means not only worthy of "awe" but also loathsome, "just terrible." "Awe" is in fact a characteristic Bronk word: "World, world, I am scared / and waver in awe before the wilderness / of raw consciousness, because it is all / dark and formlessness" (*LS* 27-8). And for Bronk, the experience of awe shades into the awful, in all senses of that term:

> Here,
> at the center—it is the center?—only the sound
> of silence, that mocking sound. Awful. Once,
> before this, I stood in an actual ruin, a street
> no longer a street, in a town no longer a town,
> and felt the central, strong suck of it, not
> understanding what I felt: the heart of things.
> This nothing. This full silence. To not know. (*LS* 44)

At the center—but how can we know where the "center" is?—lies a nothing, a silence. And to find oneself alone, sucked into that silence, is awful.

Characteristically, the encounter with the Real, the silence at the heart of things, evokes in Bronk a mix of positive and negative emotions. In "Virgin and Child with Music and Numbers," he addresses the Virgin Mary, reminding her how "the pledge / the angel gave you, the songs you exchanged in joy / with Elizabeth, your cousin," have, with the slaughter of the innocents, given way to "meanness, the overhanging terror, and the need / for flight." But

> Still, the singing was and is. Song
> whether or not we sing. The song is sung.
> Are we cozened? The song we hear is like
> those numbers we cannot factor whose overplus,
> an indeterminate fraction, seems more than the part
> we factor out. Lady, if our despair
> is to be unable to factor ourselves in song
> or factor the world there, what should our joy
> be other than this same integer that sings
> and mocks at satisfaction? We are not
> fulfilled. We cannot hope to be. No,
> we are held somewhere in the void of whole despair,
> enraptured, and only there does the world endure. (*LS* 45)

Taggart, commenting on the last lines of this passage, focuses on the denial of fulfillment, the "void of whole despair" in which we find ourselves (Taggart 36). But as we turn across the line-break, we find ourselves, not only in despair, but also "enraptured," and only in this mix of despair and rapture does "the world endure." So too, earlier, "joy" is balanced against "despair." Both are present within the song. We despair because we cannot factor the song into what belongs to us and what belongs to "the world"; however we work out the equation, there seems to be something we cannot account for, an uncanny "overplus." But our joy, too, can arise only from and in the song of the world, which sings itself whether we will or not.

Nevertheless, I would also take issue with those critics who want to read Bronk as a poet of religious faith. Undoubtedly, the supernal light that we met in "Metonymy as an Approach to a Real World," and that recurs in dozens of Bronk's poems, has a distinctly divine aura. In one of the few moments in Bronk's poetry that I would call truly mystical, he tells us how

A light, this side of the hills toward Argyle,
flowed like fog through the hollows, rose to the depth
of the hills, illumined me. I faded in it
as the world faded in me, dissolved in the light.
No one to know and nothing knowable.
Oh, we know that knowing is not our way. . . . (*LS* 126-27)

For a moment, Bronk enters the Cloud of Unknowing, and as he gives up knowing the gap between Self and Other dissolves. But while the Bronkian light is always a blessing, a manifestation of a wholly unmerited grace, Bronk is careful to keep the light as indeterminate as possible: rarely if ever does he link the light with God or with traditional religious symbolism, and he particularly relishes the "winter light," which reminds us that "we see the light but we live in the cold and the dark" (*MF* 23). Admittedly too, Bronk is sometimes willing to invoke a traditional religious vocabulary in talking about the mystery that stands over against us, but the status of this vocabulary seems equivocal. As an experiment, I looked through the collection *That Tantalus*, collecting explicit religious references. The word "God" appears four times in this sequence and "Christ" once; but one use of "God" and the use of "Christ" are exclamations, "Dear God" (*LS 108*) and "Good Christ" (*LS 103*), while one "God" is a heartfelt "God help us" (*LS* 112). One use of "God" is heavily ironic: the poem titled "Of the Several Names of God" actually invokes none of those names and says nothing about God. And one is clearly negative: "it was plain that there never was to be / the City of God" (*LS* 117). More interestingly, in one poem Bronk invokes the passage in Exodus in which God speaks to Moses out of the burning bush. But what interests Bronk here is God's tautological (and thus logically absurd) self-definition, which invites our poet to a characteristic variation on the void, as God (whose name does not, indeed, appear in the poem) tells us, "I am the nameless one. I am who am. // Not one of those. Not given. Not anywhere" (*LS 115*).

More often, furthermore, Bronk denotes the mystery that stands over against us, not as "God," but as "reality" or "the world" or even simply as "it": "It is something like the weather—intentions unknown / to us, should it have intention and that unknown / also but we apparently none of its / intention, in no way its reference / but just the same happening to us. . . ." (*MAF* 17). The person who talks about God generally implies that there is Someone out there Who is listening to us, so that to hope for a reply isn't entirely foolish. And only the rare believer is immune from the temptation to conclude not only that God has certain intentions for us but that the "chosen" among us can know what those intentions are and can help carry out God's will on earth. But in the quoted poem, as again and again throughout his work, Bronk emphasizes that we don't and can't know what "its" intentions are, or even whether it has any. Bronk's shifting, equivocal gestures toward the Other emphasize that *any* label for the nothing, the silence, the void out of which the song issues is necessarily a human construct, even the word "God." Again and again, Bronk hammers home the same point: the "is" is Unspeakable. "Ideas are always wrong," he flatly declares in "Blue Spruces in Pairs, a Bird Bath Between" (*LS* 34). Or, no less categorically in "On *Credo Ut Intelligam*": "Reality is what we are ignorant of" (*LS* 89). To Bronk, anyone who claims knowledge of the "real" is guilty of idolatry: the worshipper of God is always worshipping an image constructed by the human will—and therefore false. Not only shalt thou not make a graven image of God, Bronk tells us; thou shalt not even make a *verbal* image. The poetic tradition of the Sublime, in Bronk as in his predecessors back at least to Wordsworth, may represent, in T. E. Hulme's words, "spilt religion," but it is important to remember that for the poets religion *is* "spilt": Milton's grotesque heavenly patriarch, renamed by Blake "Old Nobodaddy," demonstrated that poets had to find an alternative to "God," and they found it in the Sublime. Over the last two centuries, the Sublime has had a twisty history; but if we are to read Bronk aright, I believe it is important to see his work within this poetic lineage.

But to grasp Bronk's relationship to the Sublime, it is important to acknowledge not only his skepticism but also the hunger that drives him, again and again, to reach out toward the emptiness of What Is. Here we might return to the statement by Eagleton that I have placed at the start of this essay: as the Sublime "inscribes itself as the cautionary limit of all mere ideology, of all complacent subject-centredness," Eagleton says, it evokes within us "the pain of incompletion and unassuaged desire." The voice that speaks to us within Bronk's poetry is precisely this voice of unassuaged desire (cf. Finkelstein "World as Desire"). In a short essay titled "Desire and Denial," Bronk himself emphasizes the centrality of desire in his poetry: "Desire is our door into the world. We see shapes there and want them and we go after them into the world. But desire is our door out again also when the shapes we saw leave our desires unsatisfied. . . . How uneasy our lives are: we are denied those shapes and spaces of desire by our desire which rejects them" (VSC 51). Bronk titles one of his sequences *The Force of Desire*, and throughout his work he returns again and again to the experience of desire, need, lack:

I come in from the canal. I don't know anything.
It is well and good to ask what we need to know
as if it were all, as if we didn't need.

Well, I need. I may never know anything
—but I need. One sees desire not
as something to satisfy but to live with. (*LS* 126)

The ambiguity of the penultimate sentence in this passage ("even though I don't know anything, nevertheless I feel need," or "I don't know anything except that I need") underscores the central position of desire in human experience. Ultimately, it makes little difference whether the absolute for which we hunger is a black void or a plenitude of transcendent splendor: in either case, our human condition is defined by our finitude, our insatiable hunger for the wholeness that we lack.

III

I want to circle back now to the distinction that I drew earlier between the Dynamic or Metaphoric Sublime and the Mathematical or Metonymic Sublime, and between the two traditions in twentieth-century poetry that I have associated with these two forms of the Sublime. Bronk began his literary career as a disciple of Stevens, the great twentieth-century heir of the tradition of the Metaphoric Sublime. However, as Burt Kimmelman argues, Bronk departs from Stevens at a crucial point: "Stevens will finally assume that the world is, after all, illusory, and that his only hope for rescuing a truer world than that of his illusion-bound perception lies in embracing subjectivity—as he does in his Supreme Fiction. Bronk has another, firmer plan, which grows out of the conviction that, like illusion itself, subjectivity is helpful only so long as there remains an awareness of it final unreliability" ("Centrality" 119-20). The central issue here, I would propose, is the recuperative metaphor, which allows the poet, in pursuit of the Dynamical Sublime, to create a new balance between the power of the imagination and the absolute Otherness of the Sublime, by drawing the Other metaphorically into the Self, and by simultaneously regrounding the Self in the Transcendent. To Harold Bloom, for example, Stevens represents the "culmination of the American Sublime, or even of the Sublime in modern poetry" (Bloom 293), because he overcomes his "isolating metonymies" through a (metaphoric) "re-imagining of the First Idea" (Bloom 288-9): "For Stevens, the truth necessarily is a fiction, the fiction that results from feeling, or the re-imagining of the First idea" (Bloom 287). Stevens's pervasive irony deflects any too-easy equations of inside and outside, and his metaphors are usually "meta-metaphors," deliberately, even flamboyantly proclaiming their fictionality. But they also claim to create a habitation for the human spirit in an otherwise alien universe: "Soldier, there is a war between the mind / And sky, between thought and day and night. It is / For that the poet is always in the sun, // Patches the moon together in his room. . . . // The soldier is poor without the poet's lines, / His petty syllabi, the sounds that stick. . . . // How simply the fictive hero becomes the real, / How gladly with proper words the soldier dies, / If he must, or lives on the bread of faithful speech" (*Collected Poems* 351-2).

But Bronk refuses the Supreme Fiction, which patches the world together, offers us the nourishment we need to go on—but also sends the soldier off to die. And in practice he refuses the implicit claim of metaphor to close the gap between "I" and the Other. To be sure, there are metaphors in Bronk's poetry: two recurrent metaphors, for example, are the comparison of the makeshift worlds that we piece together to houses or other structures, or to various kinds of linguistic maneuvers. In the sequence *Silence and Metaphor*, for example, metaphor itself becomes a metaphor. In this sequence Bronk equates reality with silence: "*Here is the silence; it is everywhere. / Because it has always been, there is no time. // . . . . Under the noise, silence is what we hear: / final, always, wherever. Silence is all.*" (LS 151). In the face of the silence, we make metaphors, as the first poem in the sequence suggests:

> Everything is, almost in the utterance,
> metaphor—as we measure miles, and miles
> are meaningless, but we know what distance is:
> unmeasureable. But there are distances. (*LS* 152)

To speak at all is (or "almost" is—the qualifier puts yet another gap between the signifier and the signified) to make metaphors; but if everything we say is metaphorical then the category begins to seem meaningless. The words we use are always "made up," like our units of measurement: a mile is 5,280 feet because we agree to say it is, and the number of feet is purely arbitrary. But if our units of measurement (and, by the same token, our metaphors) are arbitrary, what they seek to describe is still irrevocably *there*, "unmeasureable," telling us that all of our categories of understanding are wrong.

The third poem in the *Silence and Metaphor* sequence, "The Signification," returns to the issue of metaphor:

> I will not say that metaphor is the great
> thing. How should I? Metaphor is a way
> to handle, signify, designate;
> we do not handle the great things, though we try.
>
> All right. Still metaphor. What is it we signify?
> We say lies as if they were not lies, as if
> we believe. And, indeed, we do believe. No;
> we know the metaphor is wrong. And yet—(*LS* 152)

The first stanza returns to a by-now-familiar Bronkian theme: the great things lie always *beyond*. Metaphor is a way of "handling" the things of this world, and we do not lay our hands on the great things, for they are "untouchable," "uncanny," "taboo." Metaphors are, in the Heideggerian sense, tools; "being" lies beyond. But even as he critiques metaphor, the poet is still *in* metaphor. The middle lines of the second stanza invite two readings: "We tell lies as if they were true, as if we believed them." But also: "We say, 'That's a lie,' as if it were possible not to lie, as if there were something true that we believed." And the poem then ends with a series of flip-flops. We *do* believe, but then, no we *don't*. We know the metaphor isn't true, and yet. . . . On this equivocal note, the poem, like so many others in this sequence, opens toward silence. "We know," says Bronk in "Misspoken," "that nothing needs our saying; there is nothing to say. / I want to sit silent, listening" (*LS* 160). This willingness—even determination—to give silence the last word distinguishes Bronk from such poets of the American Sublime as Whitman and Stevens, who instead seek to fill the silence with the resonances of their speech. But in refusing to close the gap between Self and World through a metaphoric subsumption of the Other into the Self and a resultant regrounding of the Self in the transcendent Other, Bronk's goal is, not to deny the Other, but to honor it in its absolute Otherness. Thus in reaching out toward the silence with his empty hands, Bronk is decidedly *not* turning aside from the Sublime. For what is the Sublime if not that Silence itself?

IV

The links between Bronk's poetry and what I have called the Metaphoric Sublime seem readily apparent: throughout his career Bronk was able to write, whenever he wished, poetry in the magisterial meditative mode that we associate with Wordsworth or Stevens, even as his work challenges this mode in the ways discussed above. But less obvious are Bronk's links to the Metonymic Sublime, which I have associated with the Pound tradition in twentieth-century verse (on Bronk and the metonymic tradition, see Kimmelman, "Pound, Stevens, Bronk," esp. 48ff). Formally, Bronk's poetry seems much more constrained and orderly than the work of poets writing in the Pound tradition. Poets like Pound himself, Williams, Olson, and Duncan like to splatter words over the page, whereas Bronk's poems look like traditional lyrics. In any given poem, the lines are likely to be more or less the same length, and usually we can count five stresses per line. Pound set out to "break the back of the iamb," but Bronk clearly feels no such impulse. Furthermore, Bronk's lines are usually grouped in relatively symmetrical stanza patterns, and several of his books employ the same form (a pair of quatrains, a single quatrain, a triplet) throughout lengthy sequences. Bronk even retains a lingering loyalty to the sonnet: as late as 1972 he published a sonnet sequence, *To Praise the Music*. All of these facts might suggest that we are dealing with a neo-formalist, rather than with an experimental poet in the Pound tradition. Furthermore, poets in the Pound tradition regularly stretch or even deliberately flout the rules of "normal" syntax to create open verbal fields; and the latest generation of poets within this tradition, the "Language" poets, have carried this tendency to an extreme, as in many of their poems bits and scraps of language come together more or less at random. Bronk's words, on the other hand, fall into conventional syntactical patterns, to form sentences that only rarely challenge the decoding powers of the reader. In eschewing the "open" syntactic and poetic modes of the poets in the Pound tradition, Bronk perhaps tacitly implies that these poets missed the point. They were trying to make their language mirror the world: a world made up of discrete particulars would find its reflection in a radically disjunctive language. But if language cannot touch the "real," then perhaps we may allow language to continue to play by its own rules? Certainly the traditional structures of syntax and poetic form are arbitrary. But perhaps the quest for new forms that will be "truer" to our experience is futile? If *all* the habitations that we erect are arbitrary, then what difference does it make if we choose to inhabit traditional syntactic and poetic structures? Aren't these structures as "true" as any others that we might construct?

Nevertheless, Bronk also shares some affinities with the Metonymic tradition in modern poetry. First, despite the tacit relativism suggested by his approach to poetic form, Bronk at times expresses a hunger for a language that will, by opening itself as wholly as possible to the mystery of What Is, take on some of the existential immediacy of the "Real" itself. Here is the conclusion of an essay that Bronk published in 1970, under the title "The Lens of Poetry," and republished in 1984 as a small pamphlet titled *The Attendant*:

Poetry is about reality in the way that a lens is about light. It is best when it is clear and transparent, when it is least there, in the sense of calling the least attention to itself. If it distorts, the nature of the distortion may even be multiple, so long as it doesn't muddle, so long as it releases the light that it gathers, so long as the light it gathers does not die there, absorbed, but is released to illuminate reality. The lens of poetry. . . . makes nothing, it changes nothing, but it focuses on reality, on what there is. . . . It is serious and unevasive as few activities are. It may seem evasive, though, since it is the nature of the reality, of what there is, that it evades all statements of it, even the statement a poem makes. Speaking of poetry, we found it resisted definition. Speaking of what there is, we find it resists all statements, and direct statement most or all. Are there two perceptions here, or are they one? One might say, for trial, that poetry is a statement about what there is, so attentive, so scrupulous, that it partakes of the nature of its subject: what there is, is poetry; it is not made; it is attended to.

Is it not also true that it is the nature of what there is, closely attended to, that it cries out for the directest kind of statement? It is my conviction and practice that this cry, these statements, are poetry also, impossibly so, but so, nevertheless.

The position that Bronk defines in "The Lens of Poetry" suggests that the syntactic simplicity and the transparent, all-purpose formal patterns of Bronk's poetry are ways of keeping the focus, not on the words, but on the light shining through the words. Bronk wants a poetic language that will call as little attention to itself as possible; and it now seems that he may be suspicious of formal experimentation precisely because it calls too much attention to itself. "Watch me make it new," shouts a Pound;

but from Bronk's perspective, Pound is simply showing off. Yet the quoted passage from *The Attendant* also suggests that Bronk shares with many poets in the Pound tradition a hunger for a language that will take on the materiality of the "real" itself. If Objectivism sought, as Zukofsky insisted, to move beyond Imagism by making the poem, not simply a description of the Thing, but a Thing in its own right, an Object *in* the world, then Bronk appears to share this goal. The Bronkian word, like the Poundian or the Zukofskian word, is trying to reach out to the Real, to touch it. And insofar as the word can make itself transparent to the Real, it will, perhaps, take on the ineffability of the Real. Conversely, Bronk suggests, perhaps the Real is itself a cry that comes to us, out of the silence, so that poetry is What Is, and What Is is, "impossibly," poetry. At this point the differences between Bronk and the poets of the Pound tradition seem to become more strategic than substantive.

If Bronk, like other poets in the Pound tradition, wants to—adapting the title of a poem discussed above—move metonymically toward a real world, what strategies does he employ to this end? The most important of these strategies, I think, is his consistent reliance on a dialogic poetic voice. As Ruth Grogan has argued, Bronk characteristically presents himself as a speaker engaged in a serious but direct and colloquial dialogue with a "you." This dialogic dimension of Bronk's poetic discourse "opens" his apparently "closed" poetic forms to counter-voices, both actual and implied, and thus the poem itself becomes radically contingent:

> To say I only listen isn't true
> but neither is it conversation really: in the end
> whatever is said is theirs. If I hold back,
> their stubborn assurance, their patience, waits for me. (*LS* 131)

The relationship between the "I" and the "you," speaker and listener, also proves radically contingent, for there is no "originary word" in Bronk's universe, no voice that can claim authority. Rather, it seems, we are all listeners:

THE BODY OF THIS LIFE:

Reader, listen: I use the I and you
in order to tell you we are, neither, there,
speaker nor listener. No: listener yes;
we listen or miss it. However. There it is. (*LS* 140)

What "is," finally, is not the speaking subject of the Romantic poem.
Again and again, Bronk repeats Rimbaud's radically effacing gesture, "je
suis une âutre," leaving us, not with authentic selves in relation, but
simply the process of dialogue itself:

I, you; you, I: do you believe this?
I don't. So, who is asking, who speaks?
It is as though, sometimes, we are two and talk
as if to one another: say *you*, say *love*. (*LS* 186)

An explanation here begins to emerge for the sheer volume of
Bronk's poetic production, especially in his later years, and for his
interest in recurrent poetic forms. A good many observers have
noted—sometimes with considerable displeasure—that all of Bronk's
poems seem to be "saying the same thing." Every reader of Bronk must
have asked at some point, "How many different ways can he find to tell
us that none of the worlds that we construct is the real world, that the
real lies somewhere beyond? That, nevertheless, we love the worlds we
construct? But that, still, we also want the real?" Bronk's characteristic
mode of discourse is a series of flat, categorical proposition. Each Bronk
poem seems to address us with an aura of definitive finality, so that the
poem seems to be saying exactly what needs to be said, once and for all.
And yet the poet also seems to feel a need to come back to the same set of
issues, again and again and again. He can never, it seems, get everything
quite right. But the problem is language itself. Only through speech can
we move toward silence. And the moment that we speak, we have created
another of those verbal cages that we use to shelter ourselves from the
terrible Otherness of What Is, to hold the Silence at bay. So each Bronk
poem seeks to self-destruct, to move through a series of categorical
propositions, toward a moment when these propositions will cancel one

another out. But we cannot remain in the Silence. By definition, we can only point toward it, and so the whole operation must be repeated, again and again. Throughout his career, Bronk seems to have composed not simply individual poems but books, and he often underscored the sequential character of his writing by employing the same verse form throughout a book. The sense that the point is, not the individual poem, but the reiterative process itself becomes especially strong in these sequences. Bronk may not have offered his life work as a single long poem, in the ways that Pound, Olson, Duncan, Blackburn, Ginsberg, and Creeley have done, but his need to begin again and again suggests that he shares with them a sense of the finitude of language, as he reaches, metonymically, toward the "impossible" Real.

Finally, and again in common with the work of many other poets in the Pound/Williams lineage, many individual Bronk poems reach toward the "now," in an attempt to reach an impossible experience of total immediacy. Following Barnett Newman, Jean-Françoise Lyotard has equated what he calls the "indeterminate Sublime" with the *now*. The *now*, says Lyotard,

> is one of the temporal 'ecstasies' that has been analyzed since Augustine's day and particularly since Edmund Husserl, according to a line of thought that has attempted to constitute time on the basis of consciousness. [Barnett] Newman's *now* which is no more than *now* is a stranger to consciousness and cannot be constituted by it. Rather, it is what dismantles consciousness, . . . it is what consciousness cannot formulate, and even what consciousness forgets in order to constitute itself. What we do not manage to formulate is that something happens, *dass etwas geschieht*. (Lyotard 90)

For Bronk, too, the *now* seems to promise access to the Real, in part simply because it is gone the moment that we grasp it: the moment that we say "now," the *now* is already a *then*. A remarkable number of Bronk poems end with a simple deictic act of pointing: "The now! Has there ever been, will there ever be, / not now? No, always. Only now!" (*LS* 81).

"Invention everywhere, / but something exists. We come as we can to this" (*LS* 86). "There is the real / It is there. Where we are: nowhere. It is there" (*LS* 100). "Going somewhere. Moving again so as not / to have time for here, not to be stuck with it. / With here. Look at it! At here. Let's go!" (*LS* 108). "But the unbelievable, which nothing believes, / says something. Listen. Says itself. / As if it were my voice. As if it were now" (*LS* 121). "I don't know what we can do. There isn't a way. / Some things are there, though. We have to say that" (*LS* 124). "What sweetnesses! Here, / there are wonders that grace us. Holy God! // Where do they come from? Not possible / to come from this or even from near this. / Here they are. I am here. In this place" (*LS* 132). "There is a real world which does make sense. / It is beyond our knowing or speaking but it is there" (*LS* 136). "Here, though, is the world now. It is here" (*LS* 157). At these moments, Bronk enacts the characteristic Sublime gesture, as he passes from naming to, simply, pointing—in terror or wonder or, rarely, in something like religious ecstasy; but whatever the feeling-tone of the moment, we have passed beyond words, as we reach toward the Here, the Now.

V

As the language of this essay has perhaps made evident, I feel a greater sympathy for the tradition of the Metonymic or Mathematical Sublime than for the tradition of the Metaphoric or Dynamic Sublime, simply because the poets of the first tradition, intentionally or not, always end by "giving themselves away," acknowledging the impossibility of the enterprise in which they are engaged. In contrast, the poets of the Metaphoric Sublime sustain through a figurative displacement the fiction that there is for us at least a momentary habitation in this world. Of course, by naming this habitation a fiction, by demanding that we watch him as he invents his tropes, Stevens too acknowledges the gap between signifier and signified. Thereby Stevens (and some other poets in this tradition too) proleptically validates the work of the critics who will deconstruct these metaphoric fictions, to reveal how even in the closed poetic text presence is always deferred. But the poets of the Metonymic

Sublime open their poetic texts to the indeterminacy that a Stevens can acknowledge only ironically, and thereby they in effect deconstruct their own texts—even when, as in the case of Pound, the poet's conscious intentions are fiercely, even tyrannically dogmatic. By arguing that Bronk's work represents a critique of both these traditions, then, I do not want to imply a symmetry in his relationship with the two traditions. Bronk begins, consciously, within the Stevens tradition; but, rather like Dickinson before him, his rigorous determination to confront the Otherness of the Real leads him to push the poetics of the Emersonian Sublime to the point where it ex/implodes. At this juncture, his poetry converges, in ways that I assume he himself never recognized, with the work of Olson, Duncan, Creeley et al—the poets of the Metonymic Sublime. Yet precisely *because* he started within the Stevens camp, his poetry also resists the temptation toward magniloquent posturing that we see in poets like Pound, Olson, and—from time to time at least—Duncan. A daily dose of Bronk can build up our resistance to a variety of poetic—and thus, potentially, moral—infections. At the same time, his writing also carries forward the great task of poetry over the last four centuries: to preserve an openness to the sacred at a time when dogma and despairing skepticism nurture and feed on one another. For these gifts, the humble, stubborn sage of Hudson Falls has won for himself a place with the great forebears he so nobly salutes, Thoreau and Whitman and Melville, among the Brothers in Elysium.

Don Adams

PLEADING THE PERMANENCE OF IGNORANCE:
THE POETRY OF WILLIAM BRONK

HEN THE ANNALS OF TWENTIETH-CENTURY AMERICAN POETRY are written, William Bronk will surely be included as one of the most insistently and insightfully philosophical poets of his time. It is perhaps only fitting, then, that in attempting to understand the range and nature of the philosophical meditations in Bronk's work, we turn to the modern philosopher most attuned to the poetic, Martin Heidegger.

Taking his theme from Nietzsche, whom he calls "the West's last thinker" (*What Is Called Thinking?* 46), Heidegger in his late essays and lectures contended that modern man is in danger of losing the basic experience of existence, because of his devotion to an all-encompassing self-assertion, whereby he objectifies both the world and himself in the service of technical production (*PLT* 112-115). Even the threat of atomic energy, the philosopher claims, is merely a symptom of modem man's deluded, insistent self-willing:

> What has long since been threatening man with death, and indeed with the death of his own nature, is the unconditional character of mere willing in the sense of purposeful self-assertion in everything. What threatens man in his very nature is the willed view that man, by the peaceful release, transformation, storage, and channeling of the energies of physical nature, could render the human condition, man's being, tolerable for everybody and happy in all respects. (*PLT* 116)

In such a "destitute time of the world's night" (*PLT* 92), as Heidegger calls it, we must look to the poets to save us, for they alone have maintained a "dialogue" with "the history of Being" (*PLT* 96). Heidegger defines language as the temple or house of Being (*PLT* 132), for it is in and through language that we discover and explore the inexhaustible mystery of our existence—a mystery that is mirrored by the inexplicable nature of language, which does not exhaust itself in signifying" (*PLT* 132), but remains always a transcendent presence. Although language may always be interpreted as signifying *something,* we cannot account for the fact that language exists as meaning in the first place, just as we cannot account for the fact of our own existence as a transcendentally self-aware presence.

The poet, Heidegger contends, is he who dares "the venture with language," striving *not* to know the meaning of life—which is to ask the wrong question and to begin at a dead end—but, rather, to be *present* in what is present itself (*PLT* 133). This primal poetic singer alerts us to the fact that the world of self-assertion, which seeks to know all, and discounts what is unknowable as non-existent—this world in which modern man almost wholly resides—is not the *real* world, which is altogether other, and elsewhere.

"There is a real world which does make sense," Bronk writes, "It is beyond our knowing or speaking but it is there" (*SP* 43). Throughout his work, Bronk is continually alerting us to the existence of this unknowable and unspeakable real world and insisting on its primacy and value:

> We are imperfect concepts. Our world, besides,
> is a flawed world. Our view were hopelessness
> were there no places beyond us; these are beautiful.(*LS* 158)

Like Heidegger, Bronk considers it the poet's vocation to point us in the direction of these beautiful places beyond our flawed knowing.

In his most explicit statement regarding his vocation as a poet, "On *Credo Ut Intelligam*" (*LS* 96-7), Bronk labels this world "reality" and claims that it is "what we are ignorant of," concluding:

> How should I turn my head away to look
> at anything other than that I am ignorant of,
> it being all; or make belief invent

a world or a life besides, it being there?

It is Bronk's singular accomplishment as a twentieth-century poet to continually "disclaim the invented world . . . . which asks / our belief and offers us understanding back" in favor of the "reaches of ignorance" that lead to an intimation of reality. He is perpetually vigilant in his distrust of the all-too-certain language of our flawed world, which "means to say what we don't know" and "creates the world as if the world were" (*VSC* 48). In his illuminating and disturbing defense of poetry, "Desire and Denial," Bronk writes:

> Words are refuge and sanctuary but how they penalize us and set us apart, how they subvert our experience as though it happened only in a world and could happen only if there, could only be said to have really happened if it can be related to that world's premises and temporal schemes. As we become increasingly at home in a world and more loyally citizens of it, so our experience does seem to happen there,—within those confines. We dismiss it otherwise as of no consequence. (*VSC* 50)

Bronk contends that we take language at its word and live within its confines at our peril, for an ultimate trust in language as meaning implies the inherent unreality of our own unspeakable natures. Heidegger gives us a similar warning concerning our thoughtless trust in language as meaning in a late meditation in which he observes that "Man acts as though he were the shaper and master of language, while in fact language remains master of man. Perhaps it is before all else man's subversion of this relation that drives his nature into alienation" (*PLT* 146). In a typically terse late poem, Bronk asks, "Don't we know it all? Everything. / Language is what we lack. Neither the words / we have nor our syntax say certain things" (*AWWL* 130).

Like his great influence, Henry David Thoreau, Bronk puts his trust, rather, in the silence to which our "most excellent speech finally falls," and which "is the seat and source of our strangeness." His poems are ever tending toward this silence, implicitly guarding—in their ascetic rigor of form and theme—against the "frivolous speech, which has no reference to silence and so prevents valid speech or sound" (*VSC* 78).

I do not know of another poet of Bronk's ability and deserving stature who uses the poetic staples of metaphor, symbol, and imagery more sparingly and reluctantly. Beside his scrupulously plain and concise poems, most other poetry of our time seems gaudy, obtuse, and self-indulgent. It is as though Bronk were afraid to give in to the temptation of merely verbal success, of which he was so clearly able.

Bronk's remarkably chaste mature style bespeaks of his absolute assurance of poetic mission. Heidegger observes:

> Every great poet creates his poetry out of one single poetic state-ment only. The measure of his greatness is the extent to which he becomes so committed to that singleness that he is able to keep his poetic Saying wholly within it. (Heidegger160)

Bronk's single poetic statement might be summed up thus: The world we want is not the world we have; but the very fact of our desire implies its existence. His "anti"-poetics embody an insistent turning away from our self-created worlds, with their questionable (because knowable) truths, toward the unknowable reality intuited by desire. In poem after poem, Bronk contends that the experience of existence would tell those of us willing to listen that "We are beside the point. // No matter. Close beside. The seriousness / of desire is a voice that sings us up / and, in its singing, humbles whatever claims" (*SP* 78).

More persistently than any other poetry of our time, William Bronk's songs of desire and denial seek to silence our self-deluded self-willing in favor of the legitimate challenge to thought provided by that which is beyond our knowing. They proffer the solace "of all our awareness" as they guide us toward the "reaches of ignorance" (*LS* 97) in which we, in reality, and only there, truly exist.

Tom Lisk

Bronk's Berkeleyan Idealism

IN HIS *Life of Samuel Johnson*, James Boswell tells of a discussion with Johnson about Bishop George Berkeley, the Anglican divine who believed firmly in the reality of God and the spirit and the unreality of the world:

> After we came out of the church, we stood talking for some time together of Bishop Berkeley's ingenious sophistry to prove the non-existence of matter, and that every thing in the universe is merely ideal. I observed, that though we are satisfied his doctrine is not true, it is impossible to refute it. I shall never forget the alacrity with which Johnson answered, striking his foot with mighty force against a large stone, till he rebounded from it,—"I refute it *thus*." (Boswell 285)

William Bronk has affinities with the curmudgeonly Johnson, whose bluff common sense makes him skeptical of metaphysical claims, but Bronk 's steadfast adherence to a belief in the unknowability of the world links his work more strongly with Berkeley's. Though Johnson dismissed Berkeley without completely understanding his work—no matter how firm the stone, the spirited Johnson rebounded—Bronk's skepticism is more inquisitive.

A couple of hundred years after Berkeley, Bronk writes in "AKA" in *The Cage of Age*:

> If time is another way for space and mass
> a special face of energy, what
> otherwise unspoken, otherwise
> unheard but single word in either case
> is doubly said and doubly left not said?

What current has wave and quantum as aliases? (*LS* 97)

Bronk's essential wisdom, that there is a world beyond our knowing, is fundamentally the same as Berkeley's philosophy wedded to the non-traditional religion of modern physics where "wave and quantum" stand for what we can know of the unknowable. Berkeley, who believes that God is the author of reality, that reality is spirit and spirit is eternal, denies that there are abstract general ideas and that objects exist outside the mind. Bronk, on the other hand, seems to believe the world exists outside the mind, and he struggles to make his abstractions as particular as possible, but we can't know the world, any more than Berkeley thought we could know God. In "Ideations," Bronk says,

> Something's grace and favor allows us our mind's
> imaginings in shapes practical
> to use and find, in using them, their truths.
> But, just beyond, are truths it keeps to itself. (*LS* 96)

For several years before his death in 1999, Bronk's poems had been almost all short and aphoristic, apparently reflecting an increasing impatience with the mannerisms identified with poetry. Though it is not his last book, the 1996 volume, *The Cage of Age*, has a valedictory quality, representing his assertions in stripped-down and final-sounding rhetoric that might be characterized as abstract (for the poems are often devoid of imagery), if abstraction were not such a troubling concept in Bronk's world of uncertain certainties. Bronk recognizes but does not stop with the recognition that whatever we think we know through the senses is not the world, but consciousness. If it is to become poetry, what comes through the senses must be *processed* by consciousness and language. Without consciousness, the shiftings of matter would be of no consequence. Even to say they would be of no consequence is nonsensical since anything one might say, including the nonsensical, requires consciousness. So far, Berkeley would surely agree.

In *The Cage of Age*, as in Bronk's earlier work, general statements that seem to be at the brink of despair are transcended by the belief that there is a reality in which our being is grounded, but which we cannot know:

> All worlds are temporary. Mine and yours
> were born when we were and when we go we'll take
> along with us worlds no realer than we.
>   (*CA* 59)

Years before, in a letter to Robert Meyer, Bronk had gone a little farther down the path toward mysticism when he wrote, "The reality of this world is not to be found in this world and is not the less real for the failure. (If that last sentence seems not to have any meaning, you are probably correct)" ("*Winter Mind*" 44-45).

Long before postmodernism alerted us to the failures of languages, mystics were often challenged by the difficulties of putting their experience into words. Bronk's poem, "The Cloud of Unknowing," takes its title from the work of an anonymous late medieval mystic:

> Go all the way ignorant of whom
> you wanted to know but could only speculate
> inaccurately. And never know yourself
> either or be able to say what it is you are. (*Cloud* 61)

Bronk's earlier sonnet, "The Real World," ends "There is a real world which does make sense./ It is beyond our knowing or speaking but it is there" (*LS* 145). Neither that statement nor "The Cloud of Unknowing" would not be out of place in the work of many mystics, even in the original *The Cloud of Unknowing*, where we find, "Then will He sometimes peradventure send out a beam of ghostly light, piercing the cloud of unknowing that is betwixt thee and Him: and shew thee some of His privity, the which man may not, nor cannot speak" (*Cloud* 105). Bronk's skepticism is not at all discordant with Berkeley's Christian Platonism, though, as Burt Kimmelman has said, "Unlike in Plato's construct, Bronk's worldlessness would cease to exist if there were no world, and so

there is a stronger bond between the two then [sic] what we find between
Plato's Ideal and his world of shadow" ("*Winter Mind*"178).

The longest poem in *The Cage of Age* is "Visitors' Day at the
World," which appears on the page facing "The Cloud of Unknowing":

> . . . .You don't
> remember the old time movie palaces
> but I do. So sumptuous, they
> were, alone, the show. When the lights went down the stars
> in the ceiling twinkled. Like here. But this goes on
> and on. What we're seeing now is a little part.
> I've been to some of the other places but not
> to all of them. You wouldn't believe.

As in Bronk's earlier poem, "Loew's World," in this poem the experience
of knowable reality is likened to being in a movie house, the contempo-
rary equivalent of Plato's cave. Here is the ambiguous Platonic world of
"Loew's," the theater we all live in:

> We, in the dark, beset by love and fear,
> as by a kind of weather without terrain.
> suffer the unsourced tricks of light, as when
> at night in the summer, heat lightning thrusts from the dark
> a world which was not and is gone. (*LS* 60)

The lightning metaphor illuminates a scene we only glimpse, and meta-
phorically stands for the material reality in which we live.

Bronk has been identified as a postmodernist, in part because his
work fits so perfectly with the indeterminate universe described by
contemporary physics. As Werner Heisenberg explains the background
of his famous uncertainty principle,

> We can express the departure from previous forms of physics by
> means of the so-called uncertainty relations. It was discovered
> that it was impossible to describe simultaneously both the posi-

tion and the velocity of an atomic particle with any prescribed degree of accuracy. (Heisenberg 449)

As a result of this inability to describe particle position and velocity at the same time, Heisenberg generalized in a fashion that sounds very much like Bronk:

> We can no longer speak of the behaviour of a particle independently of the process of observation. As a final consequence, the natural laws formulated mathematically in quantum theory no longer deal with the elementary particles themselves but with our knowledge of them. Nor is it any longer possible to ask whether or not these particles exist in space and time objectively, since the only processes we can refer to as taking place are those which represent the interplay of particles with some other physical system, e. g., a measuring instrument. (Heisenberg 446)

This quintessentially modernist statement is the gateway to post-modernism. Emphasizing the relativity of the physical ground of being makes knowledge of the "real" world uncertain and further suggests the distance of language from that reality.

According to Tom Clark, the term "post-modern" was coined by Charles Olson "to describe the historical aftermath of sixteenth- and seventeenth-century world voyaging and the nineteenth-century machine age" (Clark 208). Clark goes on to say, "But the hazards of a headlong approach to cultural evolution could not always be so blithely side-stepped. His [Olson's] precipitate reactions could get him in trouble . . ." (Clark 208). In the years since Olson's death in 1970, the term has, of course, been taken up by others and stretched even beyond Olson's generous intentions.

"Postmodernism" is in fact a capacious term, a code word like "liberal" or "conservative" that may be more useful as a way of dividing thinkers into "them" and "us" than an actual theoretical position, and in fact "postmodern" might be more precisely described in terms associated with particular ideologies. Raman Selden and Peter Widdowson, however, summarize the range of postmodernist positions as being guided by two "leading contentions:" "first, the 'grand narratives' of historical progress initiated by the Enlightenment are discredited; and second, any political grounding of these ideas in 'history' or 'reality' is no longer possible, since both have become 'textualised' in the world of images and/simulations which characterize the contemporary age of mass consumption and advanced technologies" (Selden and Widdowson 174-175). The assertion, "any political grounding of these ideas in 'history' or 'reality' is no longer possible," sounds like a point of departure for William Bronk, though his work is not self-consciously political. "Reality" and "indeterminacy" are two important concepts for Bronk, and his use of the terms seems to link him to postmodernism, though as Peter Brooker has explained:

> Since the first uses of the term in the late 1950s and early 1960s, "postmodernism" has acquired an amoebic range of attributions and meanings, in academic debate and in journalism. In general terms it can be said to describe a mood or condition of radical indeterminacy, and a tone of self-conscious, parodic skepticism toward previous certainties in personal, intellectual and political life. (Selden and Widdowson 175)

As Brooker goes on to say, "'postmodernism' is used both as a descriptive and an evaluative term, and not always of the same phenomena" (Selden and Widdowson 176). The attitudes designated by the term "post-modernist" "can settle anywhere from fervid evangelicalism or faddish knowingness to resignation or resistance. Furthermore, as a relational term, *post*modernism is seen either as a continuation of, or break with, dominant features in modernism or the avant garde, about which there is also naturally much debate" (Selden and Widdowson 176).

A reviewer of *The Cage of Age* comments,

> Bronk has long labored under the influence of Wallace Stevens's intense statements and discursive meditations. But the poems in *The Cage of Age*, lacking sensory detail, resemble Stevens with-

out his imagery or imagination. Nonetheless, Bronk has tuned out experience in order to tune in the silence of the great void of the universe—"the mute deaf of the world." Joseph Brodsky once described hearing as the transmitter of both the spiritual and intellectual aspects of a poem (as in when we speak of "the poet's ear.") In Stevens's pentametric discourse and Bronk's colloquial, religious aphorisms, each poet *hears* in a form suitable for his subjects: time and space. (Biespiel, n. p.)

The reviewer, David Bielspiel, goes on to say, "If this style of writing lacks a heightened sense of detail, it's because Bronk's poems seem to be more about the poet's conviction and feeling about phenomena than the phenomena itself [sic]." In other words, Bronk's work is more about "reality" than about physical phenomena—if the two can be distinguished. For that reality is as unreachable as the soul or, as John Ernest has pointed out, as unreachable as God: "Mistrustful of the reason which would guide him, persistently examining his life for evidence of grace, Bronk is an essentially religious poet whose God is the personification of an enticingly immanent but irrevocably remote reality—"A world beyond our world which holds our world'" ("Music that Sees Beyond The World") ("Religious Desire" 145).

Partly because of his engagement with uncertainty, partly because he was friendly with Olson, and his work appeared in *Black Mountain Review* and *Origin*, journals with postmodern cachet, Bronk is often identified as a postmodernist writer. The book jacket for the first edition of Bronk's *Life Supports: New and Collected Poems* includes the oddly opaque praise from Olson, "I may have, for the first time in my life, imagined a further succinct life"*—postmodern flattery. Rather than canceling the postmodernist identification, the influence of Robert Frost and Wallace Stevens on Bronk's work may make him seem precisely postmodern in his continuing, including and going beyond modernism. Bronk's relatively early poem, "How Indeterminacy Determines Us,"

---

*According to Kimmelman (184n.), this curious encomium appears in a letter Olson wrote Bronk, 14 September 1964. The letter is in the Columbia University archives.

addresses these questions much more directly than Frost or Stevens might:

> . . . . We are left to wonder at
> and ponder our privacy and ponder this:
> we are two unknowns in a single equation, we
> and our world, functions one of the other. Sight
> is inward and sees itself, hearing, touch,
> are inward. What do we know of an outer world? (LS 65-6)

The inner world and the outer relative to what? Do quarks exist out in the world or in the physicist's mind? In "The Outer Becoming Inner," Bronk says,

> Sometimes, I could go in anywhere, not
> to see the stars, not to be as we
> are always, not only under them
> but in them. The outer spaces push against
> us, all their vastness apart, they crowd
> us. They become our world. I could go hide
> like Adam in his garden. How
> would it matter? No, we are in the stars. Not
> for us ever any familiar and definite world. (LS 53)

The identity of anything, as well as any person, seems to be analogous to a moebius band, on which it is possible to move from one side of a flat three-dimensional surface to the other without going over the edge.

Actually Olson may have been right to date postmodernism much earlier than the latter half of the twentieth century. In 1710, Berkeley wrote in *A Treatise Concerning the Principles of Human Knowledge*:

> Some there are of great note, who, not content with holding that
> finite lines may be divided into an infinite number of parts, do
> yet further maintain, that each of those infinitesimals is itself
> subdivisible into an infinite number of parts, or infinitesimals of

THE BODY OF THIS LIFE:

a second order, and so on *ad infinitum*. These, I say, assert there
are infinitesimals of infinitesimals without ever coming to an
end. (Berkeley 181)

Berkeley wrote that passage before Blake saw a "universe in a grain of
sand." It is also not far from the world of microchips and nanoseconds in
which we live today, a world deluged by the overwhelming transferability
of information, making us long for certain knowledge. Berkeley likes the
idea that "infinitesimals of infinitesimals" make perfect sense in
consciousness, but are ultimately impossible in the world of matter. And,
though physicists have gone on parsing matter into smaller and smaller
units, the ultimate infinitesimal of infinitesimals, the hard nub of reality,
still seems unreachable.

  Just as Berkeley understood that the mysterious unreachability of
material reality may encourage belief in God, Bronk maintains that the
fragility of consciousness defines our position in a world—or
worlds—we can inhabit but not understand, not know. The *idea* of
matter can be divided to infinitesimals of infinitesimals but reality itself
remains elusive. "Hence," Berkeley writes,

> as it is impossible for me to see or feel any thing without an
> actual sensation of that thing, so it is impossible for me to con-
> ceive in my thoughts any sensible thing or object distinct from
> the sensation or perception of it. (Berkeley 115)

In a statement startlingly close to Heisenberg's assertion that "natural
laws no longer deal with the . . . elementary particles themselves but with
our knowledge of them," Berkeley states his position clearly: "When we
do our utmost to conceive the existence of external bodies, we are all the
while contemplating only our own ideas" (Berkeley 124). In such a world,
Bronk's gnomic utterance in "Lite," "What we say about truth is so little
about/truth the opposite is just as true" (*COA* 19), makes perfect sense.
  Berkeley tells us,

The plainest things in the world, those we are most intimately acquainted with, and perfectly know, when they are considered in an abstract way, appear strangely difficult and incomprehensible. Time, place, and motion, taken in particular or concrete, are what every body knows; but having passed through the hands of a metaphysician, they become too abstract and fine to be apprehended by men of ordinary sense. (Berkeley 161)

In those terms Bronk at his plainest appears as both a Johnsonian man "of ordinary sense" and something of a Berkeleyan metaphysician, as in "The Plainest Narrative" from *Life Supports*:

I am William Bronk, have been raised to believe
the personal pronoun plus the verb to be
and a proper name said honestly is fact
from which the plainest narrative begins.
But it isn't fact; it comes to this. Is it wrong?
Not wrong. Just that it isn't true.
No more than the opposite is true. . . . (*LS* 113)

Never mind that this plain speech is in unobtrusive blank verse, it calls into question the simplest and plainest statements, the names for things and beings in this world. The most plain speaking slides into postmodernism near mysticism.

Berkeley's modern-sounding awareness of the limits of epistemology is, of course, grounded in traditional Christianity, so he concludes, "From what has been said, it follows, there is *not any other substance than spirit*, or that which perceives" (*LS* 117). The identification of "that which perceives" with spirit asks for a leap of faith. Without that leap, we are left with an dual uncertainty: Who knows? And what does the knower know?

It will perhaps be said, that we want a sense (as some have imagined) proper to know substances withal, which if we had, we might know our own soul, as we do a triangle. To this I *answer*, that in case we had a new sense bestowed upon us, we could only receive thereby *some new sensation or ideas of sense.* But I believe nobody will say, that what he means by the terms *soul* and *substance,* is only some particular sort of idea or sensation. We may therefore infer, that all things duly considered, it is not more reasonable to think our faculties defective, in that they do not furnish us with an idea of spirit or *active thinking* substance, than it would be if we should blame them for not being able to comprehend a *round square. (LS 184)*

The way Berkeley describes the unknowability of the soul sounds much like Bronk describing the unknowability of the world: Even if "we had a new sense bestowed upon on, we could only receive thereby *some new sensation or ideas of sense.*"

Starting with an identical premise, that a knowledge of the physical world is not a knowledge of reality, Berkeley and Bronk come to conclusions that at first appear diametrically opposed: Berkeley, belief; Bronk, unbelief. Berkeley says, "For after all, what deserves the first place in our studies, is the consideration of God, and our duty: which to promote, as it was the main drift and design of my labours, so shall I esteem them altogether useless and ineffectual if by what I have said I cannot inspire my readers with a pious sense of the presence of God . . . " *(LS 195).* Bronk says, in "Love and Terror,"

> We are in ourselves like air inside a balloon
> and the shapes of our skin is neither what we are.
> The solids of the world are pictures we make of them.
> All of it will disperse. Do not believe. *(COA 90)*

In Bronk's poetry "feeling" and "thinking" are tools for analysis of inward processes rather than discrete states of consciousness. Expressions of feeling seem at first to have been all but squeezed out of many of Bronk's poems: "Feel of course but try to know the why/of what you feel" ("Outs," *COA* 50). The result is a condensation rather than an absence of emotion, as in the book's final poem, "The Cage of Age:"

In the cage of age
days are slow
nights the same
it's all been
it won't end (*COA* 100)

Appearing in a collection published when Bronk was nearly eighty, the poem's autobiographical resonance sounds pretty grim, but the poem also suggest continuity beyond life or beyond identity, despair and a hope of transcendence: outside the cage is freedom. Years earlier, in *The Empty Hands*, Bronk wrote,

> . . . . The strength of the mind
> is just that the mind knows better. And it always does.
> The mind *knows* that this is the possible world.
> But the heart is hopeful. Do you want to call it the heart?
> Unsatisfied desire. ("The Failure to Devise a Better World," *LS* 83)

That collection took its title from one of Bronk's most beautiful poems, "The Smile on the Face of a Kouros," which ends "I tell you, death, expect no smile of pride/ from me. I bring you nothing in my empty hands" (*LS* 73). The fact that the speaker's hands are empty suggests the reality of death ("You can't take it with you") and at the same time hints at ambivalence about what death might be: person, place, thing or condition.

As Kimmelman has explained "Bronk's basic conundrum":

> There are two poles in his fathoming of existence. At one limit, there is a devotion to the present and/or to its simple physicality, at the other, a devotion of equal commitment to a reality existing beyond any present, past, or future world Bronk can know—to a *worldlessness*. All Bronk can say of this reality is that he feels it must be somewhere, which is to say that the world he inhabits, unreal as it may seem, tells him the real world is other than there. How can one live with such an outlook—when every assump-

tion, every physical position to be adopted in order to explain life, is undermined? (Kimmelman 35)

One answer to Kimmelman's rhetorical question is obvious: Bronk did live with such an outlook. Other people do. And we are all many-minded, able to live with anguish and conradiction. But this implicitly bleak question has a more optimistic—even transcendent—answer if we accept Bronk's feeling that there is a world somewhere. Knowledge fails, but feeling intuits something beyond knowledge. That assertion, while true of Bronk, also seems true of Berkeley. Berkeley is willing to identify that something beyond with a Christian God, Bronk is not.

Different from Bronk's conundrum but similar to it is the conundrum on which postmodernism founders: the fact that the statement, "There is no truth," becomes the ultimate truth. Bronk goes beyond that to say, "If there is a truth, we can't know it." Some days he feels there is such a truth, other days not. Thus, in a self-mocking state of mind, he produces "Nice Try:"

> One of the riotous jokes the world tells
> us is about us and the fixes we make to restore
> an order to the world: it never had one to restore. (COA 63)

In such poems, Bronk seems most postmodern and farthest from Berkeley. We are one of the world's jokes because we insist on trying to restore an order that never existed. "Restore" repeated as the end word of two of the three lines of this three-line poem takes a jab at conservatives of all stripes, whether it is anti-postmodernists trying to restore the orderly study of literature they believe existed before modernists led to post-modernists, or Newtonian physicists happier with a less indeterminate understanding of "reality."

In other moods, however, Bronk can sound most Berkeleyan, as in "Looks Exchanged:"

> We know there was a world before the world
> had persons in it but even to say that

and to say as though it matters, to say before
and after whatever and to speak as well of the world's
creation, all these are to speak in personal terms
of a world existing there not otherwise
than in those personal terms as may be so.
Or else as persons we are not in the world;
we exist in unknown terms not ours but the world's. (*COA* 73)

If that poem is not exactly a Berkeleyan affirmation of a divine plan, in
its dark way it does suggest that the terms by which we live are set by a
world we can't control, and "world" here might be "God" by another
name. In the later poem, "The Unmourned," from *Metaphor of Trees*
and *Last Poems*, he says, "The god that was said to be dead was a person.
They die/ The god there is there where nothing is there" (*MOT* 73). That
sounds like the Nicholas of Cusa's definition of God as a being whose
center is everywhere and whose circumference is nowhere.[*]

In *The Cage of Age*, Bronk's "Stayover" gives heroism to identity:

Soul's the one we came with. When we go
it's on our own. Great to live with,
soul was loved and lover, the landscape.
Let's leave it at that. Get along. (*COA* 91)

If that short poem says soul is what animates the living and disappears
when the body dies, Bronk's view is less sanguine than Berkeley's: "When
we go/it's on our own." But, perhaps in a slightly different mood, in
"Deus Vobiscum," he says,

Some gods are household gods. The things they do
are little things and we are grateful for that.
But don't look to Olympus. Nobody's there.
The gods we think are Gods aren't Gods

---

[*]Nicholas of Cusa's reasoning was in fact firmly mathematical. Since an arc flattens
as a circle is enlarged, in infinity a circle must be a straight line.

but parts of the world. This one. Right here. (COA 99)

I am not proposing that Bronk overtly subscribes to a Berkeleyan world view. Rather, I am suggesting that Bronk's poems' stark engagement with the fundamental questions of reality links him with other great thinkers. Whether Berkeley's Christianity or Heisenberg's physics sets the terms, reality is elusive. If physical reality is indeterminate, ideas may take on the solidity of stone. Bronk's faith in a "real world," though it does not offer us an afterlife, redemption or even damnation, is a faith nonetheless. I see it as analogous to the Calvinism of the Puritans, who believed in the greatness of God, whether they as individuals were saved or damned. "I plead the permanence /of ignorance," Bronk says in "Credo ut Intelligam" (LS 96), a brave and a humble assertion.

Robert J. Bertholf

Hans Vaihinger, Wallace Stevens, William Bronk and the Poetry of "As If"

I

As Seen

In microphotographs, the invisible
is there to be seen as much as if it were there.
Photograph or no, many things
are 'there' in the many senses of there, the ways.
Scanning electrons: well, of course, electrons.
We thought of them and the concept is one
we can use and do make us of it. See
the detail: the invisible world, in its intricacies,
is a projection of the visible one, sharp
and intimate. We could live there
as, indeed, we do live there in the way we live
as much as if we were there, as if size
were our size and size were meaningful
as, in limited frames of reference, it is. But the range
of size is limitless; we exist
as tiniest wholes in the almost infinitely
divisible *what* there is. It is our heir
which is before and after us whose stuff
we are, becoming visible, whose stuff
we were, unseen, unknown, invisible. (*LS* 211)

W ILLIAM BRONK'S USE OF "as if," or "as though," may, might or perhaps, subjunctive structures going contrary to fact, arise from the central epistemological dilemma in his poetry: the mind sees a spiritual reality which is different from physical reality and then encounters great difficulty in describing either. To describe the physical world in the first place, the poet must use words, create a language which is not the world but represents parts of the world.

As he says directly in *The Force of Desire*:

These are invented words and they refer
to inventions of their own and not to a real world
unresembled, inexpressible. (*LS* 202)

Every effort, then, to describe the world generates a false gloss on it, another misty overlay which obscures the world the words attempt to describe. As in the photographs, the invisible is there to be seen "as if" it were there, and even though the invisible is a "projection of the visible," or an idea made up by the mind that is not in the world. It is possible to carry on our daily lives in the visible world, which we can not know, "as if" we were its masters, knowing full well that our size in the immense deepness of galactic space obviates any effect of mastering. The "*what*," however, exists as an invisible force before and after our attempts to describe it, and it is that "*what*" which appears in the poetry as silence, lights of various kinds, centers, that Bronk desires most of all to contain in words. The great Romantic dilemma is to define the invisible spiritual center in visible terms without sullying it.

Other poems approach the vision and the lexical dilemma differently:

There is Ignorant Silence in the Center of Things

Hopeless. Off in the distance, busyness.
Something building or coming down. Cries.
Clamor. Fuss at the edges. What? Here,
at the center—it is the center?—only the sound
of silence, that mocking sound. Awful. Once,
before this, I stood in an actual ruin, a street

no longer a street, in a town no longer a town,
and felt the central, strong suck of it, not
understanding what I felt: the heart of things.
This nothing. This full silence. To not know. (LS 44)

The Meaning

I think of the portion multiplied, of the world
entire so peopled and they unknown, as if
it were not meant to be more than that, as if
to tell us there is something desirable, not ours. (LS 164)

To Praise the Music

Evening. The trees in late winter bare
against the sky. Still light, the sky.
Trees dark against it. A few leaves
on the trees. Tension in the rigid branches as if
—oh, it is all as if, but as if, yes,
as if they sang songs, as if they praised.
Oh, I envy them. I know the songs. (LS 143)

Bronk has given up the idea of an eternal truth, the final definition of living and the fact of reality. He has given up on ideology, fixed definitions of belief, and the dominance of rational structures, all as determining factors. He posits himself as one person, alone and unmodified, looking at the world in an effort to make up a way of living and seeing that will satisfy his immense desire to believe in the position he has taken. Points of brilliance, pools of light, transparent light, silence, remind him of the presence of a spiritual reality which is different from the physical reality. Yet, when he tries to describe that spiritual presence, he must resort to a fallible language, a metaphoric barrier of language between the thing seen and the idea of the thing. In his presentation, the presence has light and silence and music but no form, different from, say Henry Vaughn stating of it as: "I saw eternity the other night, like a great ring of pure and endless light." His task as a poet is to create form for a spiritual presence that has no form—to create form in words, which in their fundamental operation, are not objects or ideas, but representation of objects or ideas. And to create in such a way that convinces himself that what he creates stands forth "as if" it were the presence, and convinces himself to believe in it even though what he has created is not it but an idea of it in the metaphoric medium of words. At this point, Bronk enters the dominion of the Romantic imagination, which works continuously to destroy ways of seeing and thinking in order to generate news ways of seeing and thinking. The dominion he enters manages itself on fictions—usable structures or modes of thought which make it possible for the mind to invent a world to inhabit with the clear recognition that it is accepting a version of the world not the world itself. He aligns himself with the line of imaginative fictions from Thoreau and Emerson to Whitman and Melville, and then to Wallace Stevens.

2

Hans Vaihinger in his book *The Philosophy of "As If"* discusses fictions in a way that leads directly forward to the poetry of Wallace Stevens and William Bronk. He creates a gate between strict logical structures of nineteenth-century, European thought and the emerging American pragmatism. For him, fictions are utilities of the psyche:

> The fictive activity of the mind is an expression of the fundamental psychical forces; *fictions are mental structures*. The psyche weaves this aid to thought out of itself; for the mind is inventive; under the compulsion of necessity, stimulated by the outer world, it discovers the store of contrivances that lie hidden within itself. The organism finds itself in a world full of contradictory sensations, it is exposed to the assaults of a hostile external world, and in order to preserve itself, it is forced to seek every

possible means of assistance, external as well as internal. In necessity and pain, mental evolution is begun, in contradiction and opposition consciousness awakes, and man owes his mental development more to his enemies than to his friends. (Vaihinger 12)

When the mind relinquishes the a-priori determinations of thought, then it is flooded with a massive intake of sensations from the physical world. In response to the attack of the sensations, the psyche generates useful categories as a means of organizing these sensations.

> It must be remembered that the object of the world of ideas as a whole is not the portrayal of reality—this would be an utterly impossible task—but rather to provide us with *an instrument for finding our way about more easily in this world.* Subjective processes of thought inhere in the entire structure of cosmic phenomena. They represent the highest and ultimate results of organic development . . . whole cosmic process; but for that very reason it is not a copy of it in the ordinary sense.(Vaihinger 15-16)

> All cognition is the apperception of one thing through another. In understanding, we are always dealing with an analogy and we cannot imagine how otherwise existence can be understood. Anyone acquainted with the mechanism of thought knows that all conception and cognition are based upon analogical apperceptions. The only ideational constructs by means of which existing things can be apperceived are either the corresponding general conceptions or other concrete objects. But since these are in their turn inconceivable, all these analogies only give rise to an apparent understanding.(Vaihinger 29)

Vaihinger maintains that categories of ideas are not to be used to describe reality itself, but rather to create ways of thought that make it possible to find out about reality. The main utility of this approach is through analogy, therefore, as if one set of ideas were actually describing reality when in truth the ideas are a fictional view of reality.

> The gulf between reality and fiction must always be stressed, and care must be taken to confuse neither the fiction itself nor its immediate consequences with reality. With all these precautions before us, the fiction can be regarded as a "legitimatized error," i.e. as a fictional conceptual construct that has justified its existence by its success. On the other hand, it would be wrong to argue from the success of such a logical procedure to its logical purity or real validity. Fictions are and must remain circuitous and indirect mental paths, which cannot, because they conduct us to our goal, be regarded as really valid or free from logical contradiction. (Vaihinger 105-106)

Vaihinger argues that contradictions out of necessity are part of the fictional constructs because the fictions are ideas about reality, which are used to understand reality, but not describe it. One of the largest fictional ideas is "infinity," which he argues does not exist in reality but has been useful to make mathematical calculations about the physical world. Another usable fiction in paper money.

> "Fictional value" is the name given in political economy to paper-money and such ideas as, for instance, the pound sterling, etc. The paper is regarded *as if* it had the value of metal; the computation is made *as if* we were really dealing with "pounds sterling." Our analogy has thus a real basis. (Vaihinger 160)

As merchants and shoppers we trade in paper money as if it itself had value, but we must be very careful not to confuse the idea of money, which is an idea about reality, for either value or money. The laws of nature and fictions are not compatible worlds.

> The laws which govern the organic function of thought, like those governing nature, are all indifferent to us, all work blindly.

Whether they work for our advantage or disadvantage depends upon circumstances. In themselves they are double-edged. The alteration of reality in the logical processes, the change of the given ponderous material into the light and evanescent thought which so little resembles it, involves dangers as numerous as the possibilities which it opens up for rapid mental operations. The degree of confidence we have in thought, in its work and its products is exceedingly important for our investigation. At any rate we must leave behind us the naive belief *that what is thought of really exists*, that the forms and methods of thought can be rediscovered in world as fact. (Vaihinger 162).

Fictions have a practical object but are theoretically valueless. Nonetheless fictions are necessary for thought, which then leads on to the utility of language.

> Without its aid [a fiction] it would not have been possible for thought to create any order at all out of the confusion of sensation.
>
> This assumption of a Thing would never have been possible without the assistance of language, which provides us with a word for the Thing and gives the attributes specific names. It is to the word that the illusion of the existence of a Thing possessing attributes attaches itself, and it is the word that enables the mistake to become fixed. The logical function selects a complex of sensations from the general stream of sensations and events, and creates a thing to which these sensations, possessed by the psyche alone, are to adhere as attributes. But Thing, Attribute, and the Judgment in which they are combined, are simply transformations of reality fictions; in other words errors—but fruitful errors. (Vaihinger 169)

It might be possible to turn to Bronk's poetry for a gloss, "The Substantive":

In the beginning was the word and the word was adjective.
Attribute is everything we know.
Listen. Look. Not do. It is there. (*LS* 149)

The language of a fiction ordered by rational control gives the illusion of understanding reality, when in fact only the fictions of reality come under control for the utility of comprehension.

The desire to understand the world is therefore ridiculous, for all understanding consists in an actual or imaginary reduction to the known. But to what is this "known" itself to be reduced, especially if in the end it turns out to be something "unknown."

> Our world itself is not capable of being understood but merely of being known. Philosophy can arrive only at a knowledge of the world, not at an understanding of it; it will be a knowledge of the world in its naked simplicity, after the destruction of all subjective forms of interpretation and additions, where fictions are consciously recognized as fictions, i.e. as necessary, useful and helpful conceptual aids. To want to "understand" the world as a whole is exceedingly foolish; and foolish not because human understanding is too undeveloped, but because every individual, even one endowed with superhuman capacities, must simply accept the ultimate realities which we can actually attain as the object of knowledge. (Vaihinger 172)

All events are understood in the light of these analogies which are continuously refined, and eventually become the abstract ideas that are always quite rightly recognized as analogical fictions. If then the categories have value only in practice and not in theory—namely for purposes of order, communication, and action—then philosophical systems also can have no other value, historically have never had any other. All understanding claimed for them was but a psychical illusion. Fictions have only a practical purpose and all the systems built up on elementary fictions are only more subtle and more elaborate fictions, to which no theoretical value must ever be attributed and which possess all the characteristics that we have so far always found in fictions. Theoretically they are valueless but practically they are important.(Vaihinger 173)

We presuppose here, of course, the development of language and would merely note that the communication of an event or of an impression in an intelligible manner was made possible only through the formation of a limited number of categories. By bringing reality under these categories, communication between individuals became possible in terms of some known analogy, which immediately awakened in the recipient an idea of what the speaker wished to communicate. This is related to our third point, namely that understanding is thereby engendered—from our standpoint an illusion of understanding—reality being thought of under some known analogy. The tremendous pressure of the inrushing sensations is reduced, and the tension of these impressions is removed, in consequence of their being; apportioned to different divisions. I would add at once that was only made possible *in extenso* by language; the category is immediately attached to the word and the word becomes more abstract and loses its sensory colouring. That is why language has both such a *releasing and loosening influence upon the psyche*, [my emphasis] since it was only by this means that the division of existence into categories became possible. Finally, it was only in this way that action could be determined. The psyche was no longer merely a helpless and passive spectator of the stream of existence and events, was no longer exclusively dependent upon mere reflex tendencies, but, as the pictures in this way became ordered and grouped according to categories, it was able to determine their re-entry and to arrange its activity accordingly. (Vaihinger 176)

Even though a skepticism and even a pessimism enters this world of fictions and unknowable reality, Vaihinger maintains that these excitements cause renewed attempts to formulate views of the real world. Language structures produce an intersection between reality and the fictive activities of the psyche, and in fact carry the fictions forward with the psyche's orders within it. Fictions in the end are the most accurate, but false, versions of reality that the mind (psyche) can create in response to the desire to know more about the world and in part to satisfy its own sense of creativity.

3

Stevens proposes the manner and result of the interaction between imagination and reality as the central issues of his poetry. The conflict in "The Man with the Blue Guitar" is between the inability of the guitar (imagination) to play things as they are: the imagination changes reality into its own structures, into language structures which are versions of reality, and not the central man the poem desires to find and sing purely. It was "as if the sun" (CP 75) (reality) took on new forms that the imagination could not know. The speaker in "Farewell to Florida" wonders about the domination of the landscape over the imagination "As if I lived in ashen ground, as if / The leaves in which the wind" blew (CP 117) all came from an overheated South, or that the parts of his poems were dominated by the powerful landscape of the South. The birds in "Dry Loaf" fly "As if the sky was a current that bore them along" (CP 200), or, without citing too many examples, it is safe to say that Stevens cultivated the use of "as if" as a way of making indirect remarks about reality, and as he used the proposal more and more as it turned into a means of expressing versions of reality in language, true fictions in Vaihinger's sense, that are not descriptions of reality, rather are versions of the real that the imagination used as a medium to understand reality, when he knew absolutely that reality itself could resist comprehension completely.

> The final belief is to believe in a fiction, which you know to be a fiction, there being nothing else. The exquisite truth is to know that it is a fiction and that you believe in it willingly. (*Opus Posthumous* 163)

The statement in prose has many clarifications in the poems, for example the description of the coming of a vision proceeds by piling example on example, of expanding by apposition and simile, moving from image to image all under the assumption of "as if."

Esthétique du Mal

It seems as if the honey of common summer
Might be enough, as if the gold combs
Were part of a sustenance itself enough,

As if hell, so modified, had disappeared,
As if pain, no longer satanic mimicry,
Could be borne, as if we were to find our way. (CP 316)

Stevens based his poetry on the proposals of "as if," the fictive wish of coming to terms with the spiritual meaning that he found standing out from reality in rare, and brilliant moments. He called these moments "spots of time," occasions when the tensions between the mind and reality dissolve into visionary seeing. Stevens had such spots of "imperishable bliss," flicks of feeling, manifestation of the centrality of the earth and mind. In "Credences of Summer"

It is the rock of summer, the extreme
A mountain luminous half way in bloom
And then half way in the extremest light
Of sapphires flashing from the central sky
As if twelve princes sat before a king. (CP 375)

He knows that the experience "is the visible announced" (CP 376) the central source of the energies of the imagination and reality. The analogies follow, a mountain, sapphires, twelve princes, as if he is demonstrating that he acknowledges there is no way to express in language the vision he knows but he can present approximations, collecting one after another, accumulating meanings that might, just might catch some aspect of the wonder. The whole poem is a series of analogies, proposals of "as if," extended into parables, all trying to come to a better definition than the one before it.

   The Rock

As if nothingness contained a métier
A vital assumption, an impermanence
In its permanent cold, an illusion so desired

That the green leaves came and covered the high rocks,
That the lilacs came and bloomed, like a blindness cleaned
Exclaiming bright sight, as it was satisfied,

In a birth of sight. The blooming and the musk
Were being alive, an incessant being alive,
A particular of being, that gross universe. (CP 526)

The most exhaustive demonstration of the power of the "festival sphere," or the "transparencies of sound" (CP 466) comes in the long poem "An Ordinary Evening in New Haven." Stevens comes back again and again to the same questions which generated "The Man with the Blue Guitar," the interactions of the mind and reality, imagination and reality relentlessly confronting one another, and the desire, the drive of the imagination to wrest the final meaning from a reality which will never be conquered. "We keep coming back and coming back / To the real: to the hotel instead of the hymns / That fall upon it out of the wind." (CP 471). Stevens's solution to the conflict of driving the hammer of imagination against the rock of reality is a process of conceiving and reconceiving versions, approximations, fictions of possible ways of explaining what can not be explained. The action of the poem enacting thought in language becomes the substance of the poem. The poem is not a fiction about reality, nor a commentary about some event that happened in the actual world. It is rather a fictive demonstration of the mind conceiving thought in language, or where the process of enacting thought creates an usable fiction to satisfy belief, when all another impossible forms and logics of belief have been eliminated. The poem is an event in language, the vision enacting itself in language, as a falsifying medium, no doubt, but one that sparkles with the energy of the vision itself.

It is not an empty clearness, a bottomless sight.
It is a visibility of thought,
In which hundreds of eyes, in one mind, see at once.
(CP 488)

4

William Bronk's stance as a poet is based on the observance of a spiritual presences in reality, the physical world, that exceeds the dimensions of language to define.

Where it Ends

The gentleness of the slant October light
conceals whatever else we might have thought.
It is a hard world, empty and cruel;
but this light, oh Jesus Christ! This light!

The maple leaves, passive in front of the house,
are laved in it, abandoned, green gone.
That nothing else should matter but this light.
Gentleness, gentleness, the light. (LS 161)

The complaint of not being able to know reality is a complaint about not being able to contain the light in a direct seeing of it. The light is the reality of the poems; it is the world out there that can not be known, which is other than the appearances of the physical world that can be known, yet knowing those appearances does not advance comprehension of the reality of the light in the maple leaves. He comes to accept the limits of language, and engages the fiction of language to create a substitute for the thing that he desires the most.

> All right. Still metaphor. What is it we signify?
> We say lies as if they were not lies, as if
> we believe. And indeed, we do believe. No;
> we know the metaphor is wrong. And yet—(LS 152)

Like Stevens he believes in the lies, the metaphor, knowing full what they are, fictions of the absolute angle, the revolutions of the crystal.

In the poem "The Field" from, *The Mild Day*, the lines appear:

> Desire alone attracts
> us together to make a common sense and found
> an unfounded order, a house of thought to leave
> unlived and empty almost as soon as built. (MD 33)

These lines clarify one of Bronk's persistent images as a fictive structure of the house of the mind. Desire wants "a big house of which we say / 'Yes, but what a place to put it, here'!" (LS 83). In "The Cipher"

> I had to leave that town
> as though the last not living there. As though.
> For we never lived there. No one. We played we did.
> Played house. The games of time and place. All kinds
> of games. (LS 9L)

That house of fictions was a place of imaginative acts, a place satisfaction, of fun though he certainly knew that it was a fiction and not a real house. In "Period Metaphor" from *Manifest*, he writes "Jesus, spoke, metaphorically, about houses built on rock and sand"(MAF 35), and the poem "Sojourner" from *Living Instead*:

He's hardly ever here but I have the house
and it's all I need. It does for me.
People think it's mine and I treat it so
—pay the taxes and all, keep it up—
it's not that much. Even if he never comes
other people do. And the house is here. (*LI* 50)

And in the poem "Worlds and Changes" from *Careless Love and its Apostrophies*,

The world we make ourselves seems Made for us it fits is as well.
    It took a while.

But, at times, I am locked out of my own house. I walk around
    the sides. I look at it. I have no key,

Or, as though I go in and the rooms are empty. Nothing there.
    The stove is out.

His own metaphors, fictions of the other reality, lock him out of the sustaining fiction of the house of the mind that he has constructed for many years.

There are of course many more references to houses, locked doors, corridors and windows, other parts of the fiction of the house. But there are enough here to make the point that Bronk's resolution to his life-long struggle to define the nature of spiritual reality was to accept, now and again, the fiction of a metaphor as the closest approximation to the light in the tress by the house that he would ever obtain. The elusive vision sketched at the edge of his eye, and vanishing in direct sight came to life in the fiction of language, as a reconciliation of the pessimistic struggle of the mind to bring form to formlessness, to built the grand house of the mind to live in. While the structure of his stance toward reality follows Vaihinger's description of the fictive procedure, he did not jump to Stevens's reconciliation of the contest between imagination and reality in the act of the mind conceiving language, or in the process of poetry

THE BODY OF THIS LIFE:

miming the processes of the imagination and reality. Bronk followed Stevens's habit of advancing a poem with analogy and apposition in the poems in *Life Supports*, but in the subsequent books, as the poems became shorter they became more assertive and reluctant to amplify. He held tenaciously to his exposition of knowing the vision and resisting the joy that it brought, Nathaniel Hawthorne in Hudson Falls to the end.

Joseph Conte

"NOT BY ART ALONE":
WILLIAM BRONK'S MEDITATIVE NEGATIVITY

I N A REVIEW OF WILLIAM BRONK'S WORK, Gilbert Sorrentino remarks that Bronk "writes the same poem over and over again, explaining the quality and reality of despair. Each rings a variation on his dark theme." If Bronk is, as Sorrentino suggests, "a scandalously neglected poet," it is not because so many of his poems are locked in an aesthetic battle with the nature of reality, but because their outcome is unremittingly "tragic." Nevertheless, Sorrentino notes, "the darker and more intransigent the world they inscribe, the more salutary they become" (Sorrentino 78). As evidence of the neglect that Bronk's reputation has suffered, an anonymous reviewer for the *Virginia Quarterly Review* comments that "His voice is . . . austere. I don't suppose he is for every palate, but those with a taste for the fine, tart, and clear," etc. (*VQR* 59). For Bronk, the issue is far more serious and consuming than a dispute over "taste," as if his collected poems, *Life Supports,* were a basket of Hudson Valley apples.

Those who have had the pleasure of sampling even a few poems by Bronk are aware that they articulate a persistent motif. "The world" is a reality which "we" are never able to perceive in its entirety. Because we "miss" the big picture, nothing we perceive is ever a "true" estimate. Several critics have succinctly paraphrased this central theme (one might as well say obsession) of Bronk's. Norman Finkelstein comments that "the single great constant in the poetry of William Bronk is desire; specifically desire for *the world,* which can never be known as a totality. Despite the self-limiting fact that consciousness is aware of its inability to experience this totality, it continually struggles for the achievement of its goal. Cut off from any ground of belief, secure only in its desire, consciousness therefore creates *a world,* which despite its insufficiency in metaphysical terms nevertheless allows for the rendering of form—the poem" (Finkelstein 481). Having analyzed the "constant" in Bronk's work, Finkelstein then points out that, although they move through "many essential human situations," the poems "echo each other so hauntingly that they seem like endless variations on the same theme." Indeed, Bronk's proposition of *the world* functions much as the *statement* of a fugue, a motif around which all further repetition and elaboration is built. Though it recurs in many variations of expression, this statement is the constant preoccupation of the poet. It is impossible for language to express what *it* (the real) is; but even though he knows this, the poet must struggle to approach the *real* in language. Given Bronk's epistemology, his approach to *the world,* his opinion of the efficacy of language follows: it is obviously insufficient, inasmuch as *the real* remains always inexpressible.

The poet, unable to state *the world* directly, creates *a world* in the iterative composition of the poem. Bronk expresses the heavy presence of this epistemological quandary in his poetry's intensive meditations, the turning over and over in his mind of his theme. He argues, in terms most discomforting, that "the world" *is* the absence of form, and that all the "form" which we perceive is of our own making. As he says in a late poem, "Genesis Over," "It is a makeshift world and we know it is / because we made it up" *(MOT* 24). This observation is in large part the tragic information which William Bronk conveys. But the mitigating circumstance is, as he says in "The Arts and Death: A Fugue for Sidney Cox," that "it is real / this passion that we feel for forms." And yet, "the forms / are never real. Are not really there. Are not" *(LS* 35). Bronk's negative insistence, his denial of transcendent form, can be found in his poem, "The Nature of Musical Form," which also serves as a gloss on the analogy of the fugue:

It is tempting to say of the incomprehensible,
the formlessness, there is only order as we
so order and ordering, make it so; or this,
there is natural order which music apprehends

which apprehension justifies the world;

or even this, these forms are false, not true,
and music irrelevant at least, the world
is stated somewhere else, not there. But no.

                    (LS 69)

Bronk offers several alternatives to "the incomprehensible, the formless-
ness" of the world, all of which he rejects: (1) human order, (2) natural
order, and (3) transcendent order. He recognizes that the order we make
cannot be thought to be part of the real—we cannot "make it so." What
we "apprehend" as natural order is merely an expression of our "view"
of the cosmos, rather like a Rorschach test, and such impression cannot
be said to "justify" anything. Lastly, there is the transcendental view that
the order is "somewhere else." This view stated by Robert Duncan's
"divine order," or perhaps more systematically in something like Yeats's
"gyres," must also be rejected. All three approaches to the real are false.
What makes Bronk a post-humanist, postmodern writer is his conviction
that all forms are false, artificial. We make them, and we cannot pretend
that they have a validity beyond us, in any way. So he says in "A Fugue"
that "the forms are never real," they are always the product of artifice.

The meditative poem as a genre can be located as an intermediary
type between the epic and the lyric poem. The modern epic is a "poem
including history," concerned with the interpretation of past events and
their implications for the current state of affairs. The authorial voice of
Ezra Pound's *Cantos* or Charles Olson's *Maximus Poems* pretends to
speak for the culture at-large. But the meditative poem purports to be a
product of the present state of the poet's mind; it documents the spiritu-
ality or mindscape of an individual, remaining more or less isolated from
empirical concerns. On the other hand, the lyric is the genre that has
traditionally accommodated the physical and the passionate; it demands
a personal address; and it is most comfortable in an emotive or a descrip-
tive mode. But the meditative poem must necessarily be cognitive rather
than sensual, abstract rather than particular; it seeks at least a temporary
retreat from the turbulent desires of the ego. Neither public discourse nor
intimate confession, the meditative poem has traditionally presented the
thought of the individual as that thought aspires to a more general truth.

The meditative poetry of William Bronk provides no affirmative answer to the Romantic poetics of the subject and its transcendental signifiers. It is true that Bronk's epistemological concerns find their source in the work of Wallace Stevens, whose definition of modern poetry is "The poem of the mind in the act of finding / What will suffice"(*Collected Poems* 239). At the risk of appearing to be composed of private—even solipsistic—ruminations, the meditative poem usually makes some appeal to transpersonal, or transcendental, beliefs; that what the poet thinks in his or her most private moments will ultimately be held as truth for those who read the work. In such contemplative poems as "The Auroras of Autumn," Stevens presents a figurative unity of the probing mind and the engulfing world. Both the aurora borealis and the imagination of the poet are searching and recoiling; they are "form gulping after formlessness" (*Collected Poems* 411). But as a postmodern meditative poet Bronk rejects even a tentative consideration of the identification of the human mind with an Emersonian Oversoul.

The absolute insistence on the failure of this communion of the mind with the natural world appears readily in the following poem from *Life Supports* (*LS* 1981):

The Destroyer Life

I know there are things: crystals, fossils, basalts,
certain metals, that seem as though they last
eternally and I know it is not so.
But we think of them so. I think also of logs
in the woods, tree-trunks, their bark whole
still and, inside, soft as suede, their strength,
their hard solidity wasted, years away.
I saw on the back porch a mold on a squash,
tiny magnificences yesterday
and, today, mold and squash together slime.

These poems that, once, I thought might be
support and comfort to me, come bad times,

are now an emptiness. I need to know that
all their strength is only as a strength
fills them, some strong life, and my
strong life is down as living things
show life so, do drive down.
And I hasten it: my impatiences
bristle why it takes so long, open the veins
of feeling, pulse let go, let go, let go. (LS 213)

There's an exquisite balance in this poem between the abstract language
of cogitation and the concrete, sensual description of the natural world.
This resolute opposition between the mind and the world, the resistance
to Romantic belief in the transcendental union of nature and soul, is the
central negation of Bronk's poetry. His tone is at one moment dry and at
another anguished, as the reasoning faculty and the emotional drive
contend for a fuller part in the drama. The theme of decay in life is
perhaps a *locus classicus* for the meditative poem, especially as the
contemplative act is thought to provide consolation. Though Bronk has
sought "life support" from his poetry, it does not appear to have been
enough.

The poem is evenly divided into two stanzas of ten lines apiece. The
first stanza addresses the poet's failure to fully comprehend the destruc-
tive force of the natural world; even the inorganic mineral, which seems
a permanence, is subject to decay. The second stanza reiterates the poet's
sense of deception when he finds that his own work, like the fallen log,
does not possess any resilience beyond the life that supports it. This
carefully balanced comparison rests on the repeated verbs of thinking,
seeming, and knowing. Each stanza begins with an epistemological
statement in which an apparent understanding about life is debunked.
The poet next arrives at a condition of aporia, an admission of doubt
that is more appealing than hollow sureties. And then in the final three
lines of each stanza he plunges, with the more active verbs, "I saw," "I
hasten," into a confrontation with death characterized by disgust,
"slime," or suicidal impulse, "open the veins." The rhetorical parallelism
in the poem not only depends on the repeated verbs of cognition but also

on recursive syntax, as in the lines: "I need to know / that all their *strength* is only as a *strength* / fills them, some *strong life,* and my / *strong life* is *down* as living things / show life so, do drive *down*" (my emphases). There is a degree to which syntax is thought, and a degree to which syntax alone can describe the mode of thought. Syntax provides a more literal enactment of the meditative process of the poet's mind than a dramatization of the self. Bronk's meditation insists—in the very terms of reasoned argument—on the inefficacy of the reasoning mind for apprehending the essential world. The meditative act of the poem, like the final gesture described, is practically self-canceling.

Just as Bronk negates the transcendental signifier of Romantic poetry, so too he rejects any illusion of the transpersonal in his meditative poems. Notice how unstable the collective subject "we" becomes in "Real Thinking" in *Death Is the Place* (1989):

> Reality is willing we should think
> about it: no harm. But it isn't going to be
> comprehended by our thought or even admit
> to us its being there. "Maybe I'm not,"
> it says. Ha, ha; funny type.
> Meanwhile, we doubt ourselves, too, as far
> as thinking goes, finding us just as strange,
> finding us both not any way possible. (*DITP* 10)

Reality's denial, that it can be comprehended in its totality, that it even exists in the face of our abject failure to think about it, is a familiar point of departure for Bronk. Yet reality's ventriloquized rejoinder, "Maybe I'm not," redounds upon the poet, as if in an argument between two preadolescents. We are each alone in a world of our own making. Thinking, that which should "suffice" for the meditative poet, offers no lasting resort. Just as no harm is done by the poet in making propositions about reality, so there is no harm in proposing an integral speaker or the transpersonal "we" in the poem. Yet they are merely convenient rhetorical devices; chess pieces on the board of contemplative action. The poet—and his reader—must acknowledge that the "we" or "us" that the poem ventures is no more "possible" as an expression than the comprehension of reality. There can be no surety of shared experience. Bronk's repeated, stern, and unyielding conviction that this must be so, however popular the promise of transpersonal communication may be for lyric poetry, has made him one of our most formidable poets.

David Landrey

LOVE AND SILENCE IN WILLIAM BRONK

> Great is emotional love, even in the order of the rational universe. But, if we
> must make gradations, I am clear there is something greater....By the names
> right, justice, truth, we suggest, but do not describe it. To the world of men it
> remains a dream, an idea as they call it. But no dream is it to the wise— but the
> proudest, almost only solid lasting thing of all. Its analogy in the material
> universe is what holds together this world, and every object upon it, and carries
> its dynamics on forever sure and safe.
>
> —Walt Whitman, from "Democratic Vistas"

> After searching for a long time for some form of his own, [Whitman] found that
> external form was more satisfying and splendid, and finally abandoned himself
> to the ecstatic pleasures of disintegration.
>
> —William Bronk, from "Walt Whitman's Marine Democracy"

C ALL WILLIAM BRONK'S OWN ECSTATIC PLEASURE of (or with) disinte-
gration: *love*. And, paradoxically, call love's ultimate expression: silence.

Bronk had written all of *The Brother in Elysium* by 1941, all except
the chapter on Melville. Except for one small part of his thoughts on
Melville, I'll concentrate on the sections on Thoreau and Whitman and
particularly the former, for the kinship he found with Thoreau and the
assertions he makes about him are so closely related to his early poetry
and to his recurrent sense of Love and Silence in poetry to the very end.
I've come to serious consideration of Bronk's work late, having been
moved by hearing him on two occasions: the first in 1983, in Rochester,
when he read "Silence and Metaphor" from *Life Supports* (and made a
special point of signing the first page of that section); the second at his
home when he charmed us with sausage soup and by reading all of *All of
What We Loved*. So, as I develop my understanding, I've selected pas-

sages from *The Brother in Elysium*, from the very early work, and a small number of poems from the works which first caught my attention, caught it in the heart of my own silence and my own ambiguous love for a world I so often hate.

The Whitman passage in the epigraph speaks of a binding force roughly equivalent to some combination of the Greek Eros (or perhaps Themis; or both) and the Egyptian Ma'at, forces born of Chaos whose role is to prevent falling back therein—a cosmic Love, greater, as he says, than emotional love. Yet the Bronk epigraph suggests that only a disintegrative instinct, a diffusion, enabled Whitman to achieve a form that approximates or stands for or renders that binding force. Bronk writes:

> Paradoxically, it was the urgency and desirability of form which led Whitman to cultivate his sea-like formlessness, for not only was he able by this means to project himself at liberty into forms which were attractive to him, but the very attractiveness of those forms and his yearning after them was increased almost to the point of ecstasy by his polarity with them. *(VSC* 139)

Elsewhere in "Democratic Vistas" Whitman says,

> America needs, and the world needs, a class of bards who will, now and ever, so link and tally the rational physical being of man, with the ensembles of time and space, and with this vast and multiform show, Nature, surrounding him, ever tantalizing him, equally a part, and yet not a part of him, as to essentially harmonize, satisfy, and put at rest.

Once more Bronk: "This vast similitude was the basis of Whitman's universe, in which, despite diversity there was only one substance, one reality, a single material and a single spirit" *(VSC* 132).

A host of paradoxical relations, then, informs Bronk's vision (or his vision informs paradox): the one and the many, form and formlessness, integration and disintegration, expression and silence. The last of these—so central to his thought and work—is beautifully explored in his three-part essay on Thoreau.

The subtitle of *The Brother in Elysium*, "Ideas of Friendship and Society in the United States," might be heard in the way Duncan heard Whitman: that "United States" means "united states of being." In his dedication to Sidney Cox, Bronk says, "there will be no inconsistencies to be found between our real ideas of our friends and our real political desires" (*VSC* 55). He then asserts the united state of his own craft:

> *I have wanted to write a kind of essential drama, in which each of the three characters comments on the matter at hand by his own word and deed, and so reveals himself and his subject If my book makes any statement, therefore, it must be by the relationships that are revealed, by its composition, by a form brought about to the perceptive reader; by that element which is in every line and in no single one.* (*VSC* 55)

Reading "Silence and Henry Thoreau" one often forgets who is speaking, Henry or William, so well has he mined that "element."

Bronk sounds like the Whitman of "Democratic Vistas" when, in the dedication, he adds, "Society is based on something more than economics and physical security. . . . without it, too, our political conceptions, even the most grandiose, are slight and shallow and will not last long" (*VSC* 55). Oh, that "it": should it, perhaps, be capitalized, as if uttered by Dean Moriarty? And, in the end, did Bronk think we *were* without it and would not last long?

But on to Thoreau. Bronk quotes him: "Friends do not live in harmony merely, as some say, but in melody. We do not wish for friends to feed and clothe our bodies,—our neighbors are kind enough for that—but to do the like office for our spirits" (*VSC* 68). Bronk says that, selecting harmony instead of melody, Thoreau's neighbors, "Fearful of real freedom or actual religion [and, we might add, of real friendship] . . . erected the prison of an institution around them and so had the safe and make-believe of the prison yard or . . . had Christianity bunged up" (*VSC* 97). No willingness there to abandon themselves to pleasures of disintegration. Thoreau, Bronk contends, arrived at a different idea of friendship:

> the force which motivated all the rest of the complex, friendship was an exalting and powerful love. It was a kind of love that went forth with no particular object in view and was wholly selfgenerated. It neither arose from, nor was directed toward, anything else in the world. This love without reference is the basis of friendship in Thoreau. It was the one thing in his life that never tarnished for him. (*VSC* 68)

This "love without reference" has "an all-pervasive, evanescent quality" (*VSC* 69). So how is it achieved?

It is "as likely to come upon us when alone as when in company," Bronk says, and argues, surely revealing himself more than Thoreau, that, "All men were dreaming of it and its drama which was always a tragedy was enacted daily" (*VSC* 70). Here is a powerful negative capability, achieved in silence, where being is more significant than expression: "Thoreau knew that his life was in nature, not in society, just as whatever community life as has value and is truly existent is in nature too. That, however, is not society" (*VSC* 105). But the silence! Following is a sequence of comments, again revelations of Bronk's paradoxical vision.

[1] Silence leads a man to give another the best of his wares and enables him to do so. It is the seat and source of our strangeness (*VSC* 78).

[2] Silence is the world of potentialities and meanings beyond the actual and expressed, which the meanness of our actions and the interpretations put upon them threatens to conceal (*VSC* 79)

[3] Nothing is worth saying, nothing is worth doing except as a foil for the waves of silence to break against (*VSC* 80).

[4] Silence is an asylum not because it enabled him, in any sense, to stop living, but because it made it possible for him to continue to live and always come back for more in spite of disappointments and failures (*VSC* 80).

[5] The asylum of silence was inviolable. This it was, ultimately, that prevented the finality of experience *(VSC* 80).

With these passages suspended before us, let's examine some of the poems in search of non-specific love's melody.

Hard to imagine a more stunning beginning to a life's collection than, "The Inclination of the Earth," which, I gather from the conversation with Edward Foster in *Postmodern Poetry,* was either just before or just after *The Brother in Elysium.* Bronk appears to sense that he has entered creation at a late stage of entropy. Disturbance and dissatisfaction are our very attitude, our axes all tilted in a late time. One can understand an inclination to silence in such an obliquity, but, lo, it is the beginning of a great outpouring, a "flood from our hands/held cupped to catch them in" *(LS* 11). Note that the *dissatisfactions* are flooding—well lost, perhaps, from our hands; perhaps purged in the utterance, yet still profuse, inescapable.

For me, love's melody emerges most eloquently at the beginning of his second volume, *Light and Dark,* in the meditative "Some Musicians Play Chamber Music For Us" *(LS* 25-27). Now this is clearly not *about* silence; it's about sound, about music, but it may be a fulfillment of number 3, above. What he writes and the music itself may be foils "for the waves of silence to break against." Break indeed: "But all we know are fragments of the world," fragments he invokes the music to lift so as to convince us that "we build/a design of fragments to entrap our world"—to entrap them in our silent chamber. Part III is Bronk's own abandonment to the ecstatic pleasures of disintegration. He and those others who constitute the "us" (Might the others be only the musicians? Might he be otherwise alone in his chamber?) are in sacramental communion, lifting the broken pieces of their world. It is—after the lament of part two about how good it would be if we only had guidance, had plans, knew "what something finally is"—an ecstatic celebration and captures "a true presence"—the IT Kerouac heard in the music of his time: Whitman's and Thoreau's force of disintegrative, undirected love, "composed, oh wholly and well composed." The chamber of this music is Bronk's "asylum of silence . . . that prevented the finality of experience" (#5 above); the world is "never reduced/to final elements." It is only a late stage of entropy Bronk has entered, not the end.

Consider, also, the last poem in *The World, the Worldless:*

What I want to do is shout. Happiness? No.
Outrage? No. What I want to do is shout
because we were all wrong, because the point
was not the point, because the world, or what
we took for the world, is breaking, breaking. We were wrong
and are not right. Break! Break! We are here!
What I want is to shout! Break! Shout! *(LS 72)*

Yet more abandonment to the ecstatic pleasures of disintegration. The opening poem of *Silence and Metaphor* asserts:

Under the noise, silence is what we hear:
final, always, wherever Silence is all. (LS 161)

There's certainly ample gloom in Bronk's work, and later in *Silence and Metaphor* he begins "The Revelation": "My life has no shape; I live in an old house" *(LS 168)*. The shape he has supposed would impose itself (or thought he had supposed, for he isn't even certain of that) did not, but he concludes, "I find I don't care/this didn't happen, and yet am surprised" *(LS 169)*. Silence is no solace, but it continues to be an asylum. As he said in #4 above, "it made it possible for him to continue to live and always come back for more in spite of disappointments and failures."

Perhaps all of Bronk's work illustrates Love and Silence. I'll confine myself to two more examples. First, "The Elusions of Desire" *(LS 175)*. The word "elusions" seems a combination of three words: illusion, elude, and elute. That is, desire may well be an illusion, certainly eludes us (or we it) and finally extracts something from us (or we from it). All of these choices constitute the mystery, wherein he loves Sense, but, "My eyes look out/while I stay in mystery, wanting sense." The only thing definite is that nothing is—almost a cause for rejoicing.

Finally, I offer, from *All of What We Loved,* "Worldspeak":

The world speaks none of the world's languages
multiple though they may be — lost,
some of them when their people were lost — and they
are all languages of people but the world speaks
a language of its own not understood
by any of us who don't know how it says.
But it moves us to do as the world moves. (*AWWL* 149)

Is that world not "the world of potentialities and meanings beyond the actual and expressed" in #2 above? And did Bronk not continue to "do" from within that silence?

Writing of Herman Melville in *The Brother in Elysium,* Bronk had found *Moby-Dick* "notably serene and objective . . . in spite of all Ahab's intense and bitter passions" (*VSC* 199). He continues by saying,

There is a new element in *Moby Dick,* an element which gives Melville's work the dimension of greatness, the element of wonder. As much as anything else no doubt, it sustained him through disappointment. "The great floodgates of the wonder world swung open," he said. . . . He knew that such a response to the world was a reflection of the mystery which man is within himself [and] . . . he asks, "Is it possible, after all, that spite of bricks and shaven faces, this world we live in is brimmed with wonders, and I and all mankind, beneath our garbs of common-placeness, conceal enigmas that the stars themselves, and perhaps the highest seraphim can not resolve?" (*VSC* 200)

Out of Bronk's wonderment in the vastness of Silence, he gave us "the best of his wares" and perhaps even enabled us to do so: the seat and source of our strangeness, truly.

Paul Christensen

THE HARD, SPARE GRAMMAR OF REALITY:
WILLIAM BRONK'S PROSE

W̲ILLIAM BRONK'S PROSE OPERATES AS A KIND OF WORKSHOP for hammering out the principal theme of his poetry, the fictions human beings construct about themselves and their world in order to live in this ineffable totality Bronk calls reality. Take time, for example. Each culture devises its own watch to mark the time; since that watch refers to nothing but its own internal system of monitoring, it is as valid as any other. Of Mayan time, Bronk has this to say: "If the experience of time is, on its simplest terms, an experience of change and recurrence without external reference, any ordering of that experience is as valid as another. If there is an absolute of time the Mayas had not seen it."* It is "worldlessness" one should aspire to, to escape the illusions the mind is prey to.†

Like Olson, Bronk was beginning to write in the age of McCarthyism, the propaganda battles of the Cold War; he was a teenager when Stalin began the purges that would ultimately break up the Communist Party and set back the socialist movement in the United States. Large schemes and political ideology were corrupted by the arms race and the epic battle between the state and the rising power of corporations with geopolitical ambitions. The mid-century was a wasteland of bankrupt philosophical language, now that the colonial world under Europe was disintegrating and with it the racial metaphysics that once justified imperial exploitation.

---

*Vectors and Smoothable Curves· Collected Essays. San Francisco, CA: North Point Press, 1983, p. 15.

†See his early poems on this subject in *The World, the Worldless.* NY· New Directions/San Francisco, CA· *San Francisco Review,* 1964.

The crisis wracking the West after World War II was, "Who are we?" And the answer was not forthcoming; the gap of silence greeting the question was suddenly filled by merchants and the consumer society. The corporate surpluses that would fatten the industrial populations were a distraction from the real issue—the emptiness and floating condition of western civilization itself—which was without a universal religion or a conception of self and its perils. Instead, there was materialism and an unquenchable desire to know the self through possessions and status. Bronk would have none of it and said so.

The era in which Olson and Bronk launched their literary careers was marked by widespread disillusionment and of literary visions of an absolute of emptiness and despair. Both struggled not to yield to the post-Holocaust guilt wracking France and Germany, or the post-imperial blues of England. America was bristling with new armor, but it lacked the experience to pursue world domination with grace or subtlety. It would take over with yeomanly ardor in the name of an inflated rhetoric about democracy and the free world.

Bronk was against what he might have called the longings of reason, the "conventions" it creates to make reality self-serving. He was in this sense too ardent an atheist, a man who could look down the rest of the century and see nothing but fantasies and techno-utopias coming, and a culture with easy religions, instant absolutions, redemptive giveaways. He was writing from a perspective already staked out by the Frankfurt School of Social Research exiles, Max Horkheimer, Herbert Marcuse, Theodore Adorno, and Walter Benjamin. Bronk could well have written Horkheimer's *Eclipse of Reason* (1947), with its explicit thesis that reason had lost touch with nature and become only a narcissistic tool of self-aggrandizement. As he told Olson early into their friendship,

We aren't what we conspire with one another to appear to be.
Who are we? I go to look in the mirror hoping to see us in the prism of the remote. I dont care about the primitive for its own sake. If I can suddenly see around the conventions of a remote society it would be something like our reality I would hope to see. We might as well

live with our own conventions even if we dont believe them; and even if we don't believe them they obscure us and obscure the world.[*]

He would have none of contemporary faith, but in ridding himself so passionately of all belief, he was also a seeker asking to believe in *something*.

Bronk's prose is practical, rather spare in its style, with few flourishes or ambitious turns of thought. His logic is a spider web of associations and image chains, corollaries and parallels all converging on our inability to penetrate or understand the flux of things in which we find ourselves. He uses prose to cut through the exhausted language of post-war English, which had lost much of its capacity for self-examination and become a kind of mirror to desire, the way skyscrapers began using mirror windows to reflect rather than absorb light.

Bronk never departs from this one centralizing premise that "we are always in some degree still nowhere in an empty vastness," and that "we tire of the forms we impose upon space and the restricted identities we secure from them" (*VSC* 29). To prove this point is the goal of all his sentences, and he can pick up almost anywhere in his meditations and follow the string back to this principal notion of our foreignness in nature, our alienation even from ourselves as things in the work of the real. Like Olson, Bronk saw himself as an artist caught between the death of Newtonianism and classical physics, and the slow and unpromising rise of a post-positivist scientific revolution. He could neither submit to the one nor embrace the other, since neither vision was acceptable to him. He tried to live without the benefit of a constructed metaphysic, which left him in the awkward situation of being the skeptic, the naysayer, as a poet. He would have to transcend the nihilism of most skepticisms and make poetry the tool for cleaning thought of its own worst vices—egotism and racial hubris.

The body of his prose consists of a relentless shake-down of three writers of the American Renaissance, Thoreau, Whitman and Melville,

---

[*] "The William Bronk-Charles Olson Correspondence," ed. Burt Kimmelman. *Minutes of the Charles Olson Society,* 22 (January 1998): 10.

in a study called *The Brother in Elysium*; a short, carefully articulated set of meditations on Mayan cities called *The New World* (1974); and a few pieces on costumes and desire the Elizabeth Press first issued as *A Partial Glossary: Two Essays* (1974). Elizabeth Press, Cid Corman's journal, *Origin*, the magazine *Grosseteste Review* published these works originally, which were reissued in a single volume by North Point Press in 1983.

The prose tradition behind these works begins with Herodotus as the first peripatetic student of ruins and oddities which he wrote down in a kind of journalistic prose; Pausanias is closer to Bronk's purpose in his 2nd century *Guide to Greece*, a source for Olson as well. Both writers are survivors of the death of civilizations, and venture into the ruins of grand schemes to take modest inventories. They are like intellectual widows at the funeral, and reminisce on a vanished greatness but also take stock of reality as it is now, without its authority. Coming upon Greek temples, stele, fragments like the famous "E" in Olson's "The Kingfisher," accord with the sort of thing Bronk does in his wanderings around the Yucatan and in central Mexico, observing and carefully absorbing the patterns of Mayan architecture and city-building, and the curious density of jungle and coral in which these things are situated. Clearly, Pound's wanderings through Provence, recorded in *The Spirit of Provence*, are also part of this tradition, as are William Carlos Williams' *In the American Grain* and Olson's *Mayan Letters*. All these works are surveys of the damage of time, and represent a kind of awe felt by those who have come after and look back partly in wonder partly in regret at the fall of once-great cultures.

Neruda's long meditative poem on Macchu Pichu, as Guy Davenport pointed out long ago, is the twentieth-century extension of the long tradition of meditation on ruins. "The Kingfisher" grows out of Neruda's poem but clearly has other goals in mind—finding the lost thread of a cultural high tradition now buried under the crassness and material wasteland of modern America. The past is instrumentalized in Olson, as

---

*Guy Davenport, "Scholia and Conjectures for Olson's 'The Kingfishes,'" *Boundary2*, II, 1 and 2 (Fall '73/Winter '74). 250-62.

it was in Pound. Both writers believed one could revive the pre-Newtonian world and live in it again, if the right argument could be made for it.

But Bronk adds something new to the tradition in the sense that he does not analyze the past as something for use now; he sees the past as a kind of theater of the vanities, as aspirations to conquer the evasive ghost of something we tentatively call reality, but which eludes language, logic, consciousness, and leaves us helplessly fabricating versions of a world we can call our own. The Yucatan is a museum of elaborate fictions, ruses and theatrical settings where a certain desire to know the real came in fiercely and then vanished with the wind.

That perception of ruins is almost unique with Bronk; Shelley may have hit upon the theme in his sonnet, "Ozymandias," but he is being ironic and full of faith in other forms of government less obviously tyrannical than that of the dictator whose statue lies broken in the desert. Bronk says at one point that the ruins of Copan reveal the presence of that ineffable thing we cannot capture, and only ruins expose it to us.

> One of the strongest impressions that we have is that under the mask and metaphor something is there though it is not perhaps man that is there. There is something which is. Nothing else matters. Copan is a liberation. It is all gone, emptied away. To see it is to see ourselves gone, to see us freed from the weight of our own world and its limitations. (*VSC* 34)

"We are in the real world as ghosts are in this world, of doubtful being," he says later. Our contact with reality is "uncertain and remote," and can never be anything more. To nail reality with a word would merely nail an illusory aspect of something already gone, slipped away. As Whitehead observed of an idea, once stated it is no longer alive in the world, its potential is exhausted.˙ So with reality for Bronk; every culture

---

˙Alfred North Whitehead, "The Eighteenth Century," *Science and the Modern World* (NY: The Free Press, 1953), pp. 70-71. This book was especially important to Charles Olson, who quoted from it and used many of its concepts in writing "Projective Verse."

names a world and leaves behind ruins that reveal that the thing below, the ineffable substrate that never dies or changes, remains intact, unabused or unaffected by the stone and mortar, the masks and drums.

If we take away purpose and theft from the value of the past, we are left with something much less tenable or useful, something akin to what Robert Creeley perceived about self and the "world"—that it is essentially mute and impenetrable. Creeley's prose comes closest to Bronk's spirit in its reluctance to admit plot, and in its desire to fall silent at almost every turn. New England is a curious kind of stony world that inspires this taciturn, often resistant speech, and Bronk has dovetailed the style to his view that no amount of human effort can do more than reveal the nature of *homo ludens*, the playful animal bent upon making things up.

To this tradition of Bronk's prose allies I would add the name of Martin Heidegger, if not for the sorts of phenomenology he argued as accesses to reality, then to his elemental distinction between earth and world, which Bronk seemed to know intimately, if only by instinct. Heidegger made the distinction between these two concepts by remarking on the curious abruptness by which Greeks posed their temples in Sicily. They were lodged precariously against a hill or a wild meadow, with no attempt to claim the immediate environment, but rather to distinguish the temple's artificial and subjective world from what was the otherness of earth, the wild and untreatable immensity on which the delicate white building was laid.[*] That notion of clashes and contradictions struck Heidegger as the root of human self-knowledge—the admission that ideas and subjective perspectives, like time, had no "outside," only internal reference for its validity or meaning.

And it is this lack of outside reference that gives Bronk his lever into the Mayan imagination. Time and space represent the precise way in which the Mayas construed things in terms of twenties, measuring vast

---

[*]Martin Heidegger, "The Origin of the Work of Art," *Poetry, Language, Thought*, trans. Albert Hofstadter. NY: Harper & Row Publishers, 1971, pp. 41-49. "World and earth are essentially different from one another and yet are never separated. The world grounds itself on the earth, and earth juts through world" (49).

amounts of time by this algorithm and no other. This is the culture that invented zero on its own, but not the wheel—and showed itself fully capable of the highest levels of invention within human limits, while failing to create an interesting religion or a lasting conception of the thing, the pure real. They abandoned their cities, he says, for no apparent reason, other than to admit they had not found any answers worth preserving.

> We are in the real world as nothing in ourselves, as a skin on that world, as a network of nerves, an awareness not of ourselves but of that world, even as though we might be that world's awareness of itself. In this act of union, the self is shed like an exoskeleton and we lie so close against the real world our identity lies there. (*VSC* 39)

"The real world is not manipulable," he says in his chapter on Copan, it is "not useable by us" (*VSC* 37). By such indirect allusions to a living Other which cannot be named or defined, he builds up slowly a sense of a spiritual reality, but one that defies any personal meaning. It is simply there, like a Comanche god buried too deep in rock to be worshiped or called forth. It is there, and it represents for Bronk the very summa by which he moves beyond Christianity into a future of possible animist worship. He won't say outright that he is post-Christian, as did Pound and Olson, and other writers of the Whitman axis. He would not venture into such dangerous terrain where to deny is to secretly affirm the same illusory certainties on which official religions are built.

He will not negotiate any terms for a possible religion and yet that is his chief and perhaps sole concern as a writer—to debunk the churches in all their forms in order to lay bare the real sense of god as a figure of such unrecognizable ugliness or unfamiliarity as to present the human being with its one absolute—the power of a spirit never to be grasped, but only to be distorted and counterfeited by the very energies driving the cultural imagination. Derived from religion are all those other forms of order, equally shadows or lake reflections, which go to make up a limited Heideggerian world, and thus miss the earth that is always there.

THE BODY OF THIS LIFE:

Bronk's vision of things reminds me of the vineyard wisdom of that part of the Rhone valley near Gigondas, where it is said that the highly bred vines of Grenache and Syrah and Cinseault get their strength from the bees roaming in the wild hinterlands that are purposely left untended. The *garrigue*, as it is called, supplies the strength of wild nature to the humanly perfected and fragile vines of human ingenuity. That is Bronk's conception of the Yucatan civilizations—their fragile ruins are the flowers of a longing to understand as the jungle leaps in to punctuate and then remove that longing in a leisurely process of silent being.

This longing to en-world reality is akin to children's fantasies, Bronk says in "Costume as Metaphor." "Children dress in scraps of costume and play at being what the scraps suggest" (*VSC* 47). That alone is the basis of a theory of language, a kind of Roland Barthes system of myth in a nutshell. But Bronk puts his own spin on this twentieth-century nostrum when he says, "They try it and let it go." That is all he derives from the Mayan moment—it was another of those attempts to invest the unknown with shapes and calendars which were let go when the game was over. It is a lesson to anyone who is attempting to build another faith from scratch, and I take it Bronk is here dismissing the idea of the long poem. For what else is a long poem but a kind of cathedral in words with a religion not yet written down in full. Bronk's poems follow from the prose as reductions, subtractions, deletions of faith from what is really there. The limits of language, as Bronk felt them in his prose, and exerted them in his poems, is to come up against the desire to believe in one's own fictions and resist them. But at the same time, Bronk admires the more crafted and modest forms of religious, metaphysical fiction he finds in the Yucatan, and is willing to say they served their purpose well.

Of Christianity and its prelates and offices, he has little good to say. It covered the ground and gave no feeling of a blank thereness underlying it. For that reason, it has no appeal for Bronk. The only truth in art is the gap in which the raw earth, unworlded and unspoken, lies there manifest in its own inarticulate boldness. Perhaps that is why he treats Whitman to a ruthless dissection, since we take this poet to be the source of American idealism and hope. Bronk doesn't. He parses everything in his chapter on "Walt Whitman's Marine Democracy," to declare that if anything the democracy he speaks of is a floating, watery shimmer of nothing's own beauty—the impossible vision. In the end, he observes, as did Edward Dahlberg in much the same way, that Whitman stands for loneliness, and for "death and love." "What indeed, he wondered, was finally beautiful except death and love!" Was finally, Bronk's key words—the skeptic's reduction of the illustrious hoper to the two certainties on which life itself must ultimately rest: disintegration and attraction.

And in Thoreau we do not find Bronk looking for some standard of self-sufficiency, or that element in him in which the mysticism of nature clarifies itself in simple material things, as perhaps Snyder does. Instead, we find Bronk uncovering the source of "Bartleby the Scrivener" in Thoreau, as if Melville had secretly modeled his ultimate resister in Thoreau's moment in "Civil Disobedience," confronted by an Emerson who would believe no matter what, and who would ultimately concede to the state things the state should never claim: conscience. Thoreau means one thing for Bronk: the capacity to say no to everything that is not of nature and the obduracy of mere earth. "I do not wish to kill nor to be killed," Bronk quotes Thoreau, obviously with relish. For here is the first plank in the obduracy of Thoreau the Scrivener (VSC 126).

Bronk bores in deeper to find in Thoreau a contempt or at least an indifference to standards or even models of behavior, least of all the one he set for himself, but not, certainly, for anyone else. "I desire that there may be as many different persons in the world as possible," quotes Bronk again, in an age in which mass behavior becomes more and more directed from corporate management. Bronk knew that in Thoreau is the source in which democracy can never be transformed into that thing it is today—a vast power grid of merchant authorities suppressing human difference to create the rational system by which Americans overconsume and underthink or underlive. Thoreau was the source of democracy's inability to form such a thing as nation, state, or "culture," if by these one man or woman has to sacrifice some element of their own difference or mere nastiness of self. Thoreau would want all of it to represent the unbuildable construct of "America," and leave it as dynamic and open-ended fields of particles, debris.

Bronk finds his words toward the end of the essay when he unveils Thoreau as the ultimate naysayer, his hero, as Bartleby and in part the rebel Christ:

> It seemed to [Thoreau] that only those whose whole beings were thwarted by the conditions against which they revolted, only those with a deep and personal conviction, testified to by the loneliness of their positions, only those who in themselves were already in opposition to the state, who had dispensed with its support, in whom, that is, the revolution had been accomplished:—only such as these, for whom the issues at stake were clear, could have it within their power to bring about a revolution within society which should be worthy of the name. (VSC)

Then he quotes Thoreau where he wants him, "When the subject has refused allegiance and the officer has resigned his office, then the revolution is accomplished." The word "allegiance" plays right into Bronk's own time, where the Boy Scout oath of loyalty to the state, the "pledge of allegiance," newly revamped by Eisenhower to include "under God" as a way of making America the Christian-sanctioned state, was the direct assault upon individual difference, the self's conscience.

A nihilistic Whitman in love with death as the only democracy, a nay-saying Thoreau, together with the Kafka side of Melville, the unblinking ambiguist of literature, comprise the trinity Bronk would enshrine as America's three-sided soul. But note that in recapturing the Renaissance spirit, much of the poetry and ideas that have developed in the twentieth century is eliminated. Wallace Stevens is out; he believed too much in the "necessary fictions" of the imagination to accept Melville; Pound is out in one way, for having accepted Thoreau's Scrivener mentality and the imperative to resist, but constructed his "home-made world" anyway, and thereby transcended the doubts of Melville and the nihilism of Whitman. Olson? He too believed in transcendence despite his many cautions early in life; his third volume of the *Maximus Poems* (1975) serenely implies a sacred universe accessible to imagination while excoriating the fallen America he finds around him in contemporary Gloucester. Only Creeley would survive the test of Bronk's triumvirate.

The hard, spare grammar of reality is not for us to know or use, or even glimpse. It is in fact the very force that makes our own efforts to articulate a life or a world inevitable and necessary. We are made to imagine the rules because they are ineffable and defy language or thought. So our literature and our history of culture are testaments of longing and willlingness to make it all up. In an age of venality such as this one, Bronk becomes the scolding prophet warning us away from vanity and illusion. He tried to tell us that we were headed for the cliff, and that money or success would not slow the fall or save us. We had best realize we lived in a strange world that refused to reveal its nature to us, only tolerated our meek existence by some logic of its own. To know that is to practice humility and vigilance and perhaps survive a little longer.

Of the three American writers he scrutinizes in *The Brother in Elysium*, only Melville measures up to Bronk's standard of the true moralist—a man who cried out "against Christianity and American freedom," and who lamented the "joyless shadow on the world" cast by the Christian church." (*VSC* 183).

> Rejecting religious doctrine as an absolute faith, Melville also rejected political doctrines. He saw his own country, America, as the best political hope of the world, but he was disturbed by deep doubts about it. In a way, America was like the church, professing what it neither believed or practiced. The system of negro slavery was a continuous denial of the American doctrine of the freedom and equality of all men. It is apparent that in other respects, he thinks of America in the same terms as he thought of Serenia, as a mistaken millennium, a relative good misjudged as an absolute. (*VSC* 184).

Melville lived in "uncertainty," Olson's coining of a term from Keats, the only possible relation to the whole truth, hence the chapter title on Melville in *The Brother in Elysium*, "Herman Melville; or, The Ambiguities." Unlike Olson who invents a new Melville for the twentieth century, and who makes him out as a mythographer, a new Homer of American experience, Bronk dismisses the myth of the whale and all else as a road to religious delusion. The path forks at this point, and Bronk goes his own way from his contemporaries, including Snyder. His refusal to believe in anything conceptual about nature is filtered through his analysis of Melville as brave enough to admit that the things most alien to human nature are the key to belief. In closing his chapter on Melville he writes,

> . . . faith, as it were, was reciprocated in a benediction. As Billy Budd stood beneath the main-yard with the rope around his neck, his only words, which he called out clearly and loudly, were, "God bless Captain Vere!" And the whole crew, helplessly and without any volition, took up the cry. It was Melville's great cry of affirmation and acceptance. For that little movement, in an irreparably evil and ambiguous world, ambiguity and evil with all their consequences were acquiesced in, and Jackson and Bland, Ahab, Claggart, and Ishmael, and the evil Whale itself, were drawn up and absorbed in a clear act of conviction and faith. Herman Melville was at peace. God bless Captain Vere! (VSC 220-221)

A key to Bronk's imminent religious vision lies in this power of faith to incorporate the anti-human into its vision; all other faiths that elevate the species above nature and empower it with specially designed gods that flatter human nature are nothing but mirrors and costumes, temples to selfhood. To remove these is the first step, but to embrace and love the very force that denies you life is to accept the earth as home. That is the hardness, spareness, the grammar of real nature for Bronk, and a road out of the century's decaying worlds.

David Clippinger

GONE, GONE, GONE BEYOND: EMPTINESS AND POETRY

W ILLIAM BRONK'S POETRY REVOLVES AROUND the issues of emptiness, silence, and nothingness, and one might say that the explicit goal of his poetry is to arrive at the truth of silence, emptiness, and nothingness. According to Bronk's worldview, emptiness is in fact the "real." And as in his "The Smile on the Face of a Kouros," Bronk recognized the "truth" of reality as the face of death.

> Now death, of which nothing as yet—or ever—is known,
> leaves us alone to think as we want of it,
> and accepts our choice, shaping the life to the death.
> Do we want an end? It gives us; and takes what we give
> and keeps it; and has, this way, in life itself,
> a kind of treasure house of comely form
> achieved and left with death to stay and be
> forever beautiful and whole, as if
> to want too much the perfect, unbroken form
> were the same as wanting death, as choosing death
> for an end. There are other ways; we know the way
> to make the other choice for death: unformed
> or broken, less than whole, puzzled, we live
> in a formless world. Endless, we hope for no end.
>
> I tell you, death, expect no smile of pride
> from me. I bring you nothing in my empty hands. (LS 66)

The poem foregrounds the focal point of this paper: the relation between form and formlessness, and, concomitantly, how the choice between one or the other is a choice between the death of form, which is a way of living, or the blind acceptance of form and thereby a living death.

Nevertheless, Bronk's admittance that he brings nothing in his empty hands has prompted some readers to perceive his work as nihilistic. Even George Oppen, Bronk's lifelong friend, remarked in a letter to Bronk (13 September 1967) that "Something beyond nihilism (is almost heroically visible) in the beauty of such a poem as the Lock on the Feeder, in the beauty of the final sections of your essay ['Copan: Historicity Gone']" (*Selected Letters* 168). Bronk responded to the suggestion of nihilism with a measured coolness, which temporally dampened their friendship. As Jim Weil remarks, "What divided Bronk and George some fifteen years later [after the publishing of *The World, The Worldless*] was George's misreading Bronk's work as nihilistic. Eventually Bronk put him straight. It took time to teach him how to read the work" (letter to the author 17 August 1999). What this paper interrogates is what needs to be learnt in order to "read" beyond nihilism and arrive at some conception of Bronk's perception of emptiness.

Building upon the fundamental premise that insists, to use lines from "The Late Agnostic," "There isn't an I / or a world to know" (*LS* 178), Bronk infuses his poetry with the depths of emptiness and nothingness. The deftly titled "There is an Ignorant Silence in the Center of Things" offers the most succinct perspective of the force of silence and emptiness within Bronk's worldview.

> . . . Once
> before this, I stood in an actual ruin, a street
> no longer a street, in a town no longer a town,
> and felt the central, strong suck of it, not
> understanding what I felt: the heart of things.
> This nothing. This full silence. To not know. (*LS* 44)

The poem invokes a familiar Bronkian dichotomy: namely, the tension between and absolute separation of "a" world (the human realm con-structed out of streets, towns, and names) and "the" world (that which cannot be reduced to human form), which is accentuated by the historicity of the ruins. The ruins are not transcendent but rather a physical manifestation of impermanence and flux—the revelation of the inadequacies of human form. As in the distinction made in the famous Bronk line, "it is always a world and not the world," "a" world (the one that is impermanent and subject to ruin) is separate from the transhistorical "the" world. "The Actual and the Real in Thoreau," presents this schism in slightly different terminology:

> The actual world is a surrogate reality and we deputize ourselves in its relationships just as our vocation there is not something we are really called to but something we busy ourselves with while awaiting a call or failing, from timorousness, to answer a call we think we have heard. (VSC 221)

The actual is a false form—an image projected onto the world in order to claim meaning for a situation otherwise devoid of value. Therefore to return to "There is an Ignorant Silence," the ruin, street, and town illuminate the lack of contiguity between the actual and the real by foregrounding the pervasiveness of nothingness, this full silence, that the listener cannot penetrate. "If the actual is a kind of fiction, a work of the imagination only, then reality can never be made actual" (VSC 222). The experience, though, also sparks an awareness of the "real," the impenetrable heart of "nothing," a "full silence," and "not knowing." Bronk's "answer" to the call of nothing and silence is the poem itself, which refuses to disclose the experience as a contained form. The silence and nothingness, therefore, remain intact in the final line of the poem, which refuses to render closure. The experience is transcendent, but its view is not an epiphany of universal vision but a recognition of primal emptiness and silence. Bronk's transcendental vision is Emerson's eyeball—blinded.

This proposition of fundamental nothingness is coupled with the meticulous description of ruin, partiality, and impermanence, and the poem strives to undercut the assumed truth of things, forms, ideas, concepts, and theories in order to emphasize their past and future state of rubble. "The Outcry," for example, clearly demonstrates this process:

THE BODY OF THIS LIFE:

What I want to do is shout. Happiness? No.
Outrage? No. What I want to do is shout
because we were all wrong, because the point
was not the point, because the world, or what
we took for the world, is breaking, breaking. We were wrong
and are not right. Break! Break! We are here!
What I want to do is shout! Break! Shout! (*LS* 64)

The desire to break the world springs from the recognition that the world
is already breaking because "what we took for the world" is false, an
invention. The thrust of the poem, therefore, offers a sustained critique
of form that argues that adhering to such *false* forms is nihilism. There-
fore, the act of shouting and breaking cleanses the vision by emphasizing
that we "see, if we saw [the world], only as the blind see braille" (*LS* 86).
On the whole, the sustained rumination of Bronk's poems unveils the
inherent limitations of form and the false pretensions upon which the
world is built. Such a critique brings the poet and reader to nothing—no
forms, no things, emptiness, and silence—but that emptiness still has a
particular "use," which is discernable *only* when the object is broken, as
Bronk explains in "Usable Things":

> Children know
> in their depredations indifferent to such intent
> as we have for things: the things we make, a world.
> Children are overjoyed: things are to break
> or to have their pretensions broken, made usable. (*LS* 47)

According to the dialectic of Bronk's poems, the image constructed of the
world is false, but if that image is broken, that act cleanses the doors of
perception so that the mind finally can hear the "calling" of the real of
emptiness, nothingness, silence. The mind, therefore, must keep in dual
focus the "Nothing that is not there and the nothing that is" to borrow
Wallace Stevens's phrase (*Palm at the End of the Mind* 54). Conse-
quently, Bronk's poetry perpetually ruminates upon the split between the
real and the actual as in "Silence. Emptiness":

How much was subterfuge and piety,
outrageous pretense to avoid the poverty
of the proposed self, including the poverty
of the outer world, if indeed there was one?

The pretension said there was and, oh, it admired
—expecting respect, at least, in return: it was part,
minor perhaps but part, of the multiplex.
Anyone ought to be proud to be part of that.

It could all have been subterfuge and piety,
no doubt was. I think I never cared,
listening, even then, to the unheard
where, only, still unhearing, I listen now,
the whole unheard my only attitude,
my eyes on the emptiness where nothing is. (*LS* 132)

The outer world and the self are part of the illusion—the subterfuge that
the self imagines in order to counter the true "poverty" of self and world.
The self creates a story full of pretensions that imposes "value" upon life
but in fact blinds the self from the true—the "unheard" and "the empti-
ness where nothing is."

Emptiness, therefore, has a particular resonance with truth, and the
poem as such has an explicit spiritual value. The true, the real, and the
divine all reside within emptiness and silence—behind a cloud of un-
knowing. The religious implications of Bronk's negative theology in
relation to Christian mysticism have been well documented by many
careful readers of Bronk's work to whom I am deeply indebted. John
Ernest in his "William Bronk's Religious Desire" and Henry Weinfield in
his "'The Cloud of Unknowing': William Bronk and the Condition of
Poetry" have already demonstrated the place of absence within Bronk's
conceptualization of spiritual poetry; and Norman Finkelstein's "The
World as Desire," which carefully explicates the dynamic exchange of
loss, absence, and desire, established the critical foundation for my
"Abnegation: Desire and Denial of Form in William Bronk." Yet, I would

like to consider Bronk's negative theology against another religious tradition—Buddhism, which explicitly foregrounds many of the same issues as Bronk: the assertion that form and the self are illusory; all things are impermanent; the primary condition of the real is emptiness; and an irreparable split exists between absolute and relative truth. While the affinities between Buddhist philosophy and Bronk's poetry are intriguing, my goal is to illuminate more fully the immense weight that Bronk places upon emptiness, silence, nothingness by reading his quest for emptiness against "The Heart Sutra," one of the most famous Buddhist scriptures.

The "Heart Sutra" revolves around the phrase "Form is emptiness; emptiness also is form" (*Entering the Stream* 155). As the sutra continues,

> there is no form, no feeling, no perception, no formation, no consciousness; no eye, no ear, no nose, no tongue, no body; no mind; no appearance, no sound, no smell, no taste, no touch, no dharmas. (155)

The repetition of "no" accentuates the falsity of form whereby the words, ideas, and theories projected upon the world are empty of the "meanings" that their forms assume. There is no contiguity between one's image of the world and the world itself. Form is empty; or in Bronk's terms, "Whatever the mind makes is not" (*LS* 125).

Yet, beyond the simple exclamation of the falsity of human form, the "Heart Sutra" adds that "emptiness also is a form," which refutes a crude conception of emptiness (and enlightenment) as an imaginable blankness. Rather, "real emptiness takes the form of things just as they are—without the conceptual overlay of being this or that, empty of emptiness as well" (154). Thereby Buddhism differentiates between "real" emptiness and "false" emptiness, which is manifest also as the split between absolute truth and relative truth or real mind and actual mind. Tulku Thondup, a Tibetan Buddhist Master, explains that "Buddhism is centered on the principle of two truths, the absolute truth and the relative truth." The absolute is peaceful, perfect, and enlightened. The relative, on the other hand, is "the whole spectrum of ordinary life," whereby the "absolute" is "obscured by our mental habits and emotional afflictions, rooted in our grasping at 'self'—[which] is not a fixed or solid thing, but a mere designation labeled by the mind" (18). All things that are conceptualized—the self, world, objects, and reality—are false ideational structures that attempt to mask the inadequacies and impermanence of the human world (what Bronk refers to as the "poverty" of self and world). These imposed forms attempt to protect the self from recognizing the truth of "ruin," death, and the complete emptiness within form. The mind, therefore, blinds the self to the real.

The schism between the absolute and the relative evolves out of the mind grasping desperately at illusions and thereby refusing to confront emptiness and strive for a totality beyond human form. As Lao Tsu writes in ways that mirror Bronk in terms of language and concept:

> The Tao that can be told is not the eternal Tao.
> The name that can be named is not the eternal name.
> The nameless is the beginning of heaven and earth.
> The named is the mother of the ten thousand things.
> (*Tao Te Ching* np).

The material world (the "ten thousand things") is distinct from the irreducible, unnamable origin (the "eternal name") of those things, and thereby remains beyond the reach of language, concepts, and logic. The names that correspond with the world are not the "eternal Tao" or Absolute truth. As Bronk remarks, "The fault lies partly in the idea of miles. / It is absurd to describe the world in sensible terms" (*LS* 53). For both Buddhism and for Bronk, there is no correspondence, no contiguity, no bridge between the two worlds; rather, one confronts only emptiness when looking into the face of truth. As Bronk depicts in "Names Like Barney Cain's," the real is nothingness.

> Two locks on the Feeder are named for him.
> I have asked and nobody knows who he is.
> Alexander, Alfred, Quetzalcoatl,
> nobody, nowhere, never, nothing. (*LS* 178)

In order to free oneself from the illusory, the mind must confront its partiality and penetrate through false surfaces in order to confront sheer nothingness.

Within Buddhism, grasping at illusions perpetuates suffering; for Bronk, such dependence upon false form obscures the impenetrable depths of the real. Therefore, the breaking of form and the frank but emphatic divulging of the truth of nothingness urges the reader and writer to recognize nothingness as truth. "About Dynamism, Desire and Various Fictions," for example, reads

> What I want
> you to know is that nothing happened and nothing can,
> that stories are fictions, truth doesn't tell one,
> that the beautiful is that, nothing more,
> and enough, no story, nothing to do or tell. (*LS* 144)

The desire to disclose nothingness, therefore, is not to destroy reality but to dissolve the fictions and press toward the "real." The defining characteristic of Bronk's poetry—as that of Buddhism—is not nihilism but its opposite, the quest for the true, the real, that cannot be attained except by a realization and reconciliation with the fullness of emptiness.

Certainly the thrust of Bronk's poetry, within this context, suggests significant affinities with the heart of emptiness in Buddhism as well as the dichotomy of absolute and relative truth.* Yet, much like his reaction to Oppen's claim that his work was "nihilistic," Bronk resists the notion of a Buddhist element in his poetry. In response to my letter that comments upon the similarities between Bronk's conception of "a" world and "the" world and the Buddhist notion of absolute and relative truth, Bronk remarks in the negative that "I am no more a Buddhist than I am

---

*Such affinities between Bronk and Buddhism may be purely coincidental, although a strong case could be made that Thoreau's transcendental vision, with which Bronk shares a great deal, was indebted to Mary Moody Emerson and her translations of Eastern sacred and philosophical texts. A lineage from Bronk to Thoreau to Mary Moody Emerson and to the East could be established. Furthermore, Thoreau also translated *The Lotus Sutra* for *The Dial* in 1844.

Christian or a Jew, an Atheist or believer in the gods of Greeks and Romans." (letter to the author, 4 January 1999). Bronk's response is understandable since it is his absolute desire to resist categorization and false form. Similarly, Bronk resists being placed in a literary historical genealogy as well. Bronk's remark to John Ernest recorded in "Fossilized Fish" that "I was surprised to note some of my claimed [poetic] cousins whom I would not have thought of claiming" (*Tribe of John* 168) also would seem to apply to the Buddhist connection as well.

Despite Bronk's opposition, the similarities between his work and Buddhism are not only provocative, they offer valuable insight into the dynamics of emptiness as the primary essence of existence as well as the role of poetry within an ideational structure predicated upon not knowing. That is, Bronk's relentless pursuit of emptiness, impenetrable nothingness, and the epiphany of silence take on a different hue within the light of Buddhist philosophy. In Buddhism, to concentrate upon emptiness is to attempt to penetrate through the falsity of human form and become awake, which is emphasized by the mantra from the "Heart Sutra," "Om gate gate paragate parasame gate Bodhi Svaha"—"Gone, gone, gone beyond, completely beyond—awakened mind, so be it" (*Entering the Stream* 154). The literal translation of the Sanskrit word "Buddha" is one who is fully awake, and thereby has transcended human form. The goal of the poem for Bronk is to break the logic that imprisons the mind and perpetuates the illusion of form. As Bronk writes in "Let Go":

> Something exists; but nothing else exists.
> The world is postulate; its time, its space.
> Something exists; it is not the world exists.
> World lost and we lost, too. Let go. Let go. (*LS* 87)

The poem in its refrain "Let go. Let go" parallels the idea of "paragate"—gone beyond—and articulates the desire to go beyond the false postulate of the world: only through such renunciation of the falsity of conceived time and space can the "something" be; only through diligence will emptiness become present and slip beyond the paradigm of dualistic logic and presence truth.

The poem is the site and the means to pursue truth, but as Bronk notes, "The truth has many forms which are not its form / if it has one. What has a form of its own / or, having, is only it? There is truth" (*LS* 195). Given the elusive un-form of truth, the poem must embrace an infinite range of forms and meanings because, as Bronk states in *The Brother in Elysium*, "truth lay somewhere in [paradoxical thinking]" (*VSC* 74). His poetry, therefore, employs a self-negating internal logic that resembles a Zen koan—an answerable conundrum intended to press the mind beyond the constraints of condition thinking and move the self closer to the realization of "real" emptiness. The ultimate goal for Bronk is the shattering of form, which annunciates the presence of truth—what Buddhists designate as the attainment of nirvana. Or to shift the paradigm back to poetry, the emptiness in Bronk's poetry is the mark of his passion to achieve nothing less than form dissolving into complete and whole being: the "real world which does make sense. / It is beyond our knowing or speaking but it is there" (*LS* 136).

Norman Finkelstein

WILLIAM BRONK AND THE CREATION OF THE WORLD: A FEW REMARKS

T|HE DIRECT AND IMPORTANT RELATIONSHIP between the poetry of William Bronk and the first few chapters of Genesis is perfectly obvious for most of Bronk's serious readers. Bronk refers to the creation story throughout his career, and though I haven't made a scientific study of it, I would bet that there isn't a single volume that does not contain some poem that either alludes to the creation or addresses the myth directly. Bronk's central metaphor of "the world" or, if you will, the dialectic of world and worldlessness that is at the heart of his work, leads him, inevitably and repeatedly, to these references and allusions. World making, in all its majesty and futility, is what Bronk's poetry is all about. The majesty is to be found in the continuous human effort to secure a world, to achieve wholeness, while its futility lies in, well, its futility. "Not / for us ever any familiar and definite world," he says in "The Outer Becoming Inner" (*LS* 53), a poem to which I will return shortly.

This sense of the world as something we cannot have, this sense of being estranged from what is (or should be) most familiar to us, is due, in part, to the poet's awareness on both existential and religious levels that the world has preceded us, and that one could readily believe it was created perfect by a perfect Creator. This awareness is grounded in nature, which, when he is so inclined, Bronk dubiously but lovingly celebrates. "Of the natural world, nothing is possible / but praise if we speak at all" (*LS* 117) observes the poet in "Of the Natural World." "We can be still," he continues, but at the end of the poem admits that "I grow impatient and practice the world's song." In the presence of the created world, one can either stand silent or praise, and in poems such as "The Tree In the Middle of the Field" (*LS* 57) or of course "To Praise the Music" (*LS* 153), that praise rises to grand heights. There are occasions in

Bronk's work when his discourse is reminiscent of Milton's great midrash on the Creation in Book VII of *Paradise Lost*, as in the beautiful "Certain Beasts, Like Cats":

> Along the river, white long-legged birds
> lift one foot slowly, pause to put it down,
> and lift the other, down, and feed, absorbed
> in certainties that never fail, though blind.
>
> Great drifts of purple flowers hold
> the roadside; patrols of purple flowers roam
> through fields and climb to overtop high banks.
> Purple is what color there is in the world. (*LS* 53)

Yet this piece also points to the limits of Bronk's praise, and therefore to his inability to rest content in the natural world. "Great world," he cries near the end of the poem, "your lives are such that we despair, / seeing the loveliness, to live our lives" (*LS* 54). The perfection of the created world poses a problem by the simple fact of its being: we judge our humanity to be inadequate, and although "men are all of these, and more than these / strong beasts, dark fish, white birds and colored flowers," our experience of ourselves in the world is ineluctably incomplete. The word that Bronk uses repeatedly for this condition is "makeshift."

One of the clearest expressions of this condition is found, with appropriate irony, in a poem called "The Creation of the World," in which "Discontinuousness / is all we really see: this, then that." Lacking the sensuous lyricism and rich imagery of "Certain Beasts, Like Cats," this poem contents itself with Bronk's more typical abstraction and understatement, which verge sometimes upon a seemingly dismissive summary of our situation. Thus,

> Stories appear
> about the creation of the world. Times, we could wish
> to believe (tired of makeshift). A created world,
> the void over, chaos calked: the world.

We wish to believe; thence the stories; thence
the belief. We begin to believe. But it doesn't stand.
Bits and pieces, not of an integral world,
not a created world. . . . (LS 75)

Bronk's poem is, in effect, a counter-myth to that of the Creation. As he
says in the beginning of the first stanza, "Bits and pieces appear"; then, in
the beginning of the second stanza, "Stories appear." It is the fragments,
the bits and pieces, rather than the coherent and comforting stories, that
truly constitute reality; it is only because we are "tired of makeshift" and
long for "chaos calked" that the stories and our belief in them take hold.
The creation of the world is another in the long list of the fictions in
which Bronk believes we indulge: makeshift is all.

Poems such as "The Creation of the World" lead me to conclude that
Bronk's relation to Genesis, at least on the level of theme or content, is
primarily negative. Although I would hesitate to place Bronk among the
gnostics, his dissatisfaction with the created world and with the stories in
our religious traditions that explain it leads him to denial and refutation
in poem after poem. For Bronk, what matters most is not existence as it
is set before us, not the world we can know. Rather, what is most impor-
tant is the "real world which does make sense. / It is beyond our knowing
or speaking but it is there" ("The Real World," LS 145). Like the hidden
god of the gnostics, the outside god of the abyss, and not the demiurge of
the Creation, Bronk's real world is simply beyond. One *knows*, but what
one knows is really a kind of ignorance. The problem for Bronk, how-
ever, is that this world beyond the world, or this life beyond life, is not
only unspeakable, it insists on being spoken, and spoken in the religious
and philosophical terms that are the only ones the poet possesses.

Thus, in "The Outer Becoming Inner," when Bronk compares
himself to Adam hiding from God after having eaten from the tree, the
loss of certainty that he describes both confirms and disputes the story in
Genesis. Here is the entire text of the poem:

Sometimes, I could go in anywhere, not
to see the stars, not to be as we

are always, not only under them
but in them. The outer spaces push against
us, all their vastnesses apart, they crowd
us. They become our world. I could go hide
like Adam in his garden. How
would it matter? No, we are in the stars. Not
for us ever any familiar and definite world. (*LS* 53)

Adam's fall from grace is a fall into moral indeterminacy, and on an even more fundamental level, into existential uncertainty. He hides from God because he knows he is naked, though we can also say he knows he is naked because he *knows*, and therefore knows he has done wrong. He is no longer at one with Creation, and cannot abide the presence of the Lord walking in the garden in the cool of day. Certainty and wholeness still exist, are still possible—but not for Adam. Or as Kafka once said, plenty of hope, but not for us.

Yet I am not content with this reading of the poem. "How / would it matter?" asks Bronk. For Adam, it obviously matters a great deal. But for Bronk, the definite line between knowledge and ignorance implied in the story from Genesis does not really apply to our situation. "The outer spaces push against / us" because "we are in the stars." That is certainly not the case for Adam, who is apart from the stars, i.e. God in his heavens, especially after his fall. Bronk is more like Pascal in that famous moment from the *Pensées*: "The eternal silence of these infinite spaces fills me with dread" (Pascal 95). Pascal believes, but what is the nature of his belief? How does he view Creation and its Creator? Permit me, if you will, to read another well-known paragraph from the *Pensées*:

Let man then contemplate the whole of nature in her full and lofty majesty, let him turn his gaze away from the lowly objects around him; let him behold the dazzling light set like an eternal lamp to light up the universe, let him see the earth as a mere speck compared to the vast orbit described by this star, and let him marvel at finding this vast orbit to be no more than the tiniest point compared to that described by the stars revolving in the firmament. But if our eyes stop there, let our imagination proceed further; it will grow weary of conceiving things before nature tires of producing them. The whole visible world is only an imperceptible dot in nature's ample bosom. No idea comes near it; it is no good inflating our conceptions beyond imaginable space, we only bring forth atoms compared to the reality of things. Nature is an infinite sphere whose center is everywhere and circumference nowhere. In short it is the greatest perceptible mark of God's omnipotence that our imagination should lose itself in that thought. (Pascal 89)

But if our eyes stop there, let our imagination proceed further: Bronk shares this willingness with Pascal, but ultimately, both of them are frustrated by nature's endless amplitude. In effect, the Creation is both a spur and a block to the imagination, and it is for this reason that both writers have recourse to the stars, to the infinite heavens. Being in the stars is a cause for both exaltation and terror; we are apart from and a part of God's Creation, a contradiction which defines us as human, which provides us with our human image.

This leads me to another poem from early in Bronk's career, "'In Our Image, After Our Likeness,'" the title of which comes from God's proposal to the angels regarding the creation of man in Genesis 1:26. The natural perfection of the human image, and presumably the divinity to be found therein, is first invoked through the art of Michelangelo:

In what image? Michelangelo
of course, his Adam, one thinks of that, of all
that flesh, serene, symmetrical, fresh
from the hand of God without intervention; one hears
the body's innocent, pleasant harmonies.
There is this to be said for it, that everywhere
his image is always in our presence: one sees
such figures, part by part, at least, and in need
of composition, but still they are always there. (LS 37-38)

A number of Bronk's typical rhetorical moves are in evidence here, gestures that he will refine with extraordinary subtlety over the course of his work. Generally speaking, the mode is that of proposition and argument with the self or the reader. Note in particular how the poet immediately poses a question, moves to assure himself with "of course," and asserts his idea with "There is this to be said for it." Yet the "innocent, pleasant harmonies" of the human form's relation to nature (or as Blake would have it, the "Human Form Divine") prove unconvincing. Within a few lines, the reassuring wholeness of Michelangelo's Adam, gracefully receiving life from God (with his equally beautiful human proportions) is demolished:

> . . . We go hungry. Man,
> your image eludes the flesh as though the flesh
> were a bad camera, or a slick craftsman with a quick,
> dashing facility and a sure eye
> for the grotesque, but little depth and out
> of fashion soon, regrettably, because
> the perfection and morality of the flesh can move us so.
>
> The moral and perfect, however, are not the point.
> The intrinsic image of man is what we hope
> to find, and while we hope are afraid to find.
> One would as soon confront God as man.

It's tempting to accuse Bronk of merely grousing here, as he is apt to do, occasionally, in some of his weaker poems. Why belittle "The Creation of Adam," which captures the grandeur of the biblical spirit perhaps better than all other works of art? Surely Michelangelo is far more than a "slick craftsman." Why can't the poet rest content in what he himself so convincingly calls "the perfection and morality of the flesh"?

The answer, I believe, lies less in the admitted genius of the painter than in the creative power that moves, presumably, through him. Bronk is chasteningly direct: "The moral and perfect, however, are not the point." What we see in Michelangelo's Adam, and what we see in God's creation of man in Genesis, reaches to the moral and the perfect in a way that "the intrinsic image of man" which Bronk would find simply fails to do. Thus we seek that image but equally fear it. What man truly is in terms of morality and perfection remains tactfully unstated, and this silence is one of the poem's great strengths. Instead, Bronk "would as soon confront God as man." More than Michelangelo, God is that "slick craftsman" with "a sure eye / for the grotesque." It is difficult to imagine a more severe review of divine art.

So far my remarks have centered on poems from Bronk's early career, the period of *Light and Dark* (1956)and *The World, the Worldless* (1964). As Bronk develops his central themes, Genesis and the creation story are never far from his thoughts. Why is there form instead of formlessness? What is the nature of the creative act? What exactly do we perceive when we regard the shapeliness of a made thing, whether it comes from the hand of nature or of man? Even a poem like "The Nature of Musical Form," which would appear to have nothing to do with Genesis per se, seems to be in dialogue with the biblical text and its divine protagonist, for everything that Bronk says of music in that poem could be observed of the original creation as well. And this dialogue does not cease throughout Bronk's writing life. It may even intensify in the years after the publication of *Life Supports* in 1981, for in the ten volumes which appear after the collected poems, we find a series of gnomic pieces which continue to look back upon the first seven days and the void which preceded them. It is as if Bronk, in writing what we may regard as a great coda to his poetic opus, looks upon *his* creation by returning to *the* creation. But unlike God, he cannot judge it good and rest content. Here, for instance, is "I Am," from *Living Instead* (1991):

Sense in the world what was the world before
the creation of the world. Not the world but the world's
intention is the true world. We feel it here:
the uncreated still. The rest will go. (*LI* 39)

This poem is an expression of what Bronk elsewhere calls "unsatisfied desire," the force behind creation that is perpetually unsatisfied with the created. What is so appalling about this force, or as he calls it here, this "intention," is that it is totally incommensurate with the world that it has brought forth. Itself uncreated, it resides forever in the uncreated: "The rest will go." "I Am That I Am," says God to Moses, "Ehyeh Asher Ehyeh." In his great translation of the Five Books of Moses, Everett Fox translates the phrase as "I will be-there howsoever I will be-there." Not a name per se, it is rather an assertion of God's omnipresent Being. Capable of being everywhere in the created world, this world-force is actually not a part of the world we know at all. And yet it is the true world, the world which endures: transitory, ephemeral, creation cannot contain such truth. Or as the Talmud says, "He is the place of the world, but the world is not His place."

Bronk's point, of course, is that we cannot bear to know this, and indeed, we do not truly know it, merely intuit it and express it clumsily, given the limits of thought and speech. Two last poems which I will share with you indicate the typically contradictory human desires to seek sheltering and protective limits to the truth and to go beyond limits, regardless of the consequences. Both poems come out of Genesis. The first, from *Some Words* (1992), is actually called "Genesis":

> In the beginning, the Priests said, It
> was without form and void. They knew what that
> experience was—the pull that horror had.
> Its sweet inducement feared, they shied away
> and told of created forms, easier
> to live with: even bad ones were limited. (*SW* 31)

The second comes from *Our Selves* (1994), and is called "How To Be Human":

> Genesis isn't sure what tree it is.
> First it was knowledge, then maybe life itself.

The Garden all innocence, where was the harm?
Put out, all innocence gone, is it different?
We still inquire about the unknowable
and look for ways we shouldn't ever die. (*OS* 9)

Ronald W. Collins

Science and the Poetry of William Bronk:
A View of the Influence of Science
on the Thinking of William Bronk

W|ILLIAM BRONK HAD AN EVOLVING AFFAIR with the philosophical underpinnings of relativity theory, quantum mechanics, cosmology and the various branches of mathematics, but there was one thing that he never wavered on, that there was a fundamental It, a Real World, that scientist and poets detected but could never actually know.

The lack of absolute frames of reference that result from Einstein's theory of relativity, the inherent limitations of knowledge of the real world from quantum mechanics, the incompleteness of our math and logic as a consequence of Gödel's work, and finally the total connectedness of all things from Bell's Theorem form the foundation of the greatest intellectual triumphs of twentieth-century Science. Similarly, these same ideas are central to much of the poetry of William Bronk, and a poem such as "On Credo Ut Intelligam" in *The Empty Hands* states, "I disclaim the invented world / of which we say there might be ultimate things / unknown about it, not wholly understood/ but we have the fundamentals anyway. . . . Reality is what we are ignorant of" (*LS* 88). strongly echoes relativity, the uncertainty principle, and the limitation of descriptive systems, their incompleteness. Bronk believed there were Fundamentals but that they were unknowable; and his poetry, like the theories of Einstein, Heisenberg, Godel, and Bell interrogated the nature of those Fundamentals and their relation to the inherent limitations of human understanding.

Before turning to Bronk's poetry, though, it may be prudent to offer a brief discussion of the pertinent principles of physics in order to better illuminate the relationship of Bronk's poetry to these pillars of modern science.

In brief, relativity theory states as a fundamental principle that there is no privileged frame of reference. That is, all experiences are relative to where, when, and under what circumstances we experience the phenomena. There is no center of the Universe; there is no viewpoint that is paramount or absolute. In one stroke Einstein brought into question all homocentric, heliocentric, religiocentric views, and after nearly a century of testing, Einstein's denial of absolute reference frames has been confirmed each and every time.

Heisenberg, following Einstein by two decades, demonstrates two fundamental limitations of human knowledge. He shows that it was not possible to know exactly both the location where an event occurred and the time it occurred. Second, he demonstrates that it was not possible to know exactly both the energy involved in an event, and the speed at which it occurred. Together, these limitations are called the uncertainty principle. Heisenberg's discovery was that there was a fundamental limitation to what we can know about the real world, Bronk's IT. The Heisenberg uncertainly principle led to a starling conclusion: we can not even observe the world without interacting with it, and therefore changing it from a state it would have been in if we had not observed it. We are, therefore, part of, and a partial determinant of what we observe. We cannot be an objective observer, which limits, in principle, our knowledge and our ability to predict specific events. In a strict empirical sense, we are no longer passive observers of an objective reality that pays no attention to our subjective preferences. Or in Bronk's words, "Geometers, all measures measure themselves, / none measures the world" (from "On Divers Geometries" in *The Empty Hands*, LS 93)

Gödel's Incompleteness Theorem explored this issue to a deeper level. There is an unanswered, and unanswerable mystery as to why mathematics applies to the Real World. Why should a (human created), arbitrary set of axioms, and conclusions derived from those axioms, have any correlation to the Real World? Einstein said "as far as Mathematics is exact, it is not about the real world, as far as it is about the real world it is not exact." Math in its purity of form and logic is unique amongst human creations in that every strangely concocted branch of math has found an analogy, or an application, in the physical world of science.

Why should that be? At first people thought that math was so pure that it was a branch of logic, but Russell and Whitehead, much to their chagrin, proved that concept to be false. Imagine the turmoil when Gödel demonstrated math's impurity, its incompleteness when he proved that there was a true statement that could be said in arithmetic that could not be proven. This is the Incompleteness Theorem: in any axiom based system of math or logic, there is something that is true, i.e. correct within that mathematical system or logic system, that can not be proven within that system. Logic itself was questioned. The axioms of logic were examined, and tested for consistency. One of the axioms of logic is called the "Law of the Excluded Middle" which states that it is not possible that both A and not-A are true. It was discovered that if all of the axioms of logic are used, except for the Law of the Excluded Middle, you still had a consistent and non-contradictory logic. This logic came to be called non-intuitive logic. It found a use in quantum mechanics when it was demonstrated that if you have a box divided into two halves and put one electron in that box, it is not the case that the electron is either on one side or the other. There were other conditions (called quantum states), that allowed for the electron to be on both or neither, as well as, on one side or the other.

Collectively, these three men challenged some of the most fundamental concepts of absolutes. Einstein—everything observed depends upon the viewpoint of the observer. Heisenberg—we can not observe anything exactly as it is, and when we do observe anything we change what we were trying to observe to some other state. Gödel — the math and logic we use to describe our observations can say things, which are true but not provable. Further, there are multiple systems of internally consistent logics that apply to various aspects of observation but which are mutually exclusive.

Bell confounds the matter even further. Usually overlooked, rarely understood, and only recently confirmed by rigorous testing, Bell noted in the mid-1960s that according to quantum mechanics when particle creation occurred, e.g. an electron and its associated anti-electron, the interdependency of the created particle pair resulted in a strange paradox. Bell's Theorem states that what happens to one particle of a particle-pair creation, must have an immediate resultant change in the other particle. About 1972 it was demonstrated empirically, and again about three years ago,

a physicist separated a particle into two of its quantum states and then actually separated, in space, the two quantum states from each other. And when he changed one quantum state the other was observed to change as well. All fundamental quantum entities (particles is the wrong metaphor) can be in many quantum states and the Heisenberg Uncertainty Principle says you can never pin-point exactly where and when, and in what state, a particle is in. Further, quantum mechanics says that it is possible for a particle to be in state A, or state B or both simultaneously. That is, the logical assumption that something is either true or false does not apply to quantum mechanics because it is possible for something to be A and not-A at the same time, non-intuitive logic as you recall. The experiment referred to above put the quantum entity into two of its many possible states, separated the states in space and then demonstrated that if one of the states is perturbed that the other also changes INSTANTANEOUSLY, i.e. faster than the speed of light, in fact infinitely faster. The implications are staggering. For example, if the two states were separated to opposite sides of the universe and one is modified, the other would react instantaneously. Further, because of Heisenberg, if a person know where the states are in space then the uncertainty of when they are in time must increase proportionally so as to keep $(dt \times dx) \geq h/4\pi$, i.e. the space accuracy times the time accuracy must be greater than or equal to the Heisenberg uncertainty. That means that the entire universe could be nothing more that the sum of all existing states of a single quantum entity. It means that a single entity could exist simultaneously in a nearly infinite number of states everywhere in the universe. Creation could have been nothing more than the flux of a single fundamental entity and a set of quantum laws (from a letter from Ronald Collins to William Bronk dated 8 June 1996).

Our relativity-based view of the world assumes that phenomena are separated by time and space and that no influence can travel faster than the speed of light. Bell's Theorem, now usually called quantum non-locality, proves that these assumptions are incorrect at some fundamental level, and that there is a principle of holistic interconnectedness operating at the quantum level which contradicts the localistic assumptions of relativity. Thus relativity and quantum mechanics are incompatible, and as such, these two fundamental theories of modern physics can't both be right.

Quantum nonlocality shows that at a deep level of reality the speed of light, as a limiting factor, is irrelevant because phenomena are instantaneously connected regardless of distance. Something connects them that isn't restricted by relativity. Quantum nonlocality is a fact of nature that has now been experimentally verified. Alain Aspect's experiments in 1982 at the University of Paris/South proved the existence of quantum nonlocality. These experiments have been refined and repeated many times since.

The result of Bell's Theorem, i.e. quantum nonlocality, and its verification, is the undeniable fact that at the quantum level, instantaneous actions occur at a distance. Two particles that are part of a single system continue to act in concert with one another no matter how far apart they appear to be separated by space-time. Nonlocality is asking us to revise completely our ideas about objects, to remove a pervasive projection we have upon nature. We can no longer consider objects as independently existing entities that can be localized in well-defined regions of space-time. They are interconnected in ways not even conceivable using ideas from classical physics.

"Nature has shown us that our concept of reality, consisting of units that can be considered as separate from each other, is fundamentally wrong. For this reason, Bell's theorem may be the most profound discovery of science" Kafatos, 64-5). "Bell's theorem itself leads to the inescapable conclusion that if the statistical predictions of quantum theory are correct, then our commonsense ideas about the world are profoundly deficient" (Zukav 261).

Quantum nonlocality proves that "particles that were once together in an interaction remain in some sense parts of a single system which responds together to further interactions." Since the entire universe originated in a flash of light known as the Big Bang, the existence of quantum nonlocality points toward a profound cosmological holism and suggests that "If everything that ever interacted in the Big Bang maintains its connection with everything it interacted with, then every particle in every star and galaxy that we can see 'knows' about the existence of every other particle" (Gribbin).

What then is the nature of the universal "laws of physics," which seem to be the same everywhere. Do the laws of physics presuppose some type of nonlocality? Does the very concept of "the universe" as one thing imply a form of cosmological holism and nonlocality? Bronk thought the answer to this was "yes," and his responses—via his poems—are a good indication of the degree to which these issues weighed upon his poetry.

I came into Bronk's life just before *The Empty Hands*, and his world-view, for the most part, predates our discussions. Nevertheless, in *The Empty Hands* his positions in 1968 are expressed in "Euclidean Spaces: Linear Time" where he sees "the endless world" and in "The Now Rejects Time And Eternity" his starting position on time "I want to throw the idea of time away . . . time and eternity are wrong. . . . Only now!" (*LS* 81) At this time he had read some of Einstein's, Heisenberg's, Gödel's work and some things on non-Euclidean geometry. He was convinced that the World was eternal and unchanging, i.e. the fundamental aspects of the Real World never change, and have been as they are now forever. The concepts of past and future, for Bronk, are only relative to now, and relative to our position in the world as there are no external absolute references.

Shortly after this, I was in the midst of a letter exchange with Heisenberg while working on my dissertation, "The Axiomatic Foundations of Quantum Theory." In one letter Heisenberg told me that the great limitation that I was going to encounter was the limitation of language to express reality. We were limited to metaphor. I showed this letter to

THE BODY OF THIS LIFE:

Bronk, and I remember him laughing and saying "of course." We debated if math or science was a better way than language to describe the World, and the notion that math and science are only other languages attempting to do the same thing as natural language. The result was "Let Go" with "The best model of the world is the world. How else? / It is not compressible or summable. / It equals itself in each of its disparate parts" (from "Mystery Transcendent," *LS* 87). The world "is not compressible or summable" and so no language or descriptive system of science or mathematics will ever be able to compass it. This limitation of all human descriptive efforts leads at best to metaphor and analogy, the Real World is so much more that it would take the World to represent the World. If a person is limited to 300,000 words in a language or to what can be derived from a handful of axioms and theorems, how can anyone ever hope to express or describe accurately something with near infinite variation. Our inability to describe the World with the languages of math or science, or with natural language, has the problem that we need to see the world more clearly than our languages can express in order for us to use languages to describe it. This is Incompleteness in Language that is analogous to Gödel's Incompleteness Theorem for mathematics.

By the late 1970s Bronk was going through a period when many of his fundamental beliefs were conflicting. It is painful and disorienting to force oneself to the knowledge that everything one thought one knew was wrong, philosophical vertigo sets in, and a sense of being lost. Bronk started that process before I knew him, but with our discussions of Heisenberg, Einstein, Gödel, and Bell, and my confirming his interpretation of their discoveries, the process accelerated. I had been invited to Bronk's home just after his birthday for dinner; it was in early March 1969, I think. Bronk had been going through a tough period. He was agitated enough that he wanted to read some new poems before dinner, which was very unusual, as they were nearly always an after dinner treat. He read "Mystery Transcendent," "I Am," "The Aggrandizement," "The Use-Unuse Of Us," and "The Unbelievable," all of which appeared in *That Tantalus*. Bronk's despair at the losses of reference is clear in these poems. "Do you know why? / I gather you may. That it isn't only time, / that all the issues clearly drawn are, dread / shall we say? Are horror?

Are terrible?" (from "Mystery Trascendent," *LS* 118). And "Despair / which neither / was / nor will be / but is / all"(from "The Unbelievable," *LS* 119). "We are made afraid not to believe the fraud / of this world: believe or be lost." from "The Unbelievable," *LS* 120). And finally in "The Continuance" we have "The rules / change. It is uncertain what they are. We go on" (*LS* 112). Bronk never more clearly reveals the influence of science on his thinking than in these last lines. The rules by which we describe this world have changed greatly since the advent of relativity and quantum mechanics, and they are not a complete description of the world and never will be, nor will any new set of rules, such as string theory, that may replace these, but we go on because we must, and if all our efforts fail, as Bronk believed they will, no matter, it is all we will ever have.

By the time that Bronk was writing the poems that became *To Praise the Music*, he had accepted the unknowable nature of the World, as conclusive, whereas before, he had felt that the world was unknowable, but allowed, or hoped, that he could be wrong. After Einstein, Heisenberg, Godel, and Bell, though, the hope of being wrong was gone: "Well I need. I may never know anything / but I need. . . . Oh we know that knowing is not our way: / but, the choice ours, would make it our way, would leave / the world for the same world made knowable" (from "The Ignorant Lust After Knowledge," *LS* 126). "We smile, though, in a world we can neither invent / nor imagine, a world beyond thought, no thinkable world. / Thought is what we think and then shed: / we turn and look back on thought, lamenting it" (from "Beatific Effigies," *LS* 128). Bronk's lamentations did not last long; he was too strong for that. He faced the limitations of this world, and though never rejoicing in them, at least accepted them, which sounds clearest in "The real world is no world though without / our knowing it may well be. We can't / say anything about it: how it is / or why, what way it may, but it is there. /. . . There is a real world which does make sense / It is beyond our knowing or speaking but it is there" (from "The Real World," *LS* 136).

While recognizing the limits of human endeavors, Bronk still yearned for the lost innocence of belief. "In the end, is the want still and only the want, / done, then, with the doing, and the form done" (from "The

Fiction Of Shape," *LS* 136). "The loss—help us—how shall we say the loss? / It's still there. Not so; not ever there. / What can we lose but illusions. . . . / Truth, what shall I have in taking you? / Give me the nothing, that all that is" (from "The Importuning Of Truth," *LS* 138). Yet even as he pondered these limits, he was drawn back to the issues of Teleology, i.e. the use of ultimate purpose to explain natural phenomena. "The unpurposive lights in the sky at night, far / from telling us what purpose is as, say, / there is no purpose (as may, perhaps, be so) / say only how we don't know what it is" (from "The Limits Of Knowledge," *LS* 155). "My point is what is all this stuff / other than what we are as if we were / something? My point is we can't make a case, / given even all that, for what we are" (from "Looking At It," *LS* 161).

Bell's Theorem says that all entities in this Universe are connected in some fundamental way. Bronk felt to his marrow that this was true, and recognized that in some fundamental way everything is interconnected. Bronk's position (very similar to Einstein's) is stated real clear in the lines "And you, my lord, unable to other be, / be all only" (from "who Feels It," *LS* 173). More, "The biological life is not the life / of the universe. Is the large splendor of stars / only to ornament or illuminate / us? No, their life is the main show." (from "Where Are We," *LS* 174). Einstein's conception of God was very similar, and we discussed Einstein's famous quote "my God is Spinoza's God" which meant that Einstein saw God as the totality of all aspects of the universe, and in that sense, we are all parts of God in small. Bronk's believe was similar, " I am more than I was. / . . . . The world? /No asking. We are one or together. Call it the world. (from "The Way Of The World," *LS* 71).

To delve deeper into Bronk's worldview another small discussion of quantum mechanics is needed. Quantum Mechanics has been given

---

*Benedict (Baruch) Spinoza (1632-1677) composed his greatest work, *The Ethics*, in 1663-1665. In Part One, "Concerning God," after presenting a short list of definitions and axioms, Spinoza deduces thirty-six propositions which explain the nature of God. The most important of these is Proposition 14, which expresses his pantheism: "Besides God, no substance can be granted or conceived."

several "interpretations" over the years starting with the one devised by Niels Bohr called the Copenhagen Interpretation. Why "interpretations"? The math used in quantum theory does not have physical analogies that can be used by humans to form a mental image of what is happening physically. It uses matrix algebra and linear algebra combined with probability theory, and some mathematical treatments that everyone knows are wrong, but for some reason gives correct physical predictions. It gets back to the question posed earlier: why should mathematics apply to the world at all?

The multiple interpretations of quantum mechanics come from the fact that there are multiple "consistent" mathematical formulations, i.e. "models of reality," of quantum mechanics. I say "consistent" because they are not, at all levels, truly equivalent, some are actually contradictory but generate the same physical predictions.' And the "model of reality" issue is the problem that generates multiple interpretations, which becomes important when one tries to devise a completely consistent quantum theory of the universe.

In the original Copenhagen Interpretation there is a thing called a wave function or wave packet. This wave function for a quantum level event is the set of probability functions that describe all of the possible states that the event can be in. In the Copenhagen Interpretation, the event is never actually in one of the many possible states until the time the event is "observed," which suggests that the actual condition of a physical event depend upon it being observed.

'The methods which are normally used to get the usually quoted very highly accurate results of quantum mechanics contains the highly dubious and ad hoc method of "renormalisation" which gets the right results for the wrong reasons. In general these calculations are based on mathematical and physical reasoning, but when corresponding to real particles that reasoning assigns energies etc. which are infinite, then, to make the results again meaningful uses the renormalisation procedure which roughly corresponds to dividing by infinity. Even though the renormalised results are quite accurate no reasonable explanation is known why the initial results are wrong and why the renormalisation works. See for example Richard P. Feynman, QED—The Strange Theory of Light and Matter (Princeton, NJ: Princeton Science Library, 1988) 128.

In von Neumann's view consciousness has a similar but less dramatic role: "On the other hand, the situation incorporates the human observer metonymically. As John von Neumann was perhaps first to point out (although Bohr makes similar intimations), the 'cut' may be made between the brain and the consciousness of the observer, where quantum effects may in fact operate" (Plotinsky 114). Heisenberg also followed this path as he reminded me in a letter on 12 November 1973 when he told me that in preparing an experiment and describing it we need all the concepts of natural language, even such concepts as 'free will.' In Bronk's view consciousness plays the center role:

> I don't think that nothing has objective and independent reality without our consciousness. There is something *of which* we are aware not *because* we are aware. This includes and pertains to the self as well as to the non-self insofar as these are separate entities. And our awareness *need not* lead to formulating or conceptualizing; sometimes it does and that's where the fun starts. It is by our knowing the shortcomings of our concepts and formulations that we can be sure that something is which is independent of them. In an intellectual sense nothing exists — has its own existence — until we say what it is, give it shape and limits but there is something there which is what we are trying, however unsuccessfully, to shape and limit. We try to set it off from ourselves but we are all tangled upon it (as is everything else); that doesn't mean that we made it up in the attempt. What we made up was only the attempt itself. (letter from William Bronk to Ronald Collins dated 21 May 1983)

Supposing today's physics is made of relativity theory plus quantum mechanics plus other possible components, then at the least Physics itself is incomplete, and wrong at some level—at least partially—because quantum mechanics and relativity theory are not compatible. (Their incompatibility means that they cannot be both true at the same time.) "At a time when certain pundits are predicting the End of Science on the grounds that all the important discoveries have already been made, it is worth emphasizing that the two main pillars of twentieth-century physics, quantum mechanics and Einstein's general theory of relativity, are mutually incompatible. General relativity fails to comply with the quantum rules that govern the behavior of elementary particles, whereas on the opposite scale, black holes are challenging the very foundations of quantum mechanics" (Duff 54).

Bronk, of course, always assumed that since the world was unknowable, that any systemic approach to understanding the world was at best a metaphor, and at the least, wrong. "Order is what teaches us the abstract because / whatever we make of order defaults, is wrong" (from "The Things That Are Are Not," *LS* 189). Likewise, Heisenberg stated in his letter to me in July of 1973 that the inherent limitation of classical and quantum mechanical concepts was almost fundamental to the theory and an essential point in the interpretation of Quantum Theory. In Bronk's words, "These are invented words and they refer / to inventions of their own and not to a real world / unresembled, inexpressible" (from *The Force Of Desire, LS* 198).

It was certainly not the case that Bronk thought science a waste of time in trying to help us understand the world. He only thought that the possibility of science revealing the Real World is remote, but not necessarily impossible. He left room for hope.

The Age Of Science

Proven truth is something for everyman
Except for the ones who won't listen, won't learn.
We can show them but we can't make them believe
—that wouldn't be rational anyway and we don't
try. Admittedly, we don't have
the whole thing; that's what our method's about
but, at least, we have a method at last and if
it doesn't work I don't know what we can do. (*MF* 38)

Our conversations always came back to Cosmology, or led to it through various routes, and our positions by the mid-1980s was built upon the fact that we observe only from our frames of reference (Einstein), and what we observe depends upon our observing it (Heisenberg). It wouldn't exist otherwise. And all we create through our observations are interconnected from the moment of creation (Bell). What we can say about IT is limited (Heisenberg) and by necessity incomplete (Gödel), but the totality of all there is, is IT (Einstein, Spinoza). Bronk, ultimately, found confirmation for his own ideas in these various theories, all of which validated the point that his points returned to again and again: IT is unknown and unknowable, unchanged and unchangeable, everywhere and no where seen.

> Not Plato's cave upon the wall of which
> we see, he said, the shadows of reality.
> There is reality but I've never seen
> even its shadow on that or any wall.
> (from "The Natural Sciences," *LS* 175)

Sherry Kearns

Metaphor Again:
William Bronk's Real World

W HEN WILLIAM BRONK WROTE OF THE REAL WORLD, he did not mean the external, physical world. On that subject he wrote, "Of the natural world, nothing is possible/but praise if we speak at all." (*LS* 109) When he wrote about what he called the real world, he was referring to something else of which he said, "We are in the real world as ghosts are in this world, of doubtful being, almost impalpable." (*VSC* 36)

This conceit of a real world to which the rules of ordinary reality do not apply is one of the most persistent in Bronk's work. It appears first in the final poem of *Light and Dark*, published in 1956, and continues regularly and frequently through the body of his work up to and including the poems written in the last years of his life. This real world and its relation to Bronk's poetic persona occupy a central place in hundreds of his poems. The reader who wishes to understand Bronk's work may well wonder to what world the poet is referring when in a poem titled "The Real World" he calls real a world which "We can't say anything about. . ." (*LS* 136). He says further in the same poem, "There is a real world which does make sense. It is beyond our knowing or speaking but it is there" (*LS* 136).

This enigmatic world is recognized in poem after poem. Bronk establishes it first in "At Tikal" when he begins his separation in verse of the physical world from this other conceit. He writes, "And oh, it is always a world and not the world" (*LS* 32). A world refers to a fiction humans create to live in while the world, by use of the definite article, is one which is specialized in meaning as pre-eminent.

With the publication in 1964 of *The World, the Worldless*, William Bronk made public an investigation of how that real world affected meaning in its relation to humankind generally and to Bronk's poetic persona specifically. Bronk often used the first person plural pronoun in poetry to make statements about the discrepancy between the world of human created fictions we all live in and the truth of the world beyond our control or understanding which is real and which in actuality controls our lives in a larger sense. His persona says *we* to tell the reader that this real world encompasses the entire human race, not just the poet who writes of it. By that generalization, we are all worldless and the poems are about us.

Bronk begins that volume by establishing in "The Truth as Known" that we all know there is a truth about life that is unspoken and tacitly we have agreed not to speak it. A hallmark of that real world is that it is almost never spoken of in ordinary discourse. Then the poet talks about the real world as he has come to understand it. In the poem "The Annihilation of Matter" and "Metonymy As An Approach to a Real World" Bronk uses light as a metaphor for meaning in a world where what is real can't be known. He says, "Objects are nothing. There is only the light, the light!" (*LS* 36) And then, "Conceded, we make a world:/is something caught there, contained there,/ something real, something which we can sense?/ Once in a city blocked and filled, I saw/ the light lie in the deep chasm of a street,/ palpable and blue, as though it had drifted in/ from say, the sea, a purity of space" (*LS* 36).

Light and its appearance in so many of Bronk's poems as an anodyne to the ignorance we share of reality is a guide to a way of understanding what the poet is talking about when he writes of the real world. Light is often a symbol for consciousness and understanding and it is used commonly as such. One might say, "I saw the light" to mean that I understood this or that and it is a figure of speech which needs no explanation.

The title of Bronk's book *Light and Dark* states a theme of opposition, as does the title *The World, the Worldless*. If light means consciousness and understanding, the unconscious and ignorance are its opposites. If the real world is the world of the unconscious, then by definition we, conscious beings, are worldless. These are the themes presented by the symbols in the titles.

But is the unconscious that real world Bronk speaks of? It is a difficult subject to discuss because the nature of unconsciousness precludes knowing about it directly. Carl Jung made the human psyche his life study and wrote of it. In the volume of his *Collected Works* entitled *The Archetypes and the Collective Unconscious* he says, "The unconscious is the psyche that reaches down from the daylight of mentally and morally lucid consciousness into the nervous system that for ages has been known as the 'sympathetic'. This does not govern perception and muscular activity like the cerebrospinal . . . but through functioning without sense organs, it maintains the balance of life, and through the mysterious path of sympathetic excitation, not only gives us knowledge of the innermost life of other beings, but also has an inner effect upon them. In this sense it is an extremely collective system. . ." (*ACU* 19-20).

Jung is not speaking of each human being's personal unconscious which contains forgotten events as well as repressed material from each individual's life, but of a deeper layer of unconsciousness which is inborn and common to all humans. "(T)he collective unconscious . . . is sheer objectivity, as wide as the world and open to the world. There I am the object of every subject, in complete reversal of my ordinary consciousness, where I am always the subject that has an object. There I am utterly one with the world . . . (t)his self is the world if only a consciousness could see it" (*ACU* 20).

He explains further, "In the realm of consciousness we are our own masters; we seem to be the 'factors' (the makers) themselves. But if we step through the door of the shadow to the unconscious we discover with terror that we are the object of unseen factors . . . the anxiously guarded supremacy of consciousness . . . is questioned in the most dangerous way. But . . . ignorance is no guarantee of security . . ." (*ACU* 23). "Psychic life is for the greater part an unconscious life that surrounds consciousness on all sides" (*ACU* 27).

These quotes from Jung are in line with many of Bronk's poetic statements about the real world. Bronk's use of the first person plural reinforces an understanding of the unconscious as collective and common. Often the two men write on the same topic (though Bronk writes about it in symbol) and say similar things. In the poem "The Nature of the Universe" The poet says:

If there is One, and all we know is One,
and there is no other, nothing, as nightly the far
glitter of distant stars proclaims it, we
are the inner mirror of those stars, who find

only an ecstasy to outfeel
horror, and be blind to that sight that:
we are nowhere, there is no other place,
and nothing to turn to, in solitude. (*LS* 59)

In a letter Jung writes:

My consciousness is like an eye that penetrates to the most
distant spaces, yet it is the psychic non-ego that fills them with
non-spatial images. And those images are not pale shadows, but
tremendously powerful psychic factors. . . . Beside this picture I
would like to place the spectacle of the starry heavens at night,
for the only equivalent of the universe within is universe without;
and just as I reach this world through the medium of the body, so
I reach that world through the medium of the psyche. (*JSOT*
215)

Jung even sounds like Bronk when he writes, "The body's carbon is
simply carbon. Hence, 'at bottom' the psyche is simply 'world.' (*PS* 138)
This isn't the world Bronk means, however, and *The World, the World-l-
ess* ends with a poem that is a cry of distress. ". . . We were all wrong,
because the point/ was not the point, because the world, or what/ we
took for the world is breaking, breaking. We were wrong/ and are not
right. Break! Break! We are here!/ What I want to do is shout! Break!
Shout!" (*LS* 63)

Not only is the world—the world of constructed fictions—breaking,
but Bronk by recognizing the fictions and calling them that is helping in
the breakage. Yet, he has no new world to offer in place of the old.

Jung describes this break-down of the world of ego-consciousness as
follows:

In actual reality we do not have at our command any power of cool reflection nor does any science or philosophy help us. . . . We are caught and entangled in aimless experience and the judging intellect with its categories proves itself powerless. Human interpretation fails, for a turbulent life-situation has arisen that refuses to fit any of the traditional meanings assigned to it. It is a moment of collapse. (ACU 32)

Bronk's poetic relation to the unconscious, to the real world which he intuited but did not know, changed over the course of his work. This did not happen quickly. In *The Empty Hands* which followed *The World, the Worldless* and was published five years later, the same problems are still being addressed, and a new one has been added. The real world which exists beyond conscious knowing and control has, the poet now realizes, irrupted into his life instead of just going on around him. Consciousness and will have no primacy. The poet has found that the real world uses him to act out its dramas; he finds that he is used as an expression of its reality.

The manifestation of that realization begins with "The Smile on the Face of a Kouros" when Bronk personifies death which, like the unconscious, is beyond human awareness. He proposes death as the shaping force of life. "It gives us; and takes what we give/ and keeps it; and has, this way, in life itself,/ a kind of treasure house of comely form/ achieved and left with death to stay and be/ forever beautiful and whole . . ." (*LS* 66).

In "In Contempt of Worldliness" the poet sets up the divide between a world which humans cling to and the world which is unmasterable, saying to be at home in the world is to make too light of it. He says, "Strangely, the same thing makes too light/ of us, as though it mattered this world, to us" (*LS* 69). We—the human race, the poet—are the indirect objects, not the subjects of mattering.

"Whatever the world/ may be, it's not what we think it is." (*LS* 69) Having said that in the seventh poem of *The Empty Hands*, Bronk goes through that poem and the whole volume demonstrating how this statement is so. In the poem "Of the All With Which We Coexist", Bronk describes the role of consciousness the center of which is the psychic component that Jung calls the ego. That is the I that speaks: "If I am anything at all, I am/ the instrument of the world's passion and not the doer or the done to" (*LS 71*). And again in "The Way of the World": "Much/ of the time, I am nowhere, not in any world; . . . Other times, something. An outside power. Or more,/ my power. Something outside. I am more than I was" (*LS 71*). What could that power be?

In Carl Jung's model of the unconscious, he has posited instinctual patterns which he calls archetypes and which he says have asserted themselves in human life since prehistoric time regardless of race or culture. He calls the archetype "an irrepresentable, unconscious, pre-existent form that seems to be part of the inherited structure of the psyche and can therefore manifest itself spontaneously anywhere, at any time" (*MDR* 329). He says representations themselves are not inherited, only the forms; and he thinks "the real nature of the archetype is not capable of being made conscious, . . . it is transcendent . . ." (*MDR* 393). Jung states "Insofar as the archetypes act upon me, they are real and actual to me, even though I do not know what their real nature is" (*MDR* 352). Nor does he believe objective knowledge of the archetypes or psyche is possible. "Whatever it may state about itself, it will never get beyond itself. All comprehension and all that is comprehended is in itself psychic and to that extent we are hopelessly cooped up in an exclusively psychic world" (*MDR* 352). "Archetypes are complexes of experience that come upon us like fate and their effects are felt in our most personal life" (*ACU* 30).

Bronk shows the archetypes of the real world intruding into life in so many poems and so many ways. The following are only a very few examples:

If life may be said to happen, it is not to us. (*LS 96*)

The world is not our world,
and what we make for a world is simply that
not more, not less. (*LS 104*)

Do as you will.
It doesn't matter. What happens to us is not
what happens. It isn't by us. We feel it there.
Listen. Something is living. It is not we. (*LS* 106)

I am that bull they bait, this way, that way,
head down, stupid, off to the side of the ring.
Who are they? They fade to the fence whenever I charge. (*LS 115*)

To say I only listen isn't true
but neither is it conversation really: in the end
whatever is said is theirs. (*LS* 131)

Life lives / our life . . . (*LS* 215)

Life is aside from us,
though we are lived:
It uses us
Without our knowing what it means to do. (*LS* 217)

By the end of *Life Supports*, Bronk has recognized, acknowledged, and chronicled the way our lives lived aren't the result of our conscious wills. And the tone of much of Bronk's poetry is that of a man injured and disappointed. He knows that life is living out its necessities through him regardless of his ego's sense that it should be the center of life. Ego is the center of consciousness, but consciousness is not the center of life, the self is. The role of the archetypes is to bring the individual into a state of psychological development in which the center of personality shifts from the ego by integration of the unconscious into conscious life. Being consciously aware of this wholeness is what Jung called the self. It is not an easy task "because consciousness deviates again and again from its archetypal, instinctual foundation and finds itself in opposition to it." (*ACU* 40) According to Jung the archetypes "cannot be integrated simply by rational means but require a . . . real coming to terms with them." (*ACU* 40)

THE BODY OF THIS LIFE:

Published in 1985, *Careless Love and Its Apostrophes* is a volume that speaks the poet's great despair. This anguish begins with the first poem and appears throughout the book. It is the anguish of the ego, the I consciousness, aware of its incomplete and limited state, and its impotence in the face of that.

There is nothing of us to say, nothing of you,
nothing to know in all there is to say.
    (As Though Our Ways With Each Other Mattered At Last)

I don't know what I want, ever wanted.
    (Wants and Questions)

Now, near the end, I never grasped it.
I missed it all. A repeat wouldn't help.
    (Brief)

So, who says it matters? It doesn't.
    (Credulity's Wonder)

There are no places, no worlds that matter.
    (Unworldly Beauty is the Beauty of the World)

The light may be a darkness: those holes we speak of.
Light is held there condensed and heavy, can never escape.
    (Such Stuff)

In this volume, even light which was a symbol Bronk had used to great effect in previous works has lost its ability to mean for him. And the real world which he knew existed though he was excluded from it has no meaning for him whatsoever despite the facts of its existence and preeminence.

But here is the epigraph of *Manifest and Furthermore* published in 1987:

The arts have something to tell us.
It is not what we wanted to hear;
but we listen.
It is a very private communication.
It becomes our life.

These are the words of a poet who has come to terms with what his unconscious presented him with as the immutable way of life. There is no bitter tone or sense of loss, or a world offered not to have. In "What Foot" from that same volume, Bronk shows that our human relation to the unconscious remains the same.

We are shoes it wears for a time and then discards.
Nothing wears them again. Memorials,
they show for awhile what foot and where it walked. (*MF* 14)

Very different now is the poet's response to the presence of the great objective within him. He states it outright in "Out There":

I have laughed with the mind sometimes hard
and with ugly dismissal, how its last conclusions rot out
initial bases or tight lock up the mind
in a cage it cannot escape from and is held there.

But I accede; knowledge is what I am freed
from, as once I was freed from power, not
having any. Knowledge and power are what
we want until we find, at last, they are not.

There is a state outside of me, too, without
these things. Reality? The God? I apply
to it. It has my reverence and awe, my love.
I am content there where I wanted once. (*MF* 6)

That outside he speaks of is the unconscious, the outside within, where before he resented being used by life; now he is at peace. In "The House That Doesn't House" he senses

> the shelter and have no sense of wall, where there seems
> concern for us though no one there and we
> feel thankful for what we give: our temporal
> tininess and begin to love ourselves
> as worthy deservers, as though we were ones who are loved
> and go, bemused, back home. Alone there. (*MF* 9)

Now when he faces a made-up world, the fact of its fiction doesn't fill him with empty despair. Witness this in "Metaphor Again":

> Oh, make a world, OK
> but its glory will go and the stones it's built on
> will erode and frost-fracture or something else
> in warmer climates. Never mind what else
> would make the metaphor; the world is one
> itself and not to be taken word for word
> any more than other metaphors:
> pronouncements, dogmas, ideologies,
> hard facts, material truth. Give up
> and believe without, say praise, give thanks. (*MF* 60)

This is not the same praise as in the poem "To Praise the Music". (*LS* 143) There the poet praises the songs of praise that the trees sing. He is praising the natural world and its ability to praise in the condition of its own unknowing. Poet and trees are alike in their ignorance, but not in their responses created by it. The poet envies the music the trees sing. In "Metaphor Again" the poet accepts the real world for what it is—unknowable, indescribable—and is as grateful for it as the trees seemingly are for their world, though those worlds are worlds apart.

What has caused this change that Bronk's poetic persona speaks of? In *Careless Love* the poet was in the deeps of hopelessness. According to

Jung, it is "only when all props and crutches are broken, and no cover from the rear offers even the slightest hope of security, does it become possible for us to experience an archetype that up till then had lain hidden. . . . This is the archetype of meaning" (*ACU* 32) which Jung also calls the spirit (*ACU* 35). This is the self that represents the whole psyche which can not be comprehended in its entirety. It is too large for the ego to contain because it holds both consciousness and the unconscious.

What he called the real world, that of the unconscious, is one against which the poet is no longer in hostile opposition. Jung tells us "Modern man in experiencing this archetype (meaning/spirit) comes to know that most ancient form of thinking as an autonomous activity whose object he is" (*ACU* 37). The conceit of the real world and its autonomy was one of Bronk's main poetic themes all his life. His changed feeling toward the unconscious did not change its importance to him. Its existence was a verity which made itself into poems. As was Paul on the road to Damascus, Bronk was overtaken by meaning which he then made manifest. The last poem of *Careless Love* says it so:

The Wonder

Let it go unprotested we are useless, mortal and alone.
Man, you are marvelous and freed.

The Published Works of William Bronk

Light and Dark (1956)
The World, the Worldless (1964)
The Empty Hands (1969)
That Tantalus (1971)
To Praise the Music (1972)
The New World (1974)
A Partial Glossary: Two Essays (1974)
Silence and Metaphor (1975)
Finding Losses (1976)
The Meantime (1976)
My Father Photographed with Friends (1976)
The Force of Desire (1979)
*The Brother in Elysium: Ideas of Friendship
and Society in the United States* (1980)
Life Supports: New and Collected Poems (1981)
*Vectors and Smoothable Curves:
Collected Essays* (1983)
Careless Love and Its Apostrophes (1985)
Manifest; and Furthermore (1987)
Death Is the Place (1989)
Living Instead (1991)
Some Words (1992)
The Mild Day (1993)
Our Selves (1994)
Selected Poems (1995)
The Cage of Age (1996)
*Vectors and Smoothable Curves:
Collected Essays: New Edition* (1997)
*Life Supports: New and
Collected Poems: New Edition* (1997)
All of What We Loved (1998)
Some Words: New Edition (1998)
Metaphor of Trees and Last Poems (1999)

Works Cited

Anonymous. *The Cloud of Unknowing*. Original text rendered by Evelyn Underhill. Rockport: Element, 1997.

Anonymous. Review of *Life Supports*. *Virginia Quarterly Review* 58 (Spring 1982): 59.

Berkeley, George. *A New Theory of Vision and Other Writings*. New York: Dutton Everyman, 1969.

Bender, Robert M., and Charles L. Squier, eds. *The Sonnet: An Anthology*. New York: Washington Square P, 1987.

Bercholz, Samuel. *Entering the Stream*. Boston: Shambhala, 1995.

Bertholf, Robert. "A Conversation with William Bronk." *Credences III.3* (1976): 9-33.

Biespiel, David. "To Understand America," review of *The Cage of Age* by Campbell McGrath. *Hungry Mind Review*. (http://www.bookwire.bowker.com/bookinfo/review.aspx.?3722).

Blasing, Mutlu Konick. *American Poetry: The Rhetoric of Its Forms*. New Haven: Yale UP, 1987.

Bloom, Harold. *Poetry and Repression: Revisionism from Blake to Stevens*. New Haven: Yale UP, 1976.

Boswell, James. *The Life of Samuel Johnson*. New York: The Modern Library, n. d.

Bronk, William. *All Of What We Loved*. Jersey City, New Jersey: Talisman House, 1998. (appears as *AWWL* in text)

_____, ___. *The Attendant*. New Rochelle: James L. Weil, 1984.

_____, ___. *The Cage of Age*. Jersey City: Talisman House, 1996. (appears as *COA* in text)

_____, ___. *Death Is the Place*. San Francisco: North Point Press, 1989. (appears as *DITP* in text)

_____, ___. Letters to Robert Meyer. The Rare Book and Manuscript Library, Butler Library, Columbia University.

_____, ___. *Life Supports: New and Collected Poems*. San Francisco: North Point Press, 1981. (appears as *LS* in text)

_____, ___. *Lines & Smudges*. New Rochelle, NY: James L. Weil, 1999.

_____, ___. *Living Instead*. San Francisco: Northpoint, 1991.

_____, ___. *Manifest; and Furthermore*. San Francisco: North Point Press, 1987. (appears as *MF* in text)

_____, ___. *Metaphor of Trees and Last Poems*. Jersey City, NJ: Talisman House, 1999. (appears as *MOT* in text)

_____, ___. *Of Poetry*. New Rochelle, NY: James L. Weil, 1988.

_____, ___. *Our Selves*. Hoboken, NJ: Talisman House, 1994.

_____, ___. *Selected Poems*. Ed. Henry Weinfield. New York: New Directions, 1995. (appears as *SP* in text)

_____, ___. *Some Words* Jersey City, NJ: Talisman House, 1999 (appears as *SW* in text).

_____, ___. *That Beauty Still*. Providence: Burning Deck, 1978.

_____, ___. *Vectors and Smoothable Curves: New Edition*. Jersey City, NJ: Talisman House, 1997 (appears as *VSC* in text).

_____, ___. *The World, the Worldless*. New York: New Directions/San Francisco, CA: *San Francisco Review*, 1964.

Chawla, Louise. "Biography of an Antibiograph." *Sagetrieb* 7.3 (Winter 1988): 83-94.

Clark, Tom. *Charles Olson: The Allegory of a Poet's Life*. New York: W. W. Norton, 1991.

Conte, Joseph M. *Unending Design: The Forms of Postmodern Poetry*. Ithaca: Cornell UP, 1991.

Corman, Cid. *William Bronk: An Essay*. Carrboro, NC: Truck, 1976.

Davenport, Guy. "Scholia and Conjectures for Olson's 'The Kingfishes.'" *Boundary* 2, II, 1 and 2 (Fall '73/Winter '74): 250-62.

Duff, Michael J. "The Theory Formerly Known as Strings,." *Scientific American*. (February 1998).

Eagleton, Terry. *The Ideology of the Aesthetic*. Oxford: Basil Blackwell, 1990.

Edinger, Edward F. *Ego and Archetype*. Boston: Shambhala, 1991.

Ernest, John. "Fossilized Fish and the World of Unknowing: John Ashbery and William Bronk" in *The Tribe of John: Ashbery and Contemporary Poetry*. Tuscaloosa: University of Alabama Press, 1995.

_____, ___. "William Bronk's Religious Desire." *Sagetrieb* 7.3 (Winter 1988): 145-152.

Finkelstein, Norman. "Bronk, Duncan, and the Far Border of Poetry." *Sagetrieb* 12.3 (Winter 1993): 33-48.

_____, ___. "William Bronk: The World as Desire." *Contemporary Literature* 23.4 (1982): 480-92.

_____, ___. "The Singular Achievement of William Bronk." *Sagetrieb* 7.3 (Winter 1988): 75-82.

_____, ___. *The Utopian Moment in Contemporary American Poetry.* Lewisburg, PA: Bucknell UP, 1988.

Foster, Edward. *Answerable to None: Berrigan, Bronk, and the American Real.* New York: Spuyten Duyvil, 1999: 77-86.

_____, ___. "Conversations with William Bronk," in *Postmodern Poetry.* Ed. Edward Foster. Hoboken, NJ: Talisman House, 1994: 1-19.

Gilson, Etienne. *History of Christian Philosophy in the Middle Ages.* New York: Random House, 1955,

Gribbin, John. *In Search of Schrodinger's Cat: Physics and Reality.* New York: Bantam, 1984.

Grogan, Ruth A. "'Talk is what it's all about': William Bronk's Colloquiality." *Sagetrieb* 11.1&2 (Spring & Fall 1992): 85-101.

Heidegger, Martin. *On The Way To Language.* Trans. Peter D. Herz. New York: Harper & Row, 1971.

_____, ___. *Poetry, Language, Thought.* Trans. Albert Hofstadter. New York: Harper & Row, 1971.

_____, ___. *What Is Called Thinking?.* Trans. J. Glenn Gray. New York: Harper & Row, 1968.

Heisenberg, Werner. "Non-Objective Science and Uncertainty." *The Physicist's Conception of Nature* (1955). Trans. Arnold J. Pomerans New York: Harcourt, Brace and World, 1958: pp. 12-16, 28-29, 33-41). In Richard Ellmann and Charles Feidelson, Jr. *The Modern Tradition.* New York: Oxford, 1965.

Heller, Michael. "Bronk's *Manifest.*" *Sagetrieb* 7.3 (Winter 1988): 131-5.

Hillman, James. *The Dream and the Underworld.* New York: Harper & Row, 1979.

_____, ___. *Amina*. Texas: Spring Publications, 1981.

Horkheimer, Max. *Eclipse of Reason*. New Yorl: OUP, 1947; rpt. New York: Seabury Press, 1974.

Jakobson, Roman. *Language in Literature*. Cambridge: Harvard UP, 1987.

Jung, Carl Gustav. *The Portable Jung*. Ed. J. Campbell. New York: Viking/Penguin, 1984.

_____, ___. *The Structure and Dynamics of the Psyche*, in *The Collected Works*. Vol. 8. Princeton, NJ: Bollingen/Princeton, 1981.

Kafatos, Menas, and Thalia Kafatos. *Looking In, Seeing Out: Consciousness and Cosmos*. Wheaton: Quest, 1991.

Kant, Immanuel. *Critique of Judgment*. Trans. J. H. Bernard. New York: Hafner P, 1951.

Kaplan, J. D. *Dialogues of Plato*. New York: Pocket Books, 1950.

Kelly, Robert. *Mont Blanc*. Ann Arbor: Other Wind Press, 1994.

Kimmelman, Burt. "Centrality in a Discrete Universe: William Bronk and Wallace Stevens." *Sagetrieb* 7.3 (Winter 1988): 119-130.

_____, ___. "Pound, Stevens, Bronk: Phenomenology and the Postmodern Lyric." *The Journal of Imagism* 2 (Fall 1997): 34-63.

_____, ___. "The William Bronk-Charles Olson Correspondence," ed. Burt Kimmelman. *Minutes of the Charles Olson Society*, 22 (January 1998): 10.

_____, ___. *The "Winter Mind": William Bronk and American Letters*. Madison, NJ: Fairleigh Dickinson UP, 1998.

Lao Tsu. *Tao Te Ching*. Trans. Gia-Fu Feng and Jane English. New York: Random House, 1972.

Lyotard, Jean-François. *The Inhuman: Reflections on Time*. Trans. Geoffrey Bennington and Rachel Bowlby. Stanford, CA: Stanford UP, 1991.

Meyer, Robert. Letters to William Bronk. The Poetry / Rare Books Collection, University Libraries, State University of New York.

Neuman, E. *Art and the Unconscious*. Princeton, NJ: Princeton/Bollingen, 1974.

Odom, George Eugene. "Stuart Merrill." M.A. thesis, University of Mississippi, 1965.

Oppen, George. *The Selected Letters of George Oppen*. Ed. Rachel Blau Du Plessis. Durham: Duke, 1990.

Oppenheimer, Joel. *Collected Later Poems*. Ed. Robert J. Bertholf. Buffalo, New York: The Poetry/Rare Books Collection, 1997.

Pascal, Blaise. "Pensées." Trans. A. J. Krailsheimer. Penguin Books, London, 1966.

Plotinsky, Arkady. *Complementarity*. Durham: Duke UP, 1994.

Pound, Ezra. *The Cantos*. New York: New Directions, 1986.

Retsov, Samuel [Edward Foster]. "The Baroque Sound of William Bronk." *Talisman* 2 (1989): 91-92

Ross, James B., ed. *The Portable Medieval Reader*. New York: Viking, 1961.

Selden, Raman, and Peter Widdowson. *A Reader's Guide to Contemporary Literary Theory*. Third Edition. Lexington: U Kentucky P, 1993.

Sorrentino, Gilbert. "William Bronk." *Something Said*. San Francisco: North Point P, 1984: 77-80.

Spicer, Jack. *After Lorca*, in *The Collected Books of Jack Spicer*. Ed. Robin Blaser. Santa Barbara, CA: Black Sparrow P. 1980.

Stein, Gertrude. "Composition as Explanation," in *Selected Writings of Gertrude Stein*. Ed. Carl Van Vechten. New York: Vintage. 1972.

Stevens, Wallace. *The Collected Poems of Wallace Stevens*. New York: Knopf, 1954.

_____, ____. *Collected Poetry and Prose*. New York: Library of America, 1997.

_____, ____. *The Palm at the End of the Mind*. New York: Vintage: 1967.

Taggart, John. *Songs of Degrees: Essays on Contemporary Poetry and Poetics*. Tuscaloosa: U of Alabama P, 1994.

Tulka Thondup. *The Healing Power of Mind*. Boston: Shambhala, 1996.

Vaihinger, Hans. The Philosophy of 'As If': A System of Theoretical, Practical and Religious Fictions of Mankind. Trans. C. K. Ogden. London: Routledge & Kegan Paul, 1929.

Weinfield, Henry, ed. "A Conversation with William Bronk." *Sagetrieb* 7.3 (Winter 1988): 17-43.

_____, ____. "'The Cloud of Unknowing': William Bronk and the
Condition of Poetry." *Sagetrieb* 7.3 (Winter 1988): 137-144.

Weiskel, Thomas. *The Romantic Sublime: Studies in the Structure and
Psychology of Transcendence*. Baltimore : Johns Hopkins UP, 1976.

Whitehead, Alfred North. "The Eighteenth Century." *Science and the
Modern World*. New York: The Free Press, 1953.

Zukav, Gary. *The Dancing Wu Li Masters: An Overview of the New
Physics*. Suffolk: Fontana / Collins, 1982 (1979).

Zukofsky, Louis. *Prepositions: The Collected Critical Essays of Louis
Zukofsky*. London: Rapp & Carroll. 1967.

Library of Congress Cataloging-in-Publication Data

The body of this life : reading William Bronk / edited by David Clippinger.
    p. cm.
  "Essays and memoirs by Don Adams, Robert J. Bertholf, Joseph Conte, Paul Christensen, David Clippinger, Ronald W. Collins, John Ernest, Norman Finkelstein, Edward Foster, Burton Hatlen, W. Sheldon Hurst, S.M. Kearns, Jack Kimball, Burt Kimmelman, David Landrey, Tom Lisk, Michael Perkins, Paul Pines, Gerald Schwartz, Rose Shapiro, Henry Weinfield, and Daniel Wolff."
  Includes bibliographical references.
  ISBN 1-58498-019-2 (acid-free paper) -- ISBN 1-58498-018-4 (pbk. : acid-free paper)
  1. Bronk, William--Criticism and interpretation. I. Clippinger, David, 1967-

PS3552.R65 Z59 2001
811'.54--dc21

                    2001027362

Designed by
Samuel Retsov

Text: 11 pt Sabon

acid-free paper

Printed by
McNaughton & Gunn